Grading
Teachers,
Grading
Schools

Grading Teachers, Grading Schools

Is Student Achievement a Valid Evaluation Measure?

Editor
Jason Millman

CORWIN PRESS, INC.
A Sage Publications Company
Thousand Oaks, California

For information:

Corwin Press, Inc.
A Sage Publications Company
2455 Teller Road
Thousand Oaks, California 91320
E-mail: order@corwin.sagepub.com

SAGE Publications Ltd.
6 Bonhill Street
London EC2A 4PU
United Kingdom

SAGE Publications India Pvt. Ltd.
M-32 Market
Greater Kailash I
New Delhi 110 048 India

Printed in the United States of America

Library of Congress Cataloging-in-Publication Data

Grading teachers, grading schools: Is student achievement a valid
  evaluation measure? / edited by Jason Millman.
    p. cm.
  Includes bibliographical references and index.
  ISBN 0-8039-6401-3 (cloth: acid-free paper). — ISBN
0-8039-6402-1 (pbk.: acid-free paper)
    1. Teachers—Rating of—United States—Case studies. 2. Teacher
effectiveness—United States—Case studies. 3. Academic
achievement—United States—Case studies. I. Millman, Jason.
LB2838.G63 1997
371'.14'4—dc21   97-21050

This book is printed on acid-free paper.

97 98 99 00 01 02 10 9 8 7 6 5 4 3 2 1

Production Editor: Michele Lingre
Editorial Assistant: Kristen L. Gibson
Typesetter: Rebecca Evans
Cover Designer: Marcia R. Finlayson

Contents

About the Authors   ix

℘ PART I ℘
Origins and Underpinnings

1. Beginnings and Introduction   3
   Jason Millman and *H. Del Schalock*

℘ PART II ℘
The Oregon Teacher
Work Sample Methodology

2. The Oregon Teacher Work Sample Methodology:
   Rationale and Background   11
   Bill Cowart and *David Myton*

3. Teacher Work Sample Methodology as Used at
   Western Oregon State College   15
   H. Del Schalock, Mark Schalock, and *Gerald Girod*

4. Oregon Teacher Work Sample Methodology:
   Potential and Problems   46
   Peter W. Airasian

5. Oregon Teacher Work Sample Methodology:
   Educational Policy Review   53
   Daniel L. Stufflebeam

6. Reflections on Comments by Airasian and Stufflebeam   62
   H. Del Schalock, Mark Schalock, and *Gerald Girod*

✑ PART III ✑

The Dallas Value-Added
Accountability System

7. In the Beginning   75
   Luvern L. Cunningham

8. The Dallas Value-Added Accountability System   81
   William J. Webster and *Robert L. Mendro*

9. Value-Added Productivity Indicators:
   The Dallas System   100
   Yeow Meng Thum and *Anthony S. Bryk*

10. On Trial: The Dallas Value-Added Accountability
    System   110
    Gary Sykes

11. Little Practical Difference and Pie in the Sky: A
    Response to Thum and Bryk and a Rejoinder to Sykes   120
    *William J. Webster, Robert L. Mendro, Timothy Orsak,
    Dash Weerasinghe,* and *Karen Bembry*

✑ PART IV ✑

The Tennessee Value-Added
Assessment System

12. The Impetus for the Tennessee Value-Added
    Accountability System   133
    Patricia E. Ceperley and *Kip Reel*

13. The Tennessee Value-Added Assessment System: A Quantitative, Outcomes-Based Approach to Educational Assessment   137

    William L. Sanders, Arnold M. Saxton, and *Sandra P. Horn*

14. The Tennessee Value-Added Assessment System: A Challenge to Familiar Assessment Methods   163

    Richard B. Darlington

15. Assessment Requires Incentives to Add Value: A Review of the Tennessee Value-Added Assessment System   169

    Herbert J. Walberg and *Susan J. Paik*

16. Response to the Reviewers   179

    William L. Sanders, Arnold M. Saxton, and *Sandra P. Horn*

✑ PART V ✑

The Kentucky Instructional Results Information System

17. Historical Background: The Kentucky School Accountability Index   185

    Doris Redfield and *Roger Pankratz*

18. Kentucky's Accountability and Assessment Systems   191

    Neal Kingston and *Ed Reidy*

19. Measurement Quality of the Kentucky Instructional Results Information System, 1991-1994   210

    Ronald K. Hambleton

20. Overview and Assessment of the Kentucky Instructional Results Information System   219

    Daniel L. Stufflebeam

21. The Kentucky Instructional Results Information System
    Meets the Critics: A Little Light and Much Heat   228

    Neal Kingston and *Ed Reidy*

ഐ PART VI ൙
Synthesis and Perspectives

22. How Do I Judge Thee? Let Me Count the Ways   243

    Jason Millman

23. Toward What End? The Evaluation of Student Learning
    for the Improvement of Teaching   248

    Linda Darling-Hammond

24. The Moth and the Flame: Student Learning as a
    Criterion of Instructional Competence   264

    W. James Popham

Author Index   275

Subject Index   278

About the Authors

Peter W. Airasian is Professor of Education at Boston College. He received his Ph.D. from the University of Chicago with a concentration on testing, evaluation, and assessment. His primary teaching responsibilities include courses in pre- and in-service classroom assessment methods and teacher evaluation. He is a former high school chemistry and biology teacher. He currently is studying the ways in which teachers assess themselves.

Karen Bembry is Director of Teacher Evaluation for Dallas Public Schools and is working toward a Ph.D. in educational research at the University of North Texas. She has more than 15 years experience in public education, including 10 years in gifted education and 5 years in educational research and evaluation. She began her tenure with the Dallas Public Schools as an evaluation specialist in institutional research.

Anthony S. Bryk is Director of the Center for School Improvement and Professor of Education at the University of Chicago and is Senior Director of the Consortium on Chicago School Research. He received his B.S. from Boston College and his Ed.D. from Harvard University. He has developed new statistical methods in education that have contributed to studies of school effects. His methodological contributions have appeared in several journals. His substantive research has focused on urban school improvement. Among his current interests are the social organization of schools and school restructuring to improve student learning.

Patricia E. Ceperley is a senior manager at the Appalachian Educational Laboratory, where she directs multiple projects. She has a B.S. from Purdue University, an M.Ed. from the University of Houston, and an Ed.D. from West Virginia University. She is an educator, having taught at the secondary and college levels. She also has worked for the West Virginia Legislature and School Boards Association. Some of her selected publications at the Appalachian Educational Laboratory include *An Advocacy Coalition Approach to the Politics of Education in Tennessee* (1995), *An Evaluation of Technical Assistance Provided to Mingo County Schools by the West Virginia Department of Education* (1995), and *School Governance and Administration Exchange: The Controversy Over Tennessee Value-Added Assessment System* (1995).

Bill Cowart is Professor Emeritus at Western Oregon State College and teaches part-time at the University of Texas at Pan American. With the exception of 11 years of professional work in Oregon, his professional experience has been in Texas. He earned a Ph.D. in history and philosophy of education from the University of Texas in 1963 before accepting a teaching position at what is now Texas A&M University at Kingsville. He served as director and then founding president of what is now Texas A&M International University before accepting an appointment as provost of Western Oregon State College. While serving as provost, he became involved in research on teacher effectiveness and has continued his association with the project following his retirement in 1995, after serving as interim president of the institution for 1 year.

Luvern L. Cunningham is Novice G. Fawcett Professor of Educational Administration (Emeritus) at Ohio State University and Lead Partner at Leadership Development Associates in Gahanna, Ohio. He has a long history of combining campus-based research with field-based problem solving across the country. He currently is a consultant to large urban districts, units of state government, universities, and foundations. Germane to this book is his work on designing an urban district student assessment and program evaluation monitoring system. He also has completed the conceptual infrastructure of accountability alliances within state and youth services and juvenile courts.

Linda Darling-Hammond is William F. Russell Professor in the Foundations of Education at Teachers College, Columbia University, where she also is Co-Director of the National Center for Restructuring Education, Schools, and Teaching and Executive Director of the National Commission on Teaching and America's Future. She is actively engaged in research, teaching, and policy work on issues of school restructuring, teacher education reform, and the enhancement of educational equity. She is author or editor of seven books and has authored more than 150 journal articles, book chapters, and monographs on issues of educational policy and practice.

Richard B. Darlington has been teaching in the Psychology Department at Cornell University since 1963. He received a B.A. from Swarthmore College and a Ph.D. from the University of Minnesota. His most recent book is *Regression and Linear Models*. Besides regression and general statistics, his interests and publications include work on the long-term effects of preschool programs, the evolution of brains and behavior, culture and fair testing, and racial differences in mental test scores. He is a fellow of the American Association for the Advancement of Science. A substantial amount of his unpublished work appears on his home page at http://psych.cornell.edu/darlington/index.htm.

Gerald Girod is Research Professor at the Teaching Research Division and recently retired dean of the School of Education at Western Oregon State College. He has long been engaged in research concerning attitude assessment and the evaluation of teacher education programs. He currently is engaged in policy and program development efforts at the preservice teacher preparation level, to meaningfully connect teacher work to student learning through applied performance assessment methodology.

Ronald K. Hambleton is Professor of Education and Psychology and Chairperson of the Research and Evaluation Methods Program at the University of Massachusetts at Amherst. He earned a Ph.D. with specialties in psychometric methods and statistics from the University of Toronto in 1969. In 1993, he received the National Council on Measurement in Education's Career Achievement Award for contributions to measurement theory and practice as well as leadership in the measurement field. He is the author of more than 400 research papers, reports, and reviews. He is active primarily in two areas of research: applications of item response theory models and educational assessment practices including test development, detection of item bias, score reporting, and standard setting.

Sandra P. Horn is an Educational Consultant to the University of Tennessee Value-Added Research and Assessment Center. She has 23 years experience as a library information specialist in the Knoxville City and Knox County schools. She is a member of the Tennessee State Board of Education's Advisory Council on Teacher Education and Certification and is past state chair of the Tennessee Teachers Study Council. She was a member of the founding board of the Consortium for Research on Educational Accountability and Teacher Evaluation and now serves on its board of directors. She received her Ed.D. from the University of Tennessee, Knoxville. She has coauthored a number of chapters, articles, and booklets on educational assessment and Tennessee Value-Added Assessment System methodology, and she has presented on these topics to local, state, and national groups interested in educational assessment.

Neal Kingston is Vice President of Advanced Systems in Measurement and Evaluation, Inc. He served as associate commissioner of curriculum, assessment, and accountability for the Kentucky Department of Education from 1993 to 1995. In 1983, he received his Ph.D. in psychological measurement and research design from Teachers College of Columbia University. He entered the field of measurement in 1978 after working as a middle and secondary science teacher. During his early career, he concentrated on research on equating and validation methods, applications of item response theory, and computerized testing. While at Educational Testing Service, he was actively involved with some of the first large-scale applications of item response theory and computerized adaptive testing. He eventually moved from his focus on research to work directly with clients to dramatically improve measurement practice.

Robert L. Mendro directs the Institutional Research unit of the Dallas Public Schools. He received his Ph.D. in educational research from the Laboratory of Educational Research at the University of Colorado in 1972. He has 24 years experience in school evaluation, applied measurement, statistical applications in educational research, and computer applications in statistics. His current research interests include identification of effective schools and teachers, teacher evaluation systems, and statistical models for estimating school and teacher effectiveness.

Jason Millman has been Professor of Educational Research Methodology at Cornell University since 1960. A nationally recognized expert on many facets of educational measurement and evaluation, he has written widely on teacher evaluation including editing two handbooks, the more recent of which is published by Corwin Press. He has been editor of the *Educational Researcher* and the *Journal of Educational Measurement,* was elected five times to national offices of professional associations, has advised well over 100 government and private agencies, and in 1996 was given the National Council of Measurement in Education's Career Award for his contributions to educational measurement, particularly in the areas of criterion-referenced measurement, test development methods and procedures, and teacher evaluation.

David Myton has been Executive Secretary of the Oregon Teacher Standards and Practices Commission since 1989. Prior to that, he served as its coordinator of teacher education. He was instrumental in the development of the state's licensing system, which requires documentation of subject matter competence and teaching effectiveness.

Timothy Orsak is Evaluation Specialist with the Dallas Public Schools, where he works on statistical research, evaluation, and computing. He received his master's degree in statistics and bachelor's degree in mathematics from Texas Tech University. He will be pursuing a Ph.D. at the University of Texas at Dallas. His current interests involve hierarchical linear models.

Susan J. Paik is a doctoral student in Educational Psychology and Program Coordinator of Early Outreach at the University of Illinois at Chicago, where she coordinates academic enrichment and career and postsecondary education awareness for 7th- and 8th-grade minority and underserved students. She provides educational workshops for these students and speaks on motivation in about 50 Chicago public and private schools. Independent of her university work, she founded a project that provides workshops for inner-city youths to improve their life chances. Interested in educational evaluation and international program development, she has worked in elemosynary projects in China, Honduras, Hong Kong, Korea, and Macau. In psychology, she is interested in cross-cultural studies and how family dynamics affects learning and development.

Roger Pankratz is Executive Director of the Kentucky Institute for Education Research, an independent, nonpartisan agency created by executive order of the state's governor to evaluate the impact of the Kentucky Education Reform Act of 1990 on students, schools, educators and communities. He also is Professor of Teacher Education at Western Kentucky University, where he served as Assistant and Associate Dean in the College of Education and Behavioral Sciences from 1974 to 1993. From 1989 to 1991, he was executive director of Kentucky's Council on School Performance Standards, which developed the state's learning goals and academic expectations and first recommended that Kentucky adopt a system of performance assessment for students. He holds a Ph.D. in education from Ohio State University.

W. James Popham is Professor Emeritus in the Graduate School of Education at the University of California, Los Angeles, and Director of IOX Assessment Associates, a research and development group. His earliest publications, in the late 1950s, dealt with the appraisal of teacher competence and the evaluation of instructional interventions. For most of his career, he has dealt with assessment and evaluation issues. Much of his research and writing has centered on the use of student learning as an indicator of instructional effectiveness.

Doris Redfield is Chief of Assessment and Reporting with the Virginia Department of Education, where she directs the commonwealth's student testing programs and the annual reporting of trend data on how well students, schools, school districts, and the state are achieving relative to academic standards and indicators of school success. Her previous experience includes that of classroom teacher, school psychologist, university professor, senior research associate with the U.S. Department of Education's Office of Educational Research and Improvement, and visiting professor and project director at the UCLA CRESST (National Center for Research on Evaluation, Standards, and Student Testing). Her Ph.D. is in educational psychology, her M.Ed. is in school psychology, and her bachelor's degree is in music.

Kip Reel is Director of Business for Maury County Public Schools in Columbia, Tennessee. His background includes classroom teaching as well as administration and supervision in rural public schools. He had primary responsibility for organizing the Division of Accountability in the Tennessee Department of Education and served as deputy commissioner of education for the state of Tennessee. His academic background includes a B.S. from the University of Tennessee and an M.Ed. from Tennessee State University.

Ed Reidy is Deputy Commissioner for the Bureau of Learning Results Services of the Kentucky Department of Education. His professional interests include curriculum and professional development "learning-driven" assessment, program and policy evaluation, and organizational development. After doing his undergraduate work in liberal arts, he obtained a doctorate in educational research, measurement, and evaluation from Boston College in 1978. Prior to coming to Kentucky, he was the director of instruction for the West Hartford Public Schools in Connecticut. He came to Kentucky in 1991 as Associate Commissioner for curriculum, assessment, and accountability.

William L. Sanders is Professor and Director of the University of Tennessee Value-Added Research and Assessment Center. He has been a statistical consultant for more than 25 years to researchers in the social, biological, agricultural, and engineering sciences. His primary areas of interest are experimental design and analysis of data from a general linear mixed-model point of view. He was an early contributor to the development of SAS, the most widely used statistical software system in the world. Recently, he has been an adviser to the developers of PROC MIXED, a new mixed-model procedure now available within the SAS system. Over the past 10 years, he and his colleagues have completed research demonstrating that educational effects can be measured fairly, reliably, and objectively from student achievement data by using statistical mixed-model techniques.

Arnold M. Saxton teaches statistics, provides statistical support for faculty and graduate student research, and is directly involved in several research projects on topics such as genetic selection technologies at the University of Tennessee, where he also has been a major contributor to the development of the mixed-model software used in the Tennessee Value-Added Assessment System. After receiving a Ph.D. with emphases in statistics and quantitative genetics from North Carolina State University in 1983, he was a faculty member in the Department of Experimental Statistics at Louisiana State University. There, interests in statistical computing and quantitative genetics led to codevelopment of GLMM, a mixed-model program for personal computers. He moved to the University of Tennessee in 1992.

H. Del Schalock is Research Professor at the Teaching Research Division at Western Oregon State College. He has been actively engaged in educational research, development, and improvement in Oregon for more than 30 years. His current professional interests span teacher preparation and licensure for standards-based schools, the redesign of student and teacher work in standards-based schools, and grounded theories of teacher effectiveness, as well as theories of teaching and learning generally, within the context of standards-based schools.

Mark Schalock is Assistant Research Professor at the Teaching Research Division at Western Oregon State College. He has been involved in educational research, development, and evaluation activities at the local, state, and national levels for the past 14 years. His previous work has focused on both individual and institutional improvement and accountability based on measures of impact. He currently codirects a project that aims to meaningfully connect teacher work to student learning through applied performance assessment methodology.

Daniel L. Stufflebeam is Director of the Evaluation Center and Professor of Education at Western Michigan University. He chaired the national Joint Committee on Standards for Educational Evaluation, which issued professional standards for program evaluation and personnel evaluation, and headed the federally funded national Center for Research on Educational Accountability and Teacher Evaluation. He has authored or coauthored 12 books and about 100 journal articles and book chapters on evaluation theory, methodology, and standards as well as on testing. He is coeditor of the Kluwer Academic Press book series "Evaluation in Education and Human Services," is Associate Editor of the international journal *Studies in Educational Evaluation,* and serves on the editorial boards of several other journals. He is included in *Who's Who in America.*

Gary Sykes is Professor in the Departments of Educational Administration and of Teacher Education in the College of Education at Michigan State University, where he specializes in educational policymaking with particular emphases on professionalism, teacher education and development, and educational standards.

Yeow Meng Thum is Director of Analysis for the Consortium on Chicago School Research. He received a B.A. from Columbia University and a doctorate from the Committee on Research Methodology and Quantitative Psychology at the University of Chicago. His research focuses on multivariate, multilevel models of educational and psychological change and growth. Together with Anthony Bryk, he currently is analyzing longitudinal student achievement data from the Chicago Public Schools system. He formerly was a statistical consultant on behavioral and educational issues.

Herbert J. Walberg is Research Professor of Education at the University of Illinois at Chicago. He served as chairman of the technical committee on international education indicators for the Organization for Economic Cooperation and Development. He completed a term as founding member of the National Assessment Governing Board, whose mission is to set subject matter standards for American students. Formerly an assistant professor at Harvard University, he has written and edited more than 50 books and has contributed more than 380 articles to educational and psychological research journals on topics such as educational effectiveness and productivity, school reform, and exceptional human accomplishments.

William J. Webster heads the Research, Planning, and Evaluation Division of the Dallas Public Schools, a position he has held for 26 years. He received an M.A. from the University of Michigan and a Ph.D. from Michigan State University. His academic specialization includes measurement research design and applied statistics. His research interests are varied and include research on statistical models for identifying effective schools, principals, and teachers as well as models for evaluating educational programs. He has authored more than 50 professional journal articles, mostly in the areas of evaluation and applied statistics.

Dash Weerasinghe is Evaluation Specialist with the Dallas Public Schools, where he works on statistical research and computing. He has a bachelor's degree in engineering and a master's degree in computational mathematics, and he currently is writing his doctoral dissertation in mathmatical statistics at Texas Tech University. After receiving his master's degree, he taught as a college-level instructor for 5 years. His research interests are statistical modeling of instructional effects, biostatistics, and stochastic analysis.

PART I

Origins and Underpinnings

CHAPTER 1

Beginnings
and Introduction

JASON MILLMAN

H. DEL SCHALOCK

In a wide-ranging and extensive historical review of teacher and school evaluation, Shinkfield and Stufflebeam (1995) claim that "there is no topic on which opinion varies so markedly as that of the validity of basing teacher effectiveness on student learning" (pp. 1-15). The disagreement is not whether student learning is an important goal of teaching. Student learning is. Rather, the split is over how best, in high-stakes contexts, to evaluate how well teachers and schools accomplish this task. Usually parents and legislators support the use of gains in student achievement as the criterion of student learning. The vast majority of educational professionals favor measures of teacher knowledge and skills as preferred criteria of the likelihood that student learning is taking place.

Dead and Buried

Until the second half of this century, teacher evaluation was sporadic and informal (Shinkfield & Stufflebeam, 1995). Efforts to use student learning as the basis for teacher or school effectiveness were not well received. For example, in England in the late Victorian era, the British government introduced a payment-by-results system that corrupted the educational program and outraged the public (Travers, 1981). As a second example, during the early 1900s there was a strong movement to apply industrial techniques and concepts of business efficiency to education and to measure the success that was expected to follow these applications with achievement test results. The movement never gained momentum.

Dying

Efforts in the United States during the past 50 years to connect pupil learning meaningfully to teacher work have followed many paths. Most of these have been pursued by researchers concerned with teacher or school effects. Others, however, have been pursued by practitioners or policymakers concerned with enhancing the productivity of teachers and schools. An overview of five major efforts that have focused on one or the other of these goals is provided in Table 1.1.

Although anchored to pupil learning, none of these efforts has made a dramatic difference in the effectiveness of schools, and all have helped shape a legacy that has led both researchers and practitioners to doubt whether school-based learning can ever be connected meaningfully to the work of teachers. It should come as no surprise that teachers are skeptical, and often openly hostile, to the use of externally developed measures to determine their effectiveness as professionals in high-stakes contexts. Although feedback about learning gains can be helpful in teachers' efforts to improve instruction (the formative evaluation use [Millman, 1981]), the use of learning gains can be indefensible in the efforts of administrators, legislators, and the public to hold teachers and schools accountable (the summative evaluation use [Glass, 1990]). Psychometric reasons for the extremely negative view of high-stakes uses of learning gains are well presented by Berk (1988) and Haertel (1986). Briefly, the context in which the teaching takes place is assessed too inadequately, and teachers' effectiveness is measured too unreliably for a fair evaluation to take place.

In addition to being suspect for methodological reasons, previous attempts to connect student learning to teacher efforts carried with them features of schooling that are inconsistent with many of the current initiatives teachers are encountering. Increasingly, teachers working in today's schools view textbooks as resources for learning rather than as definers of what is to be learned; include reasoning, problem solving, and other forms of knowledge and skill acquisition as important student outcomes; emphasize "authentic" means of assessment whenever possible; and view curriculum, instruction, and assessment as interdependent components of effective teaching.

Alive and Kicking

Four contemporary approaches to using learning gains to evaluate teachers or schools are the Teacher Work Sample Methodology as used at Western Oregon State College (see Part II of this book), the Dallas Value-Added Accountability System (Part III), the Tennessee Value-Added Assessment System (Part IV), and the Kentucky Instructional Results Improvement System (Part V). Collectively, they focus on addressing major weaknesses of their predecessors, namely insufficient attention to context (e.g., factors not under a teacher's control) (Oregon, Dallas), unreliability of the measurement of teacher or school effectiveness (Tennessee), and measures of student achievement educationally compatible with contemporary views of schooling (Oregon, Kentucky).

Each of Parts II-V of this book opens with a brief accounting of the birth of the system, typically written from the perspective of a stakeholder. Individuals (called "warriors" here) closely involved with developing and implementing the system describe it not as it was initially conceived but rather as it has been refined over its history. Two outside reviewers evaluate the system from a technical and a comprehensive (e.g., educational, political) perspective, respectively. A rejoinder from each group of warriors concludes each section. Part VI offers some generalizations about the evaluation approaches and presents different perspectives on the viability and validity of making teachers and schools accountable by assessing their students' achievements.

Are the warriors in search of the Holy Grail doomed to the fate that usually awaits those on such expeditions? Or are these valiant efforts not perfect but still fairer and more valid than alternative approaches of ensuring accountability?

TABLE 1.1 Efforts to Link Learning Gains to Teacher and School Effectiveness

Focus of the Effort	Purpose	Dominant Methodology/Design	Accomplishments	Unintended Consequences
Research on *teacher* effects, particularly "process/product" research	Identify teacher characteristics, behaviors, or patterns of behavior consistently associated with large gains in student learning	Correlate teacher characteristics and behaviors with learning gains	With few exceptions, no meaningful correlations consistently found, laying to rest the idea of one best way to teach	Gave credence to the idea that student performance on *district-administered* standardized achievement tests taken at the end of a school year can be looked to as defensible measures of a teacher's effectiveness and, in so doing, helped galvanize teachers' criticism of such measures
Research on "school" effects	Identify school characteristics or conditions consistently associated with large gains in student learning	Identify conditions that discriminate schools that consistently demonstrate large learning gains from schools that do not	Identified conditions that discriminate schools that do consistently demonstrate large learning gains from schools that do not, although these conditions vary to some extent for elementary, middle, and high schools	Gave credence to the idea that improving a school as a place for learning was a reasonably straight-forward task and that it could be done by attending to factors other than the competence of teachers

Teacher evaluation for merit pay or career ladder advancement	Enhance the professionalization of teaching and reward outstanding teaching	State- or district-designed merit pay or career ladder systems, some of which have required teachers to provide evidence of success in fostering student learning but often leaving the specifics of how this is to be done to individual schools or teachers	With few exceptions, efforts to incorporate data on student learning into merit pay or career ladder systems have either failed outright or treated learning data in ways that have minimized its utility	Added to teacher skepticism and growing criticism of attempts to link learning gains to teacher work
School evaluation for accountability and organizational control	Enhance the productivity of schools by focusing teacher and administrator attention on student learning	Usually state-designed accountability systems that connect mandated curriculum and assessment components with district or school reporting requirements showing student progress toward goal attainment; accompanying financial rewards and sanctions sometimes are included	Too soon to tell; most components of these systems are still being developed or are in the early stages of implementation	Added to teacher skepticism and growing criticism of attempts to link learning gains to teacher work
Teacher and school evaluation as a central feature of performance contracting	Enhance the productivity of schools by linking private-sector contractor pay to student learning	Private sector-designed accountability systems of the kinds described above and implemented on a pay-for-results basis	Bombed; no single contractor has been able to produce outstanding results under controlled conditions	Added to teacher skepticism and growing criticism of attempts to link learning gains to teacher work

NOTE: Millman and Sykes (1992) offer details on some of the efforts shown in the table. Not included are evaluations that focus on programs (e.g., Head Start) rather than on teachers or schools.

References

Berk, R. A. (1988). Fifty reasons why student achievement gain does not mean teacher effectiveness. *Journal of Personnel Evaluation in Education, 1*, 345-363.

Glass, G. V. (1990). Using student test scores to evaluate teachers. In J. Millman & L. Darling-Hammond (Eds.), *The new handbook of teacher evaluation* (pp. 229-240). Newbury Park, CA: Sage.

Haertel, E. (1986). The valid use of student achievement measures for teacher evaluation. *Educational Evaluation and Policy Analysis, 8*(1), 45-60.

Millman, J. (1981). Student achievement as a measure of teacher competence. In J. Millman (Ed.), *Handbook of teacher evaluation* (pp. 146-166). Beverly Hills, CA: Sage.

Millman, J., & Sykes, G. (1992). *The assessment of teaching based on evidence of student learning: An analysis* (Research Monograph No. 2). Washington, DC: National Board for Professional Teaching Standards.

Shinkfield, A. J., & Stufflebeam, D. L. (1995). *Teacher evaluation: Guide to effective practice.* Kalamazoo, MI: Center for Research on Educational Accountability and Teacher Evaluation.

Travers, R. M. W. (1981). Criteria of good teaching. In J. Millman (Ed.), *Handbook of teacher evaluation* (pp. 14-22). Beverly Hills, CA: Sage.

PART II

The Oregon Teacher Work Sample Methodology

The Oregon Teacher Work Sample Methodology

Rationale and Background

BILL COWART

DAVID MYTON

Student learning is the stated objective of schooling. Historically, the only people who argued differently were those who believed that public education could never accomplish a great deal more than provide a sophisticated child care supervision service. These people have been joined more recently by those who are convinced that the disintegration of the American family will soon force the modification of the mission of public education from one primarily concerned with the cognitive development of the child into an agency that becomes the focal point for the delivery of a multitude of social services. Although some effort would be continued toward the development of the child intellectually, it would cease to be the primary focus of schooling.

As funding becomes more limited and the competition for tax dollars increases, it will become increasingly important for the American public to clarify the objectives for public education. Student learning is the only defensible objective for the public schools in their current configuration. Boards of education, since their inception, have identified the teacher as their principal agent to design, deliver, and evaluate student learning. The development of a specific connection between these two critical elements in the educational process is essential to address the current demands for increased accountability and to renew the public's confidence in its educational system.

Several developments in the state of Oregon within the past 7 years illustrate this premise. "We decided that education is too important to leave to educators, so we passed the Mentor Teacher Act," stated Vera Katz, speaker of the Oregon House of Representatives. She was speaking to 250 teachers assembled at Western Oregon State College who were training to be mentors for the 1988-1989 crop of novice teachers. Before she left the legislature to become mayor of Portland, Katz also pushed through the state's controversial Education Act for the 21st Century during the 1991 legislative session. Katz's success in reformation of public education was due, in part, to support from colleagues in the Democratic party such as Senate President John Kitzhaber, now governor, and Phil Keisling, now secretary of state. However, in 1995, the legislature conducted a major review of the Education Act for the 21st Century in both houses of the legislature, which are now controlled by Republicans. Although numerous changes were made that make implementation of certain provisions of the bill permissive rather than mandatory, the major components remain intact.

By 1987, the Oregon Board of Higher Education directed the State System of Higher Education's six schools and colleges of education to discontinue undergraduate teacher education programs within 4 years. The Teacher Standards and Practices Commission (TSPC) agreed to establish new standards for approval of teacher education programs to measure teacher candidate performance rather than the number of courses a teacher had completed.

The TSPC had instituted the California Basic Educational Skills Test 3 years earlier amid fierce criticisms from college faculty, minority groups, teachers, and others opposed to standardized testing. The decision in 1988 to substitute tests of subject matter and professional knowledge for prescribed courses in these fields came easily by comparison. Because 5th-year preservice programs were being designed for cohorts of teachers, extension of student teaching to 15 full-time weeks was accepted by colleges and school districts. The Mentor Teacher Program, although intended for 1st-year teachers, positively impacted the quality of school district supervision of student teachers as well.

In retrospect, the most powerful element in the reform formula was adopted with the least fanfare: the Teacher Work Sample Methodology (TWSM). Work samples are 2- to 5-week units of study drawn from the classroom curriculum. The student teacher assesses the pupils' knowledge and skills and plans a series of lessons to increase pupil achievement. After teaching the unit, the student teacher evaluates learning gains, prepares an interpretive essay on the degree to which objectives were met, and proposes subsequent steps in the instructional sequence. Both the college supervisor and the district's cooperating teacher must sign off that the student teaching experience has been successful for the candidate to be recommended for state licensure.

It is coincidental, but important, that a team of individuals with a common research interest in teacher effectiveness emerged at Western Oregon slightly before the reform movement gathered full momentum. The initial motivation of the group was to develop criteria and procedures that could be used to predict effective performance in teacher education candidates in a preservice program. TWSM became a major component of this research effort, and the procedures developed for the collection and use of data such as these for programmatic decisions within the teacher education program at Western Oregon have provided important support for the overall state reform agenda.

The significance of TWSM increased as the state's Education Act for the 21st Century was hammered out in 1991. In 21st-century schools, children will begin schooling at an earlier age and will be served in multiaged classrooms enriched by social and community services. Middle-level students will attend integrated courses that parallel career opportunities and include field-centered learning experiences. High school students will specialize in one of several occupational strands: arts and communications, business and management, health services, human resources, industrial and engineering systems, or natural resources systems.

The Education Act for the 21st Century also sets higher standards of performance for each school. Site councils, composed mainly of teachers and parents, will monitor learning gains and will be empowered to adapt programs and curricula to local needs. Statewide testing of pupils and reporting of results will assist site committees to gauge their success. Ultimately, the teachers' abilities—individually and collectively—to assess learning gains will spell the success or failure of these bold reforms of elementary and secondary education.

The fact that professional educators have always "assumed" that an effective teacher can foster learning in his or her students is not the question. This question arises from their failure to include this as an essential criterion of effective teaching. The failure to do so is related more to the difficulty that both the practicing profession and the research community have encountered in documenting learning and assessing responsibility than it is to a serious disagreement over whether effective teaching should be related to student learning. Basically, the problem revolves around the inability to account for all of the variables that affect learning and the resulting fear of doing disservice to both teacher and student that has restricted progress. So schools have continued to offer curricula and teachers have continued to teach without establishing an appropriate defensible relationship between student learning gains and the performance of a teacher, the principal agent responsible for designing, delivering, and evaluating instruction. When the public reverted to the use of student performance on nationally standardized tests as a criterion of teacher and school success, the profession was unable to respond. The result has been a general indictment of the American school system.

The establishment of a responsible link between teacher performance and student learning is essential to effective schooling. It is the next major step in the professionalization of teaching and awaits only the initiative, the courage, and the commitment of the profession to ensure its appropriate design, development, and implementation. Furthermore, only through a proactive agenda of this magnitude can the profession hope to regain the preeminent role that it once held in the eyes of the American people.

CHAPTER 3

Teacher Work Sample Methodology as Used at Western Oregon State College

H. DEL SCHALOCK

MARK SCHALOCK

GERALD GIROD

This chapter describes Western Oregon State College's approach to Teacher Work Sample Methodology (TWSM), how it works, the rationale underlying it, and the kinds of applications it has had thus far. We also delineate how TWSM differs from other strategies pursued for linking student learning to teacher work and present illustrative evidence in support of its merit. As further background to our particular design for TWSM and the conceptual/theoretical underpinnings on which it rests, we add briefly to the description provided in Chapter 1 by Millman and Schalock of past efforts to link student progress in learning to teacher work.

AUTHORS' NOTE: The Oregon Teacher Standards and Practices Commission has adopted work sample methodology as a means of documenting a beginning teacher's ability to manage instruction within the context of a standards-based approach to schooling and within this context document pupil progress in learning. Western Oregon State College played a central role in developing the methodology prior to its adoption by the Commission in 1988 as a vehicle for teacher preparation and licensure, and it has refined and extended the methodology since that time through an ongoing program of research on teacher effectiveness. The description of the methodology here pertains to its current use at Western Oregon.

More on Forerunners, Traces, and Paradigm Shifts

Two features of the various research and development efforts described by Millman and Schalock have combined to limit their contribution to school improvement and feed the suspicion of skeptics about the defensibility of linking the learning of students to the work of teachers. One is the heavy reliance on standardized tests of achievement to measure student progress in learning, even though the limitations of these measures as defensible indicators of school-based learning have been known for decades.[1] A second is that most such efforts have failed to take into account the *conditions* under which teaching and learning occur—and often the characteristics of students being taught—leaving these critically important determinants of learning to be "controlled" through elaborate statistical procedures that have little or no meaning to most who read them.

These conditions combine to make such measures of student progress in learning largely immune to individual teacher effects. They also make such measures so distant and "decontextualized" from the conditions of teaching and learning that they have little meaning or value to a teacher or to a teacher's students and their parents. Under these conditions, it should come as no surprise that teachers are skeptical, and often openly hostile, to the use of externally developed measures to determine their effectiveness as professionals.

As new state assessment systems come on-line, these circumstances may change, but great damage already has been done. Both researchers and practitioners now hold the view—and with good reason given the nature of the data typically collected on student progress in learning—that attempting to connect learning gains to the work of individual teachers is indefensible.

Western Oregon's use of TWSM is designed to overcome the limitations in data and design that have led to this conclusion. First, TWSM procedures used to assess pupil progress in learning are linked specifically to the learning outcome or outcomes a teacher is attempting to accomplish. Second, the measures used are criterion referenced rather than norm referenced. Third, pre- to postinstructional gain scores are calculated on a student-by-student basis, with separate analyses required for initially high- and low-scoring pupils. Fourth, descriptors of classroom, school, and community context variables accompany all measures of learning gain. Through a combination of these means, TWSM becomes a "close-to-a-teacher's work" methodology that reflects the realities of a teacher's work with meaningful indicators of its consequences (Chapter 22).

Although TWSM carries limitations from the perspective of traditional psychometric theory, we believe that these are offset by the potential it carries for overcoming the kinds of problems that have plagued this area of inquiry in the past.

In addition to being suspect for methodological reasons, previous attempts to connect student learning to teacher work carried with them features of schooling that are inconsistent with many of the current emphases teachers are encountering in "restructured" schools. These features included teaching and learning dominated by textbooks; learning outcomes centering on factual knowledge or basic skills; pupil learning assessed through multiple-choice, true-false, or other short-answer paper-and-pencil tests; and performance on teacher-administered examinations used primarily for purposes of grading rather than of evaluating instruction or the improvement of learning. Increasingly, teachers working in today's schools view textbooks as resources for learning rather than as definers of what is to be learned; outcomes of importance for students include reasoning, problem solving, and other forms of knowledge and skill *application* as well as their acquisition; "authentic" means of assessment are emphasized whenever possible and appropriate and are merged with more traditional approaches to assessment in portfolios of student work; and curriculum, instruction, and assessment are viewed as *interdependent and aligned* components of effective teaching rather than as components to be thought about separately and often independently.

TWSM, as used at Western Oregon, is designed to accommodate these features of school restructuring and thereby add to its sense of appropriateness and meaningfulness to teachers working in today's schools. It also is a methodology designed to serve training and research functions as well as evaluation and licensure functions.

Western Oregon's Design for
Teacher Work Sample Methodology

In the parlance of the day, TWSM is a complex, "authentic" applied performance approach to assessment that can be tailored to fit the particular learning goals and styles of a teacher working with a particular group of students in a particular classroom, school, and community context. It is a methodology that is anchored in an "outcome-based and context-dependent" theory of teacher effectiveness[2] and is consistent with Oregon's design for 21st-century schools.[3] It also carries with it the aim of *improving instruction and learning* that is common to the alternative assessment movement (Chapter 10) (Gearhart & Herman, 1995; Gitomer, 1993; Herman, Aschbacher, & Winters, 1992; Wiggins, 1988, 1989, 1992, 1993; Wolf, 1993; Wolf, Bixby, Glenn, & Gardner, 1991).

An Overview of the Methodology

TWSM has been developed as both a vehicle for teaching and an approach to measurement. As a vehicle for teaching, it is intended to give prospective teachers experience in designating learning outcomes to be accomplished through a 3- to 5-week unit of instruction; developing plans for instruction and assessment that are *aligned* with the outcomes desired; and then collecting, interpreting, and reflecting on evidence of student progress toward outcome attainment. When used in this way, TWSM is designed to force teachers to think about the following issues and bring them into alignment:

- What are the learning outcomes I want *my* students to accomplish?
- What activities and instructional methodologies are appropriate or necessary for *these* students to achieve *these* outcomes?
- What resources and how much time do I need to implement these activities or methodologies?
- What assessment activities or methodologies are appropriate for these students and these outcomes when using these instructional methodologies?
- How successful was I at helping my students achieve the outcomes desired?
- What went right? What went wrong? Why?

As an approach to measurement, TWSM has been designed to portray the learning progress of pupils *on outcomes desired by a teacher and taught by a teacher* over a sufficiently long period of time for appreciable progress in learning to occur. It also has been designed to let teachers accompany the information they provide about student progress in learning with information about the *context* in which teaching and learning occur and to interpret information about learning in light of information about context. In this contextually grounded portrayal of teaching, measures of student progress in learning tend to be viewed by teachers as meaningful and a reasonable indicator of their effectiveness.

Steps Involved in the Methodology

Regardless of the stage in professional development, and irrespective of the use to be made of work sample information, there are eight distinct steps in Western Oregon's teacher work sample design. These combine to define the essential features of a standards-based approach to teaching. *They also reflect a significant change in the design of a teacher's work.* These steps are described briefly in Table 3.1.

Measures Derived From the Methodology

Each of the steps involved in the work sample process yields products or performance amenable to evaluation. Variables such as time and subject areas sampled, outcomes to be accomplished, descriptions of a teaching and learning context, and descriptions of instruction and assessment plans provide logical and easily accessible foci for evaluation. TWSM provides a rich and ready context for the evaluation of a teacher's knowledge and skill as well as a one-of-a-kind context for evaluating a teacher's effectiveness and/or productivity.[4]

Western Oregon's educational faculty derive seven broad categories of measures from these various steps, all of which are used for purposes of teacher preparation and licensure decisions as well as research:

- the complexity of the learning outcome(s) to be accomplished and the quality or appropriateness of measures used to assess outcome attainment;
- the characteristics of the context in which teaching and learning occur, including the preinstructional knowledge and skills possessed by pupils relative to the outcome or outcomes to be accomplished;

TABLE 3.1 Steps in a Teacher's Preparation of a Work Sample

Steps	*Notes on Related Tasks and Design Decisions*
1. Defining the sample of teaching and learning to be described	This is crucial to all that follows. It requires a decision on what unit of time (1 week? 1 month? 1 term?) and what portion of the curriculum are to be sampled. Guiding principle: Make the sample of time and curriculum large enough to provide a meaningful picture of one's work but not so large as to be overwhelming or difficult to understand by others.
2. Identifying learning outcomes to be accomplished within the work to be sampled	This listing of outcomes desired defines the focus of all that follows and determines in large part how difficult it will be for a work sample to be carried out successfully. Because of the interdependence between outcome complexity and work sample demand, Western Oregon has developed a *taxonomy* of outcome complexity that student teachers use in designing their various work samples.[a]
3. Aligning instruction and assessment with outcomes to be accomplished.	This step involves the creation of an instructional plan that will lead to outcome attainment by *all* of one's pupils and an assessment plan that will allow the continuous monitoring of progress each pupil is making toward the outcomes desired. Both instruction and assessment need to be consistent with each of the outcomes pursued, and both need to be sufficiently flexible to allow adaptation to the wide range of learners and uneven progress in learning that characterize classrooms.
4. Describing the context in which teaching and learning are to occur.	This is an essential and unique feature of Western Oregon's approach to teacher work sample methodology. Currently, Western Oregon's methodology provides four levels of context description: classroom, school, community, and the prior-to-instruction status of pupils with respect to outcomes desired.
5. Adapting outcomes desired, and related plans for instruction and assessment, to accommodate the demands of context	Formally assembling information about one's teaching and learning context prior to instruction nearly always leads to some level of adaptation in either the outcomes desired through instruction or the instruction/assessment plan leading to them.

Steps	Notes on Related Tasks and Design Decisions
6. Implementing a developmentally and contextually appropriate instructional plan	Once adaptations to context demands have been made, a teacher preparing a work sample needs to carry out his or her instructional plan as amended. Further adaptations in the amended plan will be needed as instruction and learning progress, but in most cases these will not be major.
7. Assessing the accomplishments of learners and calculating gain scores	This step in the work sample process centers on the formal (summative) evaluation of pupil learning at or near the completion of a unit/semester of instruction and the calculation, on a pupil-by-pupil basis, of the learning gains made between pre- and postinstructional measures. A measure of the competence demonstrated by a teacher in monitoring/assessing the progress of his or her students *as they progress through a unit or semester of study* (formative evaluation) is provided through the observation/evaluation of on-line teacher performance as outlined in Step 6.
8. Summarizing, interpreting, and reflecting on assessment information	Following the completion of Step 7, individual pupil gain scores are summarized in table form and interpreted on accompanying pages in a way that (a) helps parents, pupils, and colleagues understand the information presented and its implications for both a teacher and his or her pupils and (b) offers insight into why the progress made by pupils in their learning—or the lack thereof—appears as it does.

a. We have found in our work with TWSM at Western Oregon that Bloom's and Krathwohl's widely used taxonomies are inadequate to the demands of work sample methodology on two counts. First, not all levels in these taxonomies are clearly and easily amenable to classroom assessment. Second, the outcomes specified are not fully in keeping with those now being demanded of 21st-century schools. To meet these demands, we have created a taxonomy that combines the strength of the Bloom and Krathwohl designs but goes beyond them. It involves a 4×4 matrix, with categories on the vertical axis identifying *types* of outcomes (foundational knowledge, procedural knowledge, conceptual knowledge, personal and interpersonal behaviors/attitudes) and categories on the horizontal axis identifying the *levels of cognitive demand involved in a particular outcome* (awareness/recognition, comprehension/understanding, application/problem solving, reflection/evaluation/reformulation). Measurement methodologies suitable for use in classrooms have been paired with each cell in the matrix to help teachers bring to their work sample a proper alignment between assessment procedure used and learning outcome desired.

- the quality and appropriateness of the instructional plan that is to lead to outcome attainment;
- the quality or appropriateness of the manner in which the instructional plan is implemented, including creating and maintaining a classroom that is conducive to learning; engaging pupils productively in planned learning activities; and evaluating, acting on, and reporting pupil progress in learning;
- the timeliness and appropriateness of a teacher's "in-flight" decision making while implementing an instructional plan;
- evidence of success in fostering pupil progress in learning; and
- valued aspects of professionalism demonstrated during the course of a work sample.

A total of 23 "construct-defined" measures come from these broad categories of inquiry, with many constructs carrying submeasures. These are listed in Table 3.2 and are described briefly, including subscales where appropriate, in the Appendix.[5]

Evaluating Work Sample Performance

Although TWSM provides a rich context for evaluating a teacher's knowledge, skill, and effectiveness, *it carries no specifics about evaluative procedures or performance standards*. This is the case for *all* of the measures derived through the methodology. Evaluative criteria and performance standards have to be provided by those who choose to use TWSM as a data source. Because of the emphasis Western Oregon has given to pupil learning in its use of the methodology, however, and the theory-anchored view that progress in learning always is context dependent, a reasonably detailed description is provided in the next few paragraphs of how we deal with the twin issues of evaluative criteria and performance standards.

Calculating Learning Gains by Pupils Taught

Starting with preinstructional data on pupil learning, a student teacher calculates a "percentage correct" score for each pupil in his or her classroom. Using these scores, the teacher then (a) tabulates, from highest- to lowest-scoring pupil, the range of preinstructional scores; (b) sorts these scores into high-, low-, and middle-scoring groups; and (c) calculates the mean scores for each of the groups

TABLE 3.2 The 23 Construct-Defined Measures That Western
Oregon Faculty Derive From Applying Teacher Work
Sample Methodology to the Initial Preparation and
Licensure of Teachers

Construct	*Measures*[a]
Complexity of outcomes pursued and quality of measures used to assess outcome attainment	1. **Complexity of learning outcomes to be accomplished by pupils**[b] 2. **Quality of measures used by a student teacher to assess pupil learning**
Characteristics of the context in which teaching and learning occur	3. **Characteristics of the classroom** 4. **Characteristics of the school** 5. **Characteristics of the community served by a school** 6. **Preinstructional knowledge and skill possessed by pupils relative to learning outcomes to be accomplished**
Teacher compe-tence in planning instruction that leads to progress in pupil learning	7. *Clarity and appropriateness of learning outcomes to be accomplished and of the measurement strategies to be used in assessing outcome attainment* 8. *Aligning instructional methods, learning activities, and time for learning with outcomes to be accomplished and measures of outcome attainment* 9. *Adapting all the above to accommodate the demands of one's teaching context, as articulated in Measures 3-6*
Teacher compe-tence in imple-menting a standards-based instructional plan	10. **Establishing a classroom conducive to learning** 11. ENGAGING PUPILS IN PLANNED LEARNING ACTIVITIES 12. *Evaluating, acting on, and reporting pupil progress in learning* 13. *Mastery of content and of strategies for helping students master content reflected in all the above*

(continued)

TABLE 3.2 Continued

Construct	Measures[a]
The quality of a teacher's "in-flight" decision making when implementing an instructional plan	14. TIMELINESS AND APPROPRIATENESS OF CLASSROOM DECISIONS 15. CONCEPTUAL AND SITUATIONAL "GROUNDING" OF CLASSROOM DECISIONS
Providing and interpreting evidence of success in fostering pupil progress in learning	16. **Postinstructional status of pupils with respect to outcomes to be accomplished** 17. **The percentage of pupils in one's class who demonstrate appreciable progress in learning** 18. **The learning progress made by special groups of pupils, including low- and high-scoring pupils on preinstructional measures** 19. *The analysis, interpretation, and reflection on learning gains—or lack thereof—reported in Items 17 and 18*
Exhibiting valued aspects of professionalism as an accompaniment to work sample preparation	20. *Sensitivity to school policies and practices* 21. *Personal mannerisms and interpersonal relationships* 22. *General professional demeanor* 23. *Potential for leadership*

a. Many construct-defined measures are made up of or contain submeasures. These are described in the Appendix.

b. Measures listed in bold type are measures currently in use. Those listed in italicized type are existing measures currently in the process of refinement. Those listed in all capital letters are new measures currently being developed.

formed and for the class as a whole. These preinstructional groupings provide the structure for both the analysis of postinstructional measures of outcome attainment and the calculation of gain scores.

As in the case of preinstructional measures, a percentage-correct score is calculated for each pupil on the postinstructional measure and is matched with the pupil's preinstructional score. Gain scores are then tabulated for the high-, low-, and middle-scoring groups based on the preinstructional measure. Mean gain scores also are tabulated for each of these groups and for the class as a whole to obtain a general impression of the learning gains that have been made by particular groups of pupils as a consequence of instruction received.

Using these data as a point of departure, the teacher can then proceed to refine them to bring a *level of standardization* to the teacher-designed and curriculum-aligned measures of pupil learning used. This is done by calculating an Index of Pupil Growth (IPG) score for each pupil. The IPG is a simple metric devised by Millman (1981) to show the *percentage of potential growth* each pupil actually achieved. The metric is calculated as follows:

$$\frac{(\text{Post \% correct}) - (\text{Pre \% correct})}{(100\% - \text{Pre \% correct})}$$

Multiplying this metric by 100 results in a score that can range from −100 to +100, where a negative number represents a lower score on the posttest than on the pretest, 0 represents no change from pre- to posttest, and +100 represents a perfect score on the posttest regardless of pretest performance. A negative score is rare, with most scores falling in the +30 to +80 range.

Establishing Work Sample Performance Standards

The issue of performance standards for learning gains by one's pupils is particularly complex and contentious. It is complex because gain scores are a function of many things, only one of which is a teacher's knowledge and skill. It is contentious because teachers are keenly aware of the contextual dependence of pupil learning and resist pressures to be held accountable when they are not able to control all factors affecting it. TWSM does not provide a totally satisfactory solution to these issues, but it has permitted Western Oregon faculty to move a long way toward their resolution by taking into account context factors when establishing expectancies (standards) for pupil progress in learning.

The matrix appearing as Figure 3.1 illustrates our first attempt to develop performance standards that take into account both the complexity of the learning outcome or outcomes to be accomplished and the demands of the context in which instruction and learning occur. As a place to begin, we are basing these performance standards on the mean IPG score for a teacher's class as a whole, but we plan to explore other alternatives as well. The IPG "expectancies" shown in Figure 3.1 are for illustrative purposes only and do not reflect actual expectancies.

In looking at the rows and columns in Figure 3.1, we anticipate that as a teacher moves across any one row from left to right or down any one column, the expected level of learning gains by pupils taught will decrease by some factor. That is, for any particular level of classroom demand, the higher the level of complexity of the learning outcome addressed, the lower the level of learning gains expected. Overall, we expect significantly higher levels of learning gains to be achieved by teachers falling in the upper left-hand cells than in the lower right-hand cells.

Several years of trial and error, and some reasonably sophisticated statistical analyses, will be required to fine-tune and make acceptable to the teaching community a set of expectancies for pupil progress in learning that are realistic, yet appropriately demanding, for the context and learning tasks a teacher faces. As part of this work, we explore the use of *work sample profiles* to help clarify visually the relationships among a teacher's context, his or her performance in it, and learning gains achieved by pupils.

Ensuring Prerequisite Knowledge and Skills

The preparation of a work sample by a teacher is a demanding task and requires a level of knowledge and skill—as well as time and personal investment—that goes beyond what teachers ordinarily are asked to do to demonstrate their competence and effectiveness as professionals. This means that if TWSM is to be used for evaluative purposes with either beginning or experienced teachers, then steps need to be taken to ensure that the teachers involved have the knowledge and skills needed for their preparation. At Western Oregon, this has meant a significant restructuring of preparation programs leading to the *initial* teaching license, with the *alignment* of learning outcomes, instructional plans, and assessment procedures at its core. We are not yet sure of the program restructuring that will be required for work with experienced teachers, but we do know that many practicing teachers currently are not able to make such alignments without additional training and support. Once teachers understand the

Complexity of Learning Outcome to Be Accomplished

Context Demands	Level 1 Recognition/ Recall	Level 2 Under- standing	Level 3 Application/ Problem Solving	Level 4 Critical Thinking/ Evaluation/ Reflection
Minimal[a] (3.0 or lower on Western Oregon's CCD Scale)	A mean classroom IPG of 75	A mean classroom IPG of 65	A mean classroom IPG of 55	A mean classroom IPG of 45
Moderate (3.1 to 4.5 on Western Oregon's CCD Scale)	A mean classroom IPG of 70	A mean classroom IPG of 60	A mean classroom IPG of 50	A mean classroom IPG of 40
Considerable (4.6 to 5.5 on Western Oregon's CCD Scale)	A mean classroom IPG of 65	A mean classroom IPG of 55	A mean classroom IPG of 45	A mean classroom IPG of 35
Great[b] (5.6 to 6.0 on Western Oregon's CCD Scale)	A mean classroom IPG of 60	A mean classroom IPG of 50	A mean classroom IPG of 40	A mean classroom IPG of 30

Figure 3.1. A Proposed Matrix of Mean Classroom IPG Expectancies/ Standards for Progress in Pupil Learning That Takes Into Account Learning Outcomes to Be Accomplished and Characteristics of the Context in Which Teaching and Learning Occur

NOTE: The expectancies shown here for illustrative purposes are based on the time constraints faced by student teachers in preparing work samples around a 2- to 5-week unit of instruction. If longer periods of time (a term or semester) were available for instruction, then these expectancies would be higher. IPG = Index of Pupil Growth; CCD = Classroom Context Demand.

a. For example, a small class, able and motivated pupils, few pupils on individualized education plans, adequate resources, supportive parents, and school conditions that emphasize and support high levels of learning.

b. For example, a large class, many troubled and unmotivated pupils, a sizable number of pupils on individualized education plans, a sizable number of pupils who have English as a second language, and school conditions that are disruptive or nonsupportive of high levels of learning.

alignment process, however, and the utility of information coming from it—especially the utility of interpreting information about pupil progress in light of the context in which learning occurs—they lose much of their initial reticence about engaging in work sample preparation. Many, in fact, have declared it to be the "best professional development experience" of their careers.

Adapting Measures and Methodology to Data Use and the Job Demands of Teachers

Although TWSM is unusually robust as a measurement methodology in that it can be applied to any teacher in any context, adaptations are required in specific measures, instructional strategies, and outcomes sought to accommodate the demands of broad differences in job assignment. It also can be argued that adaptations in the methodology generally are needed to fit differences in purpose served, for example, licensure versus research. For the most part, however, we have rejected this argument in our own work, as we shall explain (Chapter 4).

Adaptations Required by Context

We have found that adaptations in specific measures are required to accommodate the changing nature of schools as institutions as well as the classrooms within them. The reforms enacted in the passage of Oregon's Education Act for the 21st Century, for example, have caused many changes over the past several years that we have had to account for in specific context measures. So too has the emphasis on multiaged classrooms and the ever-increasing development diversity within classrooms brought on by the inclusive education movement within special education. We also have had to adapt many of our measures to accommodate the demands of the differing contexts in which elementary, secondary, and special education teachers work.

Adaptations Required by Purpose

Most institutions in Oregon using TWSM do so for purposes of the initial preparation and licensure of teachers. Forthcoming changes in licensure requirements will require work samples for advanced licensure as well, but few institutions other than Western Oregon use work sample data for purposes of research or systematic program evaluation.

Western Oregon has taken the view that measures used for training and licensure decisions require the same level of quality and trustworthiness as do measures used for research or program evaluation. A licensure decision is a "high-stakes" decision for everyone involved, and data informing such decisions need to be as defensible and trustworthy as data supporting research or evaluative conclusions.

One measurement issue thus far unresolved does create tension between TWSM use for research and evaluation versus training: the role of teachers in the design of measures used to assess pupil learning. For training purposes, we would like to give student teachers wide latitude in developing their own measures for monitoring pupil progress in learning. For research and evaluation purposes, however, we would like to bring as much "standardization" or "comparability" to these measures as possible. We are still in the process of working our way through this issue; however, given the multiple purposes we want TWSM data to serve, it is probable that its resolution will center on a reasonably prescriptive set of guidelines for the development and administration of pupil learning measures by prospective teachers.

Some Supporting Evidence

To this point, we have developed a rational argument for the merits of work sample methodology as a vehicle for linking the work of teachers to learning gains by pupils. We believe this to be a strong argument, but we turn now to several lines of evidence that add empirical support as well. These include data that document (a) the sensitivity of our IPG metric as a measure of learning gains by pupils; (b) variation in learning gains as a function of the complexity of the context in which teaching and learning occur and the complexity of the learning outcome or outcomes pursued; (c) variation in learning gains as a function of the quality of a teacher's performance when differences in context and outcome complexity are taken into account; and (d) the capacity of the measures obtained through TWSM, when treated as independent or intervening variables, to account for an unusually large proportion of variance in IPG scores. It is our view that findings of the kind presented in Tables 3.3 to 3.6, and their interlocking support for the theoretical foundation on which TWSM rests, could be obtained only if the measures used in the research generating them were reliable and valid.[6]

The data presented in the paragraphs that follow have come from a longitudinal, predictive study that Western Oregon has initiated as part of its commitment to developing a teaching workforce that is able to implement Oregon's new design for schools effectively. The focus of the research is to determine whether it is possible to *predict* the effectiveness of teachers working within such schools from information collected prior to licensure. The research is designed to take place within the context of the institutions' teacher preparation and follow-up programs, with data collected for instructional or evaluative purposes also being used for research.

The data presented are a subsample of data collected from the 1991 fall term through the 1994 spring term on more than 400 student teachers at Western Oregon and more than 10,000 pupils taught by these teachers. The data reported in the paragraphs that follow are based on the winter 1993 through spring 1994 sample population, which includes 139 elementary and 104 secondary student teachers. This sample constitutes what we refer to as Phase 2 data in that it incorporates information on learning outcome complexity, whereas earlier data did not.

Table 3.3 presents simple descriptive data on pupil learning gains. Data are summarized by both program enrollment (elementary and secondary education programs) and classroom level in which student teachers were placed. It is clear from these data that the range of IPG scores is large for each of the databases presented and is comparable across databases, even though the numbers of teachers in some of the teaching assignment categories are relatively small. We interpret these data as offering strong support for the sensitivity and consistency of the IPG metric as a measure of teacher effects on pupil learning.

The data presented in Table 3.4 illustrate the differences observed in IPG scores when teachers within any of the cells reported in Table 3.3 are reclassified into a four-cell matrix reflecting the level of demand within their classrooms and the complexity of the learning outcome or outcomes they are pursuing. We have found that in all such analyses, the anticipated pattern of learning gains holds reasonably well, and statistically significant differences are found between mean IPG scores across cells. As an example, for the 75 student

TABLE 3.3. Descriptive Statistics for Phase 2 Pupil Learning
Gain Data

Database	Maximum IPG Value	Mean IPG Value	Minimum IPG Value
By program enrollment			
All elementary student teachers (138 teachers, 3,467 pupils)	96.84	67.92	25.76
All secondary education student teachers (105 teachers, 2,586 pupils)	100	61.51	22.97
By teaching placement			
All student teachers in kindergarten through 3rd-grade classrooms (75 teachers, 1,824 pupils)	100[a]	67.38	25.76
All student teachers in 4th and 5th-grade classrooms (55 teachers, 1,434 pupils)	96.59	68.53	28.60
All student teachers in 6th-through 8th-grade classrooms (39 teachers, 1,051 pupils)	92.83	63.34	31.41
All student teachers in 9th- through 12th-grade classrooms (74 teachers, 1,744 pupils)	89.37	61.32	22.97
Total database (243 teachers, 6,053 pupils)	100	65.12	22.97

NOTE: IPG = Index of Pupil Growth.

a. Secondary teachers in some areas may obtain a K-12 endorsement, e.g., media, music, physical education.

teachers in our Phase 2 database who had Grades K-3 teaching assignments, statistically significant differences appear in learning gain scores for teachers falling in Cells 1 and 2, 1 and 4, 3 and 2, and

TABLE 3.4. Sensitivity of Mean IPG Scores to Classroom Demands and Outcome Complexity: Kindergarten Through 3rd-Grade Classrooms

	Level of Outcome Complexity	
Level of Classroom Demand	Low Complexity	High Complexity
Low demand	76.47	60.21
	1 2	
	3 4	
High demand	68.80	61.62

NOTE: IPG = Index of Pupil Growth.

3 and 4. Why expected differences do not appear between Cells 2 and 4 is unclear from the perspective of either procedure or theory, but the anticipated differences that are observed support the view that the IPG metric is indeed sensitive to both the demands of an instructional context and the complexity of the learning outcome being pursued.

Although the data presented in Table 3.4 demonstrate the ability of work sample methodology to detect differences in pupil learning due to context and outcome complexity, they do not draw specific links between the work of teachers and the learning gains observed. For this connection to be made, it also must be shown that differences exist in teacher performance between high and low learning gain classrooms *once context and outcome complexity have been accounted for.* Data presented in Table 3.5 show that this relationship does in fact exist. Although the means of the student teacher performance ratings (which are provided independently by a college and school supervisor) are unusually high, they do pattern in expected directions, and the differences observed between Cells 1 and 2, 1 and 4, 3 and 2, and 3 and 4 are, with one exception (C4 in Cells 1 and 2), statistically significant. Comparable analyses have not as yet been made for student teachers working in Grades K-3, 4-5, or 9-12 classrooms, but we expect similar patterning of teacher performance at these levels as well. More important, we expect these patterns to become even more pronounced as our measures of teacher performance are strengthened (see the Appendix) and the size of our database grows.

The fourth line of evidence to be presented in support of the trustworthiness of the various measures obtained through TWSM is

TABLE 3.5. Sensitivity of Pupil Learning Gains to the Work of
Teachers Given Context Demands and Outcome
Complexity: 6th- through 8th-Grade Classrooms

Level of Classroom Demand	*Mean Ratings of Competence of Student Teachers*	
	Achieving Low Learning Gains	*Achieving High Learning Gains*
Low-demand, low-outcome complexity	C1 = 5.25	C1 = 5.67
	C2 = 4.98	C2 = 5.51
	C3 = 5.13	C3 = 5.53
	C4 = 5.29	C4 = 5.24
	1 2	
	3 4	
High-demand, high-outcome complexity	C1 = 5.21	C1 = 5.94
	C2 = 4.74	C2 = 5.75
	C3 = 4.87	C3 = 5.88
	C4 = 5.04	C4 = 5.63

NOTE: C1 = Competence 1 (planning for instruction); C2 = Competence 2 (establishing a classroom conducive to learning); C3 = Competence 3 (implementing instructional plans [quality of instruction]); C4 = Competence 4 (evaluating, acting on, and reporting student progress in learning).

evidence that traditionally has been looked to as supporting theory-based measurement systems, namely the proportion of variance that can be accounted for in a criterion (dependent) measure of interest through theory-related measures of explanatory (independent and/or intervening) variables. In looking to such evidence, it is argued that level of support for both theory and measures increases as the proportion of variance accounted for in the criterion measure or measures increases. The rationale for this argument is fairly straight-forward: It is likely that high R^2 values will be obtained only if (a) the criterion measure or measures is sound, (b) theory pertaining to the criterion variable is sound, and (c) theory-related measures of explanatory variables are sound.

Given this line of reasoning, the R^2 data presented in Table 3.6 support the view that both the measures derived through TWSM and the theory underlying them are strong. It is hard to imagine that relationships of this magnitude and stability across independent data sets could be obtained with either theory or measures that are weak.

TABLE 3.6. Proportion of Variance (R^2) Accounted for in IPG Scores by Explanatory Variables Obtained Through Western Oregon's Teacher Work Sample Methodology

Database	Total Class IPG Score	High Pretest IPG Score	Low Pretest IPG Score
Kindergarten through 3rd-grade student teachers ($n = 75$)	.66	.76	.62
4th- through 5th-grade student teachers ($n = 55$)	.76	.77	.71
6th- through 8th-grade student teachers ($n = 39$)	.67[a]	.72	.81
9th- through 12th-grade student teachers ($n = 74$)	.56	.75	.55

NOTE: IPG = Index of Pupil Growth.

a. Because of limitations in sample size, the full set of explanatory variables included in other R^2 analyses presented here were not able to be used. As a consequence, all SCHOOL- and COMMUNITY-level variables were omitted, arbitrarily, for purposes of this analysis.

Although still far from definitive in its support of TWSM as a means of linking teacher work and pupil learning, the data presented in Tables 3.3 to 3.6 provide good reason, in our view, for thinking that definitive empirical support will be forthcoming.

Some Technical Considerations

Regardless of the supporting data just reviewed, a host of technical issues needs to be addressed when thinking about TWSM either as an assessment system or as a vehicle for training. The traditional issues of validity and reliability will not go away, and emerging issues around applied performance ("authentic") approaches to measurement appear to complicate rather than simplify these concerns. Issues of reliability and validity are further complicated by suggesting that work sample data be used for differing purposes, for example, in support of teacher licensure decisions, research on teacher effectiveness, or the evaluation and improvement of teacher preparation programs. Space does not permit a systematic treatment of these various issues, but a number of observations about them are offered in the following paragraphs.[7]

Traditional Concerns

In traditional psychometric theory, issues pertaining to the reliability and validity of measures, and to the fairness and consequences of their use, always are measure specific. From this perspective, because TWSM represents a general approach to measurement that employs a wide range of measurement technologies and produces a wide variety of specific measures, the technical issues of measurement need to be addressed separately for the 20 or more measures obtained through the methodology as a whole. For anyone who has been involved with the development of educational or psychological measures, this represents a very large kettle of reliability and validity estimating. When one adds to this the diversity in kind of measures obtained—for example, measures involving nominal, ordinal, interval, and ratio scales as well as measures focusing on both products and performance and both pupils and teachers—measurement specialists blanch at the prospect of dealing satisfactorily with all of the technical issues that surface when applying TWSM as we are attempting to apply it at Western Oregon.

This is not to imply that these issues cannot be dealt with or that they are not being dealt with in traditional ways. Interrater agreement studies between college and school supervisors, for example, have been conducted from the beginning of our work (they are high), and reliability estimates (pre-post correlation analyses) are calculated regularly for all learning gain scores (they are low, as we hope they will be, when using criterion-referenced measures of teacher impact on learning).

The larger issue is one of validity and an expanded meaning of reliability. Content (face) and construct validity do not appear to be a problem for most of the measures obtained through TWSM *so long as one does not wish to draw inferences about the performance or effectiveness of a teacher beyond the sample of teaching and learning represented in a particular sample of work.* If one wishes to make such inferences and there is a strong tendency to do so, then the technical issues involved become as much a matter of ensuring an adequate sample of teaching contexts and learning outcomes pursued as they do of ensuring the adequacy of measures used. This broader meaning of reliability and validity needs to be center stage when thinking about various applications of work sample methodology, for it colors the meaning one needs to give even to content and construct validity. It essentially determines the meaning one needs to give to reliability and consequential validity (Chapter 4).

It is our view that although it is necessary to bring the traditional conceptions of the reliability and validity of measurement to TWSM, these are not sufficient for dealing with all of the technical issues that accompany the methodology. We think the concepts of internal and external validity advocated by Schulman (1970) more than two decades ago need to be considered as well and that the ultimate test of our measures—and the methodology generally—needs to rest on the concept of *predictive* validity. To be genuinely powerful as a measurement methodology, TWSM will need to be able to predict the effectiveness of a teacher in a wide range of teaching contexts and for a wide range of learning outcomes to be accomplished. It is for this reason that we are engaging in the predictive research referred to previously. If all goes as planned, we should be able to report this level of validation data within the next few years.

Broader Considerations

From our viewpoint, there are as many reasons for optimism about TWSM as an approach to measurement as there are reasons for concern. There are four reasons, however, that stand out. The first of these is the *reasonableness* of the methodology from the perspective of teachers, parents, school administrators, school board members, and the public at large. It anchors to the criterion of ultimate interest (pupil learning), it links pupil learning to teacher work and the realities of the context in which teaching and learning occur, it ensures that measures of pupil learning are connected to what is taught and what pupils are expected to learn, and it provides information about the performance and characteristics of teachers assumed to be related to pupil learning.

A second reason for the optimism is that TWSM is *feasible* to implement. It is applicable to any teacher in any teaching situation, it will accommodate any and all pupils being taught, and it requires no more than a logical, straightforward approach to a teacher's work and its description (planning, teaching, assessing, analyzing, and reporting results). In the language of the day, it is "user friendly." As indicated previously, however, the methodology requires a broad and reasonably high level of knowledge and skill for its application, but it can be argued that this is a level of knowledge and skill that all teachers and supervisors or administrators should have.

A third reason for optimism rests in the capacity of TWSM to *serve multiple purposes:* it can be used as a vehicle for training beginning teachers or retraining experienced teachers, it can be used as a vehicle for evaluating the effectiveness of beginning teachers or the productivity of experienced teachers, it can be used as a data source in arriving at recommendations for teacher licensure or license renewal, and it can be used as a data source for research on teacher effectiveness and productivity or in testing and refining theory pertaining thereto (Chapter 4). While particular uses place particular demands on the methodology if these can be addressed, as we think they can, then the methodology holds immense potential for advancing teaching as a science and profession.

Finally, and most important, we believe that the major reason for optimism toward the methodology is the kind of *empirical evidence* now beginning to accrue. The significant differences shown in Tables 3.3 and 3.4, the remarkable amount of variance in learning gains we are able to account for even with our current stage of measurement (Table 3.5), the consistency of findings across replications, and the consistency of findings with theoretical expectations bode well for both the power of the methodology and the theory on which it rests. We do not see how we could obtain such findings without strong (valid and reliable) measures. We interpret these findings, which will be reported in detail in the coming months, as supporting both the internal and external validity of our measures and as unusually promising of the kind of predictive validity our field of inquiry so sorely needs.

Reflections and Implications

On balance, we believe that TWSM holds great promise as a means of defensibly linking progress in learning to teacher work. We view this to be the case regardless of the purpose the methodology is asked to serve, although the technical demands that must be met clearly differ from one purpose to another. On the basis of our experience with TWSM thus far, however, we believe its broad range of application and the power of data generated through it offer promise of a methodology that can significantly advance our current understanding of teaching and the teaching-learning process (Chapter 4).

Of equal importance from the perspective of teachers, and from the perspective of all whose lives are touched by teachers, we believe the methodology and its various applications stand to enhance the professionalization of teaching. Pupil learning is, always has been, and must continue to be the professional touchstone for teachers, and TWSM provides a means for this linkage to be made meaningfully and defensibly. If viewed in this manner and extended to its limits, we believe the methodology carries with it the potential for lifting teaching to new heights as a profession and bringing with it the level of recognition teachers deserve and to which they have aspired for so long.

Appendix: Outline of the Measures Derived From Western Oregon's Application of Teacher Work Sample Methodology to the Initial Preparation and Licensure of Teachers

Category of Measures	*Specific Measures and Their Derivation*[a]
Complexity of outcomes pursued and quality of measures used to assess outcome attainment	1. **Complexity of learning outcome or outcomes to be accomplished by pupils.** A weighting of 1 to 4 assigned to each outcome on the basis of an item analysis of the measure or measures used to assess outcome attainment. Western Oregon's Taxonomy of Educational Outcomes is used in making this analysis (see column headings in Figure 3.1), with the summary weighting assigned to an outcome representing the mean score of individual test items or assessment task weightings. Summary weightings may assume any value on the scale of 1 to 4.
	2. **Quality of measures used by a student teacher to assess pupil learning.** A conceptually anchored rating of 1 to 6 is assigned by a student teacher's college supervisor to each measure used on the basis of validity and reliability indexes prepared for each measure. The validity index involves a three-level judgment about CONTEXT VALIDITY (a low,

Category of Measures	*Specific Measures and Their Derivation*[a]
	moderate, or high degree of alignment between measure used and learning goal to be assessed). The reliability index involves a three-level judgment about the EQUIVALENCE of pre and post measures of goal attainment (identical, parallel, or nonparallel). Summary ratings are limited to whole number values and represent a supervisor's overall judgment as to the quality of a measure based on the validity and reliability indexes described.

Characteristics of the context in which teaching and learning occur	3. **Characteristics of the classroom**
	   a. Number of pupils[b]
	   b. Grade level or levels of pupils[b]
	   c. Number of pupils having individualized education plans (percentage calculated)[b]
	   d. Number of pupils having English as a second language (percentage calculated)[b]
	   e. Number of pupils in pullout or supplementary programs (percentage calculated)[b]
	   f. Number of pupils unusually demanding of time and energy (percentage calculated)[b]
	   g. DEFINING CHARACTERISTICS OF THE INSTRUCTIONAL PROGRAM WITHIN WHICH A STUDENT TEACHER'S WORK SAMPLE IS TAKEN[b]
	   h. Room organization, equipment, and supplies (good, reasonable, poor)[b]
	   i. Room noise and traffic over which the teacher has no control (quiet with few interruptions, reasonably quiet with some interruptions, noisy with many interruptions)[b]
	   j. A summary rating on a conceptually anchored 6-point Likert scale, by both college and school supervisors, that takes all the above into account in depicting how demanding a classroom is as a context in which to teach and learn[c]
	   k. A listing of specialists and other sources of assistance available to a student teacher in a classroom (e.g., instructional assistants, parents, old students)[b]
	   l. A summary rating on a conceptually anchored 6-point Likert rating scale, by both college and school supervisors, of the level of support available to a student teacher[c]

Category of Measures	*Specific Measures and Their Derivation*[a]

m. The ratio of the level of demand to the level of support within a classroom (calculated from the ratings provided through Items j and l)

4. **Characteristics of the school**[d]
   a. Number of pupils in the school
   b. Growth rate (percentage) in school size over the past 3 to 5 years
   c. Pupil-teacher ratio
   d. Pupil-instructional staff ratio
   e. Counselor-pupil ratio
   f. Teacher stability ("turnover") index
   g. Average daily attendance rate

5. **Characteristics of the community (district) served by a school**[d]
   a. Number of pupils in the district
   b. Growth rate (percentage) in district size over the past 5 years
   c. Student mobility index (district)
   d. Average daily attendance rate (district)
   e. Index of racial/ethnic diversity (ratio of non-White to White students)
   f. Percentage of pupils eligible for a free or reduced lunch
   g. Percentage of teachers with advanced degrees
   h. Average teacher salary for average number of years employed (a standard score)

6. **Preinstructional status of pupils with respect to learning outcomes to be accomplished.** The performance of each pupil in one's classroom *who is not on an individualized education plan* on a preinstructional measure of the learning outcome or outcomes to be accomplished (see Measures 1 and 2)

Teacher competence in planning instruction that leads to progress in pupil learning

7. *Clarity and appropriateness of learning outcomes to be accomplished and the measurement strategies to be used in assessing outcome attainment.* A summative rating is provided by both college and school supervisors on this aspect of standards-based instruction. The 6-point Likert scale takes both factors into account and is anchored conceptually. Ratings are provided independently by the two supervisors, although the mean score of the two ratings is used for purposes of research and licensure-related decisions.

Category of *Measures*	*Specific Measures* *and Their Derivation*[a]
	8. *Aligning instructional methods, learning activities, and time for learning with outcomes to be accomplished and measures of outcome attainment.* An assessment format and pattern of use that parallels Measure 7.
	9. *Adapting an initial instructional plan to accommodate the demands of one's context for teaching and learning.* An assessment format and pattern of use that parallels Measure 7.
	10. **Establishing a classroom conducive to learning.** Multiple indicators of quality are assessed independently by college and school supervisors, on multiple occasions, but finally are merged by each supervisor into a 6-point Likert summative rating of the kind described above. As described previously, the mean score for these two summative ratings is used for purposes of licensure-related decisions and research.
Teacher competence in implementing a standards-based instructional plan	11. ENGAGING PUPILS IN PLANNED LEARNING ACTIVITIES a. THE QUALITY OF IMPLEMENTATION FROM THE PERSPECTIVE OF TEACHER PERFORMANCE. A combination of multiple indicators of quality, followed by a merged summative rating, that parallels in form and function the measures described in Measure 10. b. THE QUALITY OF IMPLEMENTATION FROM THE PERSPECTIVE OF PUPIL RESPONSE. An assessment format, and pattern of use, that parallels Measure 10.
	12. *Mastery of content, and of strategies for helping students master content, reflected in all the above.* An assessment format, and pattern of use, that parallels Measure 10.
	13. *Evaluating, acting on, and reporting pupil progress in learning.* An assessment format, and pattern of use, that parallels Measure 10.
The quality of a teacher's "in-flight" decisions when implementing an instructional plan	14. THE TIMELINESS AND APPROPRIATENESS OF CLASSROOM DECISIONS a. MANAGEMENT-RELATED DECISIONS. An assessment format, and pattern of use, that parallels Measure 10. b. INSTRUCTION-RELATED DECISIONS. An assessment format, and pattern of use, that parallels Measure 10.

Category of Measures	*Specific Measures and Their Derivation*[a]
	15. THE CONCEPTUAL AND SITUATIONAL "GROUNDING" OF CLASSROOM DECISIONS a. MANAGEMENT-RELATED DECISIONS. A summative rating, made only by a student teacher's college supervisor, that is based on a teacher's responses ("simulated recall") to a structured interview around three critical incidents observed by the supervisor on three separate occasions. b. INSTRUCTION-RELATED DECISIONS. An assessment format and procedure that parallels Measure 15a.
Providing and interpreting evidence of success in fostering pupil progress in learning	16. **Postinstructional status of pupils with respect to learning outcomes to be accomplished.** The performance of each pupil in one's classroom on a postinstructional (end-of-unit) measure of the learning outcome or outcomes to be accomplished. 17. **The percentage of pupils in one's class who demonstrate appreciable progress in learning**. The percentage of pupils in one's class who attain an IPG of 50 or higher. The rationale for and method of calculating an IPG are discussed in the text following Table 3.2. Exceptions for the percentage of pupils in one's class who attain IPGs of 50 or higher, given the characteristics of learning outcome or outcomes to be accomplished and the context in which teaching and learning occur, are shown in Figure 3.1. 18. **The learning progress made by special groups of pupils, including low- and high-scoring pupils on preinstructional measures**. The percentage of pupils in each of three subgroups in one's class (low- and high-scoring pupils on the preinstructional measure or measures plus one additional group, for example, pupils who have English as a second language) who attain IPGs of 50 or higher. IPG data are to be tabled separately for each group. 19. *An analysis, interpretation, and reflection on learning gains—or lack thereof—reported in Measures 17 and 18.* A reflective essay in which a student teacher clarifies or elaborates on the data reported in Measures 17 and 18, explains to the extent possible why the data are as they are, and discusses what he or she would do differently if a similar unit were taught again. A conceptually anchored rating scale is used

Category of Measures	Specific Measures and Their Derivation[a]	
		by the student teacher's college supervisor to capture the level of quality, care, and insight reflected in the essay.
Exhibiting valued aspects of professionalism during the course of work sample preparation	20.	*Sensitivity to school policies and practices.* A conceptually anchored 6-point Likert evaluative rating made independently by college and school supervisors on the basis of a student teacher's performance in a field setting as a whole. The mean score from these two ratings is used for purposes of research and licensure decisions.
	21.	*Personal mannerisms and interpersonal relationships.* An assessment format, and pattern of use, that parallels Measure 20.
	22.	*General professional demeanor.* An assessment format, and pattern of use, that parallels Measure 20.
	23.	*Potential for leadership.* An assessment format, and pattern of use, that parallels Measure 20.

NOTE: IPG = Index of Pupil Growth.

a. Measures listed in bold type are existing measures. Those listed in italicized type are proposed refinements in existing measures. Those listed in all capitals are new measures in the process of being developed.

b. Provided by a student teacher and verified by the teacher's school supervisor.

c. Analyzed independently for purposes of reliability and combined, with mean score values used, for purposes of licensure-related decisions and research.

d. Taken from either SCHOOL PROFILE data reported annually by the Oregon Department of Education or STATE CENSUS data.

Notes

1. The most egregious of these weaknesses include the failure of standardized achievement tests to reflect large portions of what is taught; their construction to force peer-related (norm-referenced) judgments about student accomplishment rather than criterion-referenced judgments; their susceptibility to influences other than teacher or school effects, particularly parental education and socio-economic effects; and the fact that they usually are administered, scored, and reported in ways that meet—and on a timeline that meets—the accountability needs of districts or state departments of education rather than the instruction or learning needs of teachers and students.

2. The theory is labeled an "outcome-based and context-dependent theory of teacher effectiveness." The earliest description of the theory, and the constructs or measures contained within it, was provided in an unpublished paper by Cowart, Schalock, and Schalock (1990) presented at a meeting of the Southwestern Philosophy of Education Society in Fort Worth, Texas. An updated version of the theory appears in an article by Schalock, Cowart, and Staebler (1993) published in the *Journal of Personnel Evaluation in Education*. An overview of the current status of the theory is contained in the *Proceedings* of an invitational conference held at Western Oregon in October 1994 on recent advances in theory and research pertaining to teacher effectiveness (Schalock & Schalock, 1995).

3. This is a standards-based approach to schooling that was adopted initially by the 1991 legislative assembly and revised appreciably by its 1995 counterpart.

4. As used at Western Oregon, the *effectiveness* of a teacher is defined in terms of learning gains by pupils in *short-term* (3- to 5-week) work samples, whereas the *productivity* of a teacher is defined in terms of learning gains by pupils in *long-term* (term, semester, or year-long) work samples.

5. Further information can be obtained about each of the measures listed in Table 3.2, as well as the database that has accumulated through their use, from the authors.

6. This claim pertains, of course, only to the measures derived from the 2- to 5-week work sample that currently is used in TWSM at Western Oregon involving student teachers. Claims for the reliability and validity of such measures beyond this limited sample of work, for either beginning or experienced teachers, obviously would depend on expanded samples of work.

7. A great deal of time was spent on these matters in the invitational research conference referred to in Note 2, and we acknowledge our indebtedness to conference participants in helping us think them through. In our minds, they are far from resolved, however, and will continue to be addressed in the future. Related critiques by conference participants are reproduced as an attachment to the conference *Proceedings* (Shalock & Shalock, 1996).

References

Cowart, B., Schalock, H. D., & Schalock, M. D. (1990, September). *An outcomes-based and context embedded theory of teacher effectiveness: Implications for teacher preparation, licensure, and permanent status.*

Paper presented at the 41st annual meeting of the Southwestern Philosophy of Education Society, Fort Worth, TX.

Gearhart, M., & Herman, J. L. (1995, Winter). Portfolio assessment: Whose work is it? Issues in the use of classroom assignments for accountability. *Evaluation Comment.* (Center for the Study of Evaluation, University of California, Los Angeles)

Gitomer, D. H. (1993). Performance assessment and educational measurement. In R. E. Bennett & W. C. Ward (Eds.), *Construction versus choice in cognitive measurement* (pp. 241-263). Hillsdale, NJ: Lawrence Erlbaum.

Herman, J. L., Aschbacher, P. R., & Winters, L. (1992). *A practical guide to alternative assessment.* Alexandria, VA: Association for Supervision and Curriculum Development.

Millman, J. (1981). Student achievement as a measure of teaching competence. In J. Millman (Ed.), *Handbook of teacher evaluation* (pp. 146-166). Beverly Hills, CA: Sage.

Schalock, H. D., & Schalock, M. D. (1995). *Proceedings of a conference: Advances in theory and research on teacher effectiveness.* Monmouth: Western Oregon State College.

Schalock, M. D., Cowart, B., & Staebler, B. (1993). Teacher productivity revisited: Definition, theory, measurement, and application. *Journal of Personnel Evaluation in Education, 7,* 179-196.

Schulman, L. S. (1970). Reconstruction of educational research. *Review of Educational Research, 40,* 371-396.

Wiggins, G. P. (1988). A true test: Toward more authentic and equitable assessment. *Phi Delta Kappan, 70,* 703-713.

Wiggins, G. P. (1989). Teaching to the (authentic) test. *Educational Leadership, 46*(7), 41-47.

Wiggins, G. P. (1992). Creating tests worth taking. *Education Leadership, 49*(8), 26-33.

Wiggins, G. P. (1993). *Assessing student performance: Exploring the purpose and limits of testing.* San Francisco: Jossey-Bass.

Wolf, D. P. (1993). Assessment as an episode of learning. In R. E. Bennett & W. C. Ward (Eds.), *Construction versus choice in cognitive measurement* (pp. 241-263). Hillsdale, NJ: Lawrence Erlbaum.

Wolf, D. P., Bixby, J., Glenn, J., & Gardner, H. (1991). To use their minds well: Investigating new forms of student assessment. In G. Grant (Ed.), *Review of research in education* (Vol. 17, pp. 31-74). Washington, DC: American Educational Research Association.

CHAPTER 4

Oregon Teacher Work Sample Methodology

Potential and Problems

PETER W. AIRASIAN

The Oregon Teacher Work Sample Methodology (TWSM) is an unfinished, evolving method intended to link student learning gains to teacher performance. At present, examination of TWSM is proceeding in a number of directions including its use as a teacher education activity, measurement technique, research topic, and licensure tool. The breadth of this work provides many foci for discussion and critique, a fact noted by its developers, who have identified many of their future goals and the activities projected to meet them. Although the developers of TWSM have a good grasp of the nature of their method and its required extensions, there are some questions and issues that can be raised about their work with regard to the need for both additional supporting data and for additional reflection about the future applications of TWSM. The following examination focuses on four general areas: advantages of TWSM, critique of TWSM measures, critique of the method used to link pupil learning to teacher performance, and general comments. In addressing these areas, I recognize the evolving nature of TWSM and seek to provide a *critique*, not a criticism, of work to date in the hope of enhancing its future development and refinement.

Advantages of Teacher
Work Sample Methodology

The advantages of TWSM are many. It is performance and out-come based, providing a real, personal, and integrative experience for teachers. Its eight steps are well structured and lead teachers to think through and link objectives, teaching methods, resources, pupil needs, and pupil assessment in a logical, aligned manner. It is designed to foster both formative and summative teacher reflection and self-evaluation, both important components of teachers' professional development. It focuses teachers on pupil learning as the fundamental purpose and criterion of good teaching. It is, in short, an exceptionally useful instructional tool for both preservice and in-service teachers.

In addition, TWSM forces teachers of teachers to address issues of objective-instruction-assessment alignment and the primacy of student learning in their own courses and observations. At present, the many teacher education and professional development benefits of TWSM are its primary strength. These benefits alone are sufficient to justify the use of TWSM.

Critique of Teacher Work
Sample Methodology Measures

There are a number of concerns and information gaps associated with the tests and scales used in TWSM. One primary concern is the quality of the pre- and posttests constructed by teachers to assess their pupils' learning. We know little about the quality of the test items, the levels of pupil learning being assessed, the variability in difficulty across tests, the number of items per test, the format of the items, and the comparability of the pre- and posttests. Nor is it clear to what extent teachers select easy-to-meet objectives or teach narrowly to the specific posttest items. Although it is important to align objectives, instruction, and assessment to one another, it also is important that the objectives themselves be meaningful and worthwhile. Given that both preservice and in-service teachers generally do not receive comprehensive instruction in classroom measurement and assessment, it is appropriate to raise these concerns about the quality of the

TWSM teacher-made tests and the inferences made from these tests (Chapter 23).

The strategy of having a teacher's college supervisor rate the quality of the teacher's pre- and posttests, although useful in intent, does not mitigate the preceding concerns. Explicit rating criteria and specific information about interrater reliability among different supervisors at different grade levels and subject areas are not provided, although interrater reliability studies are reported to be high. Common rating criteria and interrater reliability are important to establish the quality of teachers' TWSM tests. In general, many of the 23 TWSM measures used to examine teacher products and classroom practices also are based on rating scales that are not explicit regarding the rating criteria and interrater reliability. Such information should be provided, especially in efforts aimed at the measurement, research, and licensure uses of TWSM.

The Index of Pupil Growth (IPG) is used to determine the percentage of potential growth evidenced by pupils from pre- to posttesting. The IPG is essentially a gain score metric with the attendant reliability problems of such metrics. The argument for the sensitivity and consistency of the IPG (see Table 3.4 in Schalock, Schalock, & Girod [Chapter 3]) would be stronger if the mean differences between elementary and secondary students on the metric were tested and discussed. Table 3.4 also is used to argue for the sensitivity of the IPG, but it is clear that high-complexity outcomes are not sensitive to differences between low- and high-demand contexts. An alternative to the IPG would involve removing the effect of pretest scores from the posttest scores and examining or testing the residuals. Regardless of the approach used, it is important to remember that the growth measure is derived from the pre- and posttests and thus is dependent on the validity and reliability of these tests.

In addressing validity, it is claimed in Schalock et al. (Chapter 3) that

> content (face) and construct validity do not appear to be a problem for most of the measures obtained through TWSM *so long as one does not wish to draw inferences about the performance or effectiveness of a teacher beyond the sample of teaching and learning represented in a particular sample of work.* (p. 35)

Content and construct validity should be important measurement concerns even if one does not wish to draw inferences that extend beyond a given TWSM sample. Interpretations of such samples would clearly be influenced by the content and construct validity of the measures involved whether they are tests or rating scales. It is difficult to envision a situation in which one would not wish to make inferences that go beyond a particular TWSM sample. A teacher would want to use the single sample to make inferences about personal strengths, weaknesses, and needs. A college supervisor would want to use the sample to suggest improvements or changes in subsequent samples. A researcher or licensing agency would be very concerned about the validity of the measures used. Why would one want to apply TWSM without making inferences of any kind? Validity will be and should be a central concern in all applications of TWSM.

Critique of Teacher Work Sample Methodology for Linking Pupil Learning to Teacher Performance

The IPG is the index used to measure pupil learning gains. It is clear, however, that raw gain scores do not provide a direct indication of the unique contribution a teacher makes to the gains. Other factors such as pupils' prior knowledge, socioeconomic status, student language proficiency, classroom resources, and the like also can influence pupil learning gains. TWSM does not yet explicitly address the link between pupil gains and teacher performance, although initial work in this direction has begun. Table 3.4 in Schalock et al. (Chapter 3) shows that a combination of some TWSM explanatory variables accounts for substantial proportions of variance in pupils' IPG scores. This finding provides support for the salient influence of these variables on gain scores, but it does not provide evidence of the unique contribution of the teacher to the gains.

To determine the latter requires the extraction from gain scores of factors that relate to pupil learning but that mask a teacher's unique contributions. Thus what is needed is a regression or regression-type analysis that successively removes from the gain score the four general, nonteacher influences on pupil performance identified in TWSM: classroom, school, and community factors as well as the prior-to-instruction knowledge level of pupils. The residual, or remainder, of the gain score after removing these influences represents the teacher's unique contribution or value added to pupil learning. At this stage, such analyses have not been done in TWSM.

Instead, what is being proposed is the development of performance standards for expected or satisfactory pupil learning gains that take into account the complexity of (a) the learning outcomes sought and (b) the contextual demands of the classroom (see Figure 3.1 in Schalock et al). The approach would set up standards or expectancies for the size of learning gains according to the complexity of a teacher's expected outcomes (recall to critical thinking) and the demands of the classroom (minimal to great). A teacher who sought high-level pupil outcomes in a classroom with great demands would be held to a lower learning-gain standard than would a teacher who sought low-level outcomes in a minimally demanding classroom.

This approach is problematic in three regards. First, it will be difficult to establish specific standards for varying combinations of outcomes and contexts. Second, it is not clear whether expectations for teacher success should vary by outcomes sought and contextual factors. Steps 5 and 6 of the 8 TWSM steps require teachers to adapt outcomes and plans to their context and to implement a contextually appropriate instructional plan. Given this expectation, should different learning standards be promulgated? Third, by establishing different standards for different contexts, one may set up self-fulfilling prophesies and lower teacher expectations for pupils.

Finally, TWSM developers should make a concerted effort to include indicators of specific teacher practices or activities that can help provide links between what teachers do and pupil learning gains. It is more useful to identify practices that enhance learning gains than to simply document such gains, and some effort should be spent on this issue.

General Comments

As described, the development and refinement of TWSM is a multifaceted, substantial undertaking. It is a tribute to its developers that it has progressed as far as it already has, both methodologically and substantively. However, to date, the main TWSM application has been in teacher education, where preservice teachers apply TWSM's integrated and comprehensive approach to improving and understanding pupil learning. The bulk of the methods discussed, data presented, and conclusions reached about TWSM flow from this primarily teacher instructional use. The preceding comments have tried to address issues and make suggestions that will refine and extend the work done to date, and it is clear from the preceding comments and the comments of the developers themselves that such refinement is needed.

However, in acknowledging the need to improve and extend TWSM, it is implied that these improvements and extensions will be relatively easy to accomplish. A number of reasons are given for having optimism about broadening the applications of TWSM, including its capacity to "*serve multiple purposes*" (p. 37; emphasis in original). "We view this to be the case regardless of the purpose the methodology is asked to serve" (pp. 37-38). "Although TWSM is unusually robust as a measurement methodology, . . . it also can be argued that adaptations in the methodology generally are needed to fit differences in purpose served, for example, licensure versus research. *For the most part, however, we have rejected this argument in our own work*" (p. 28; emphasis added). There is an implication in these statements that it will not be difficult to broaden the uses of TWSM beyond its teacher education use. Such an implication represents an overgeneralization and simplification of the present status of TWSM.

It is likely that there will be a push to use TWSM to inform a variety of policy and licensure decisions in Oregon and elsewhere. Politicians will be easily seduced by the apparent reasonableness, feasibility, and cheapness of TWSM. They will fall under the spell of face validity and the allure of numerical indexes. They will push, as they have already, to implement TWSM on a statewide basis for decisions that will have moderate- or high-stakes consequences. They will not understand that the conditions for applying TWSM for teacher education and instructional purposes are not the same as the conditions for applying TWSM for prediction, licensure, and research purposes.

In fact, these latter uses will require considerably more than a bit of "tinkering" to make them useful and defensible for policy and research decisions. Among the issues to be confronted in moving beyond TWSM as a teacher education tool are the number of subjects and samples to be examined; the quality and explicitness of the validation of the outcome, context, and process measures; the need to standardize or at least substantially narrow TWSM applications; the need to develop standards for acceptable and unacceptable TWSM performance; and the need to determine a specific and defensible procedure for leveling the contextual playing field. These issues must be confronted not for a single teacher but for large numbers of teachers who will have consequential decisions made on the basis of their TWSM performance. Much more needs to be accomplished to meaningfully extend TWSM beyond its current, largely teacher education, orientation.

The developers of TWSM are to be commended for their work, both that already accomplished and that ongoing. They have provided a methodology that, although unfinished and underexamined in many regards, holds promise for improving teaching and helping to understand teachers' contributions to pupil learning.

CHAPTER 5

Oregon Teacher Work Sample Methodology

Educational Policy Review

DANIEL L. STUFFLEBEAM

A team led by H. Del Schalock at Western Oregon State College is providing visionary, research-based leadership to help Oregon develop and carry out a teacher evaluation design for 21st-century schools. The Western Oregon team has developed an approach to preparing and evaluating teachers, labeled the "outcome-based and context-dependent theory of teacher effectiveness." The Western Oregon team has grounded its theory in study of student teachers, the contexts in which they teach, and their effects on assessed learning gains by their pupils.

The key operational aspect of this grounded theory is Teacher Work Sample Methodology (TWSM). Each student teacher develops a work sample exercise keyed to the objectives of a selected unit of instruction. The student teacher assigns each pupil to complete the work sample, teaches the unit, and readministers the work sample. The student teacher (or a Western Oregon researcher) computes gain scores for each pupil, initially high- and low-scoring pupils, and for the entire class. The student teacher then uses the analyses to reflect on results.

During this process, the Western Oregon researchers observe and rate the student teachers on performance of teaching duties and record contextual factors thought to affect pupil outcomes. The researchers have analyzed work sample data on the experiences of hundreds of student teachers. They examined pretest and posttest results as well as ratings of teaching effectiveness and descriptors of pupil, classroom, school, and community context variables. Using these analyses, the researchers evolved their theory of teaching effectiveness, developed procedures for using the work sample assessments to evaluate the effectiveness of individual student teachers, and interjected their findings into state-level policymaking.

In conducting this work, the Western Oregon researchers are closely involving many schools and the state policy groups concerned with teacher licensing and teacher education. This collaborative effort shows promise for helping Oregon's public education system use the research findings to redesign its ideas and practices about teacher preparation and licensure. This work also is of national interest in that it addresses the continuing national dilemma showing that ratings of teacher effectiveness typically have little relationship to measures of pupil achievement.

My assignment in preparing this chapter was to assess the "outcome-based and context-dependent theory of teacher effectiveness" and TWSM, as presented by Schalock, Schalock, and Girod (Chapter 3). In approaching this task, I faced a dilemma. Based on my previous study of the Western Oregon work, I had developed a favorable view of the conceptual framework, associated measuring method, and program of action research within the teacher education, relatively low-stakes setting in which this work evolved. However, the authors are considering applying the theory and methods in the much different high-stakes setting of teacher licensure and possibly merit pay. I have serious reservations about such extrapolations. In the following, I address five questions aimed at assessing the Western Oregon work sample program. These consider its value in teacher education, teacher licensing, and teacher evaluation. This analysis resulted in a dual message. My assessment of the work's applicability to teacher education and teacher self-assessment is favorable, whereas my assessment of its potential use in high-stakes decision making is unfavorable.

1. What is the importance of the proposed "outcomes-based and context-dependent theory of teacher effectiveness?"

The theory's main demonstrated value is as a framework for structuring and guiding Western Oregon's teacher education program. Western Oregon educators instruct student teachers to construct work samples and, considering context, assess their teaching effectiveness. Ongoing action research and associated theory development focused on the local situation undoubtedly are valuable to Western Oregon's teacher educators and student teachers.

The evolving theory also has contributed to state-level deliberations. Collaborators from across the state are using the framework to help focus their discussions and studies related to how best to improve policies and practices of teacher evaluation. As an advanced organizer, the theory and associated data are useful for guiding and informing meaningful discussions.

Also, researchers are using the theory to structure research on the link between teaching and learning while considering certain context variables. As described by Schalock et al. (Chapter 3), the researchers have developed tentative conclusions that certain independent variables predict pupils' work sample gain scores. For example, their data show that after accounting for differences in context and complexity of assessed outcomes, ratings of teacher performance are associated with low versus high learning gains on work sample tests. They reported findings of adjusted R^2 values between .55 and .81 for theory-derived measures regressed against pupils' learning gains in 2- to 5-week units of study.

Nevertheless, as the authors acknowledge, issues of reliability and validity in the measures employed are unresolved, and the theory is in an early stage of development. Threats to validity include the student teacher's questionable and, in any case, variable abilities to construct sound work samples that reliably measure higher order knowledge and skills; teaching the test, which is inherent in the method; and the student teacher's opportunity to bias results. TWSM and the supporting theory do not yet provide a defensible basis for formulating teacher evaluation policies related to high-stakes decisions or for solid research on teacher education. The theory is useful in the teacher education setting in which it was developed but is less useful in broader policy, research, and teacher evaluation arenas.

2. To what extent does the "outcomes-based and context-dependent theory of teacher effectiveness" meet the requirements of a sound theory?

According to one dictionary definition, a sound theory should provide a coherent set of conceptual, hypothetical, and pragmatic principles forming a general framework to guide investigation of a field, such as teacher evaluation. The Western Oregon researchers have made important strides in this direction. Overall, however, the theory needs to be strengthened.

The presented theory still is conceptually narrow. Although labeled a context-dependent theory, it omits key variables that influence measures of teacher effectiveness. One of the most important omitted context variables is "teaching the test," especially in the face of anxiety-provoking conditions. This variable will become critically important if the state or school districts use TWSM results to make high-stakes decisions about teachers such as licensing, tenure, or merit pay. The importance of the teaching-the-test variable is confirmed by failures of systems that neither considered nor controlled it. A prime example is Kentucky's use, in the 1980s, of scores from the Kentucky Essential Skills Test (KEST) to evaluate schools and teachers. When Kentucky made teaching and administrative jobs dependent on the quality of pupil KEST scores, the practice of teaching this supposedly secure test became rampant. The state no longer could trust KEST scores and so terminated this testing program. I believe the Western Oregon researchers should further develop the conceptual base of their teacher effectiveness theory. They especially should address the full range of threats to valid measurement, including teaching the test.

The theory as currently instrumented also has difficulty in fully passing a second test of a good theory: to examine relevant hypotheses. The hypothesis testing completed so far is based on weak "work sample criterion measures." TWSM is standardized only at a general level. Its application is idiosyncratic to teacher, class, unit of instruction, level of objectives tested, and period for instruction. This is both a strength and a weakness of the method. Much of the method's value is in serving the student teachers. It gives them experience in developing work samples fitted to their situations, receiving critiques of the work samples, improving them, and using them to assess effectiveness under low-stakes conditions. However, the student teachers control the development of the work samples. The dependent variable criterion information can be no better than the quality of the measurement procedures used to produce it. These measures are vulnerable to manipulation by the student teachers and thus are suspect. This would be especially true if the findings were used to inform high-stakes decisions. Student teachers might also develop poor work samples. It matters little whether ratings of teacher performance are associated with pupil gains in work sample performance if the student teachers employ biased outcome measures or assess low-level knowledge and skills (Chapter 23).

The Western Oregon teacher effectiveness theory has important strengths related to a third test of a theory. It is well grounded in experience with student teachers and includes practical guidelines for applying the Work Sample Method in a relatively low-stakes teacher education setting. However, to apply TWSM to high-stakes decisions about teachers, users will need much more rigorous guidelines and controls. To ensure comparable data across student teachers and between pretests and posttests, the researchers must develop strict application guidelines and high-quality work sample exercises for assignment to teachers.

Despite these shortcomings, the theory development effort is laudable for its student teaching orientation, participatory approach, consideration of context and outcome complexity, and focus on pupil outcomes. It makes sense to continue developing and applying the theory to study and improve student teachers' abilities to construct and use examinations to assess and improve their teaching.

3. What is the value of TWSM for formative/developmental purposes?

Teacher educators can use this approach to help student teachers improve and assess pupil learning. Student teachers undoubtedly benefit from developing and using work samples to assess how well their pupils develop particular knowledge and skills. This procedure helps student teachers clarify instructional objectives; obtain experience in developing performance assessment devices; align objectives, instruction, and assessment; obtain evidence of pupil progress; and consider whether they are effectively teaching all the pupils.

On the other hand, TWSM's utility is limited, even for formative/developmental purposes. It provides too few points to help the student teacher monitor his or her pupils' progress during an instruction unit. As implemented so far, it considers only a small amount of the student teacher's instruction. Also, the student teacher uses the pretest as the posttest, which is bound to yield an inflated assessment of the pupils' progress. In addition, many teacher education students have not developed work samples that assess anything above low-level knowledge and understanding. Involving student teachers in the development and use of low-level work samples to assess their teaching effectiveness may be influencing them to teach to low-level objectives. This could be an unfortunate side effect of concentrating almost exclusively on TWSM. In addition, heavy orientation to TWSM might influence teachers not to select certain teaching approaches best suited to their pupils, for example, cooperative learning and individually paced instruction. Overall, the work sample method has important, albeit limited, utility in teacher education.

4. What is the value of TWSM for informing high-stakes decisions?

TWSM, as implemented, does not produce student outcome information of sufficient validity, freedom from bias, and reliability to warrant developing state, university, or district policies on teacher evaluation; awarding initial or long-term teaching licenses; or awarding merit pay. The assessments are not standardized or controlled. Teachers greatly influence what they assess and at what level of performance. Many work samples address lower order knowledge and skills. The posttest work sample usually is identical to the pretest sample. Also, the teacher can "assist" the pupils in completing their posttest examinations. Experience has shown that many teachers will do this if the stakes are high. If Oregon uses the pretest-posttest differences in pupil scores to support high-stakes decisions, then this may direct teachers' construction and use of work samples to teaching to a biased, easy test and helping the pupils do well on the posttest. Low-level assessments are not a sufficient criterion of pupil learning and teaching effectiveness in a high-stakes decision application.

On the other hand, TWSM does address Oregon's commitment to focus student teacher evaluations and high-stakes decisions on pupil achievement. Using TWSM, teachers show whether they can develop and employ respectable performance assessments. In high-stakes evaluations, the state and school districts could consider such self-assessment evidence along with a wide range of other more objectively gathered information. Teach for America and the National Board for Professional Teaching Standards have successfully followed this approach.

Also, as the authors have discussed, state officials and test developers might usefully examine the large store of teacher-developed work samples to identify those that are especially interesting and good. They might then use these to develop, standardize, and employ some authentic, high-quality work samples. Using these under controlled conditions, they probably could reliably assess different teachers' effectiveness in teaching assigned units of instruction.

As a needs assessment tool, the work samples provide information for refocusing and strengthening teacher preparation. Teacher educators could periodically examine the developing pool of work samples to detect deficiencies in student teachers' abilities to write good performance examinations. Such diagnostic information provides useful direction for improving the measurement and evaluation units in preservice teacher education courses and practicums.

5. What is the value of the TWSM research program for improving teacher preparation?

This program has stirred up much activity in teacher preparation programs. The state already has enacted state education policies that provide for using work samples to evaluate teacher effectiveness. Teacher educators are using the work sample method to prepare teachers. School districts are considering using work samples to evaluate practicing teachers. Teachers also will include work sample assessments of their pupils in portfolios of teaching accomplishments.

The major advantage of enacting state policies to require the use of work samples is the increased focus on improving and assessing pupil achievement gains. However, the work sample approach has many pitfalls. Seemingly, the state has opened the door to constructive uses and abuses of the work sample method. The state probably needs to keep the use of work samples at the level of development and testing rather than of firm policy. If the state and participating schools and universities can remain circumspect and work together to improve the work sample approach, then they might avoid the negative consequences. However, this is a big *if*, especially if the state emphasizes the high-stakes use of work sample results.

In the face of this possibly premature enactment of policy to require work samples, the state's teacher education programs have an important role. They must prepare teachers to make effective, professionally responsible use of work samples. The teacher educators themselves must model appropriately cautious use of work samples in preparing and assessing teachers. I believe they also should recommend against using the approach to license teachers or award merit pay, at least until researchers fully develop and validate the approach. Inappropriate use of TWSM to license teachers or award merit pay could discredit the approach and thus impair its constructive role in teacher preparation and self-assessment.

Overall Assessment

The Western Oregon teacher effectiveness research reflects a growing and appropriate consensus that teacher evaluation should focus squarely on improving pupil achievement. The research also provides systematic means of taking account of student background and other context variables. The researchers have appropriately grounded their studies in issues related to the state's teacher education processes. They are engaging a wide range of stakeholders.

The research has a healthy theoretical and practical focus. The developing theory provides a valuable touchstone for airing and investigating teaching and learning issues. It does not yet provide a stable guide to research, merit pay, policymaking, or licensing practice. Nevertheless, the theory orientation is to be encouraged and likely will become increasingly important and useful as the effort matures.

TWSM is a promising but limited technique for use in teacher education and formative evaluation of teachers. In its present form, TWSM is best used as a tool for training teachers in how to construct performance tests and obtain feedback for improving their teaching. However, the technique is too restricted in the scope and quality of produced evidence to have much value for informing high-stakes decisions about the licensing and employment of teachers.

I predict that teacher-made work samples, if given much weight in high-stakes decisions, will produce indefensible assessments, teaching to tests, much controversy, and possibly expensive litigation. If the state decides to weight TWSM results heavily in licensing, rewarding, or sanctioning teachers, then it should assign a credible group to construct, validate, administer, score, and control the performance assessments. This would be a costly enterprise. Also, it might detract from the technique's value for training teachers to assess and improve their teaching.

Ironically, TWSM, for all its limitations, is one of the best available teacher evaluation techniques. It is more systematic and useful for assessing teacher effectiveness based on pupil outcome data than are most other practices of teacher evaluation. This is a sobering commentary on the state of teacher evaluation. It underscores the importance of systematic programs of research and development, such as Western Oregon's courageous effort to "anchor assessments of teacher effectiveness to work sample assessments of student learning."

CHAPTER 6

Reflections on Comments by Airasian and Stufflebeam

H. Del Schalock
Mark Schalock
Gerald Girod

Airasian and Stufflebeam have provided thoughtful, constructive responses to our description of work in progress. Both have read carefully the materials provided, and both have engaged previously in discussions of the methodology in conference settings. As on other occasions, we have taken and will continue to take their counsel with respect and appreciation.

Although both critiquers have been generous in pointing to the progress and possibilities of our work, both express concerns or hold views that invite further discussion. We will respond briefly to these in four sections: the progress we have made in recent months around several of the issues addressed, the confidence that can be placed in the information obtained through Teacher Work Sample Methodology (TWSM), the value that is added to the preparation and licensure of teachers through the use of TWSM, and the trade-offs that have to be balanced in using TWSM as a methodology designed to serve multiple purposes and audiences.

Progress

Airasian has labeled TWSM correctly as an unfinished, evolving methodology, and we think many of the concerns expressed by our critiquers stem from this reality. Table 6.1 summarizes the progress that has been made around several of the concerns addressed since drafting the chapter nearly a year ago. In our view, each of these steps adds to the quality of the information obtained through a work sample and thus the confidence that can be placed in it. Each step particularly adds to the confidence that can be placed in our index of learning gains by pupils, for each advance adds another degree of quality control in our efforts to *mediate* observed gains in learning by the complexity of outcomes pursued, the quality of measures used by a teacher to assess the learning progress of his or her pupils, and the nature of the context in which teaching and learning occurred.

Merit

The primary concern expressed by both critiquers centers on the quality of learning gain data generated by TWSM and thus on the defensibility of using teacher work samples as a source of evidence for high-stakes decisions pertaining to teacher preparation and licensure.[1] We think this concern is warranted; however, as expressed previously, we believe the level of concern expressed stems in part from where we are in the evolution of the methodology or, more correctly, where we were at the time the chapter was written. We also believe that some of the causes of our critiquers' concern stem from limitations inherent in *any* methodology attempting to sample something as complex and variable as a teacher's work—especially its consequences—and from the trade-offs encountered in choosing to use a methodology for purposes of instruction, assessment, and research.

The limitations imposed by the interplay of these realities on the quality of measurement probably never will be resolved to the satisfaction of psychometricians. Research studies demonstrating the reliability (generalizability) of learning gain data across work samples for a particular teacher, or studies demonstrating the predictability of a teacher's performance from one point in time or level of experience to another, would help. But the impact of context on performance in

TABLE 6.1. Progress Made During the Past Year in Addressing Concerns Expressed by Airasian and Stufflebeam

Concern	Progress
Focusing teacher work samples on "easy-to-accomplish" learning goals	Established institutional policies, procedures, and measures to ensure that learning goals and objectives pursued in a work sample will vary in both kind and complexity and will reflect the state's common curriculum goals and performance standards for pupils.
Measures of uncertain quality used to assess student progress in learning	Established criteria and accompanying rating scales for Western Oregon faculty to use in evaluating the quality of teacher-constructed measures of learning. Criteria include alignment with learning goals being pursued, clarity of directions for pupil use, attention to factors affecting the reliability of measurement (internal consistency, quality of items, breadth of coverage), variety in opportunities to demonstrate learning, feasibility of use, and developmental appropriateness.
Limited attention to the specifics of teacher behavior within a work sample	Adopted as policy at Western Oregon the following criteria for work sample design: College supervisors will formally observe a candidate's teaching performance at least once during each work sample, and both college and school supervisors will provide detailed ratings of a candidate's teaching performance separately for work sample observations and student teaching as a whole. A measure of *pupil engagement in learning* also is to be added to the observations of a candidate's performance during work sample implementation.
Lack of clarity about, or control over, the amount of assistance provided a candidate in preparing a work sample (the problems of "Whose work sample is it?")	Adopted as policy at Western Oregon the following criterion for work sample design: Although feedback always should be provided to a candidate during work sample design and implementation, increasing independence should be demonstrated by candidates in this process. A measure of both the *kind and level of assistance* provided to a candidate in work sample preparation/implementation is now being provided by both college and school supervisors.

Concern	Progress
The appropriateness and sensitivity of the IPG as a measure of learning gain	Currently reanalyzing selected subsamples of the data reported in the chapter using end-of-unit scores and raw gain scores, in addition to IPG scores and IPG "weighted" scores (i.e., IPG scores that take into account the complexity of the learning outcome pursued), to see whether differences in results occur.[a]
The lack of information in the chapter on the specifics of the many rating scales used in the methodology or on the interrater reliabilities of supervisors using the scales	Space did not permit a detailed description of our various rating scales to be presented in the chapter, although these are available on request from the authors. Our latest calculations of the percentage agreement (perfect) between college and school supervisors on the 6-point Likert scales used when summarizing measures of teacher competence and professionalism range from 85.2% to 90.9% for elementary candidates and from 81.1% to 98.2% for secondary candidates. Applying Scott's pi coefficient to correct for chance agreements lowers these scores by only 1 to 5 percentage points.

NOTE: IPG = Index of Pupil Growth.

a. We are looking at these various dependent measures along both empirical and theoretical dimensions—specifically, normalcy of distribution, range, theoretical appropriateness, performance as a dependent measure within a multiple regression framework using predetermined blocks of variables, and stepwise regression. On the criterion of normalcy of distribution, gain scores are the most normally distributed, whereas posttest scores are the least normally distributed. On the criterion of range, weighted IPG scores have the largest range, whereas posttest scores have the most restricted range. From a theoretical standpoint, we believe that the IPG score weighted (mediated) by the complexity of the learning outcome is the most valid measure, whereas the posttest score is the least valid measure. Contextual factors best explain posttest scores and provide the least explanation of gain scores. Student and outcome factors best explain gain scores and provide the least explanation of IPG scores. Teacher competence and professionalism best explain weighted IPG scores but provide the least explanation of gain scores. Both gain scores and posttest scores perform well in stepwise regression in terms of both strength and direction of relationships within final model specifications. At this stage of our analyses, we have found that no one dependent measure performs best on all dimensions. Each has its empirical and theoretical strengths and weaknesses.

studies of this kind makes their findings highly problematic. It needs to be remembered that a work sample, or any other measure of a teacher's impact on learning, provides information around the performance of *a* teacher working with a *particular* set of students toward a *particular* learning goal under a *particular* set of conditions affecting both teaching and learning!

Granting these realities and trade-offs (see subsequent paragraphs on trade-offs), we still believe that TWSM generates information that can and should be taken into account as one of many lines of evidence when considering licensure and other high-stakes decisions pertaining to teachers. Following are 10 features that pertain to the technical merits of TWSM as an approach to measurement that we think warrant this view.

1. *TWSM provides evidence of learning gains by pupils taught as the sine qua non of a teacher's effectiveness* and thus can be viewed as a breakthrough in methodology for enhancing professional standards, licensure decisions, and practice.

2. *TWSM yields measures of pupil learning that are close to a teacher's work* and thus are meaningfully and defensibly reflective of a teacher's impact on student progress in learning.

3. *TWSM includes information about the context in which teachers and students work* and thus provides a fairer and more realistic picture of the effectiveness of a teacher than if such information were not included.

4. *TWSM involves the performance of teaching tasks that mirror those required of teachers in standards-based schools* and thus is viewed as appropriate by teachers, administrators, and the public at large.

5. *TWSM involves the performance of teaching tasks that are far more complex, comprehensive, and demanding than those required of student teachers in most research universities preparing teachers* (Koziol, Minnick, & Sherman, 1996) and thus can be viewed as an advance in professional standards and practice.

6. *TWSM is grounded in both state and national policy pertaining to education for the 21st century.*

7. *TWSM is grounded in both theory and research pertaining to teacher effectiveness.*

8. *Because of all the preceding features, TWSM carries strong face and job* (professional) *validity.*

9. *Because of all the preceding features, TWSM carries strong external* (Shulman, 1987) *and consequential* (Messick, 1995) *validity.*

10. *Because of all the preceding features and the emerging empirical base lending support to our work outlined in the chapter, we believe that TWSM carries promising construct validity as well.*

Although our psychometrician friends still will insist on measure-by-measure evidence of reliability and validity—and they should continue to do so—we have become increasingly concerned with the properties of complex, performance-based, "authentic" measures as discussed by Linn, Baker, and Dunbar (1991) or "direct" measures as discussed by Resnick and Resnick (1996). Ultimately, however, we believe that we must look to the *predictive validity* of TWSM as the single best indicator of its merit. The selection and licensure of teachers has to do with *predicting* the effectiveness of teachers, and we believe that TWSM carries far greater potential for making such predictions than does any measurement methodology we have had in the past.

Worth

Although the value added to the preparation and licensure of teachers through the use of TWSM is intertwined with and depends on its merits as a vehicle for assessment, its *worth* as a vehicle for instruction rests on other criteria. Airasian and Stufflebeam have made this point and have argued that the instructional use of the methodology is its most promising strength. Because this aspect of the methodology was not elaborated in our chapter, following is a brief listing of the strengths we see in TWSM as a vehicle for instruction.

1. TWSM focuses teachers, and teachers of teachers, on student learning.

2. TWSM forces teachers, and teachers of teachers, to go beyond the knowledge, skills, and dispositions thought to be needed for teachers to be successful to how these enabling conditions

can be *integrated and applied* to foster the learning progress desired of pupils.

3. TWSM forces teacher preparation programs to attend to the *assessment* of pupil learning; to the *integration* of curriculum, instruction, and assessment when teaching; and to *interpreting, reporting, reflecting on, and making use of* pupil progress in learning.

4. TWSM provides teachers with the conceptual and procedural foundations they need to function effectively in standards-based schools.

5. TWSM provides teachers with a philosophy and methodology by which to continuously improve as professionals.

Although not addressed by Airasian and Stufflebeam, we view TWSM as having the following additional benefits:

• provides a philosophy and methodology through which teaching can gain focus and respect as a profession (Cowart, 1996);

• provides a potentially powerful methodology for use in research pertaining to teaching and learning and to the productivity of schools; and

• provides a potentially powerful methodology for use in evaluating teacher education programs or programs designed to enhance the effectiveness of practicing teachers.

Although we view these various benefits as reason for optimism about TWSM as a vehicle for instruction, assessment, and research at this juncture in the evolution of education, our critiquers are correct in their caution against overoptimism and their warning against its "seductive appeal" to policymakers.

Trade-Offs

The problem of trade-offs surfaced when we first attempted to develop TWSM as a methodology to serve multiple purposes and audiences while simultaneously attempting to remain faithful to assumptions of theory and canons of measurement. After nearly

5 years of work, the problem of trade-offs still has not gone away, but the competing demands involved have become less contentious and divisive. Following are a few of the trade-offs that have been most difficult to balance:

- the flexibility needed in the methodology as a vehicle for teacher training versus the rigor needed for evaluation and research;
- the demands of the methodology on faculty time, supervisory responsibilities, and program design versus the benefits gained by faculty, and by the institution as a whole, through its various applications;
- the threat carried by the methodology to both college and school supervisors through its emphasis on measurement and pupil progress in learning versus the challenge and sense of professionalism that its successful application brings; and
- the institutional resources required for methodological development and data analysis that could be used for other purposes.

It may well be that having to deal with trade-offs of this kind is an inevitable price to pay when teacher education programs are intended to function as contexts for research or an attempt is made to replace a researcher-specific *project* model for educational research and development with a *program-embedded* model. We are attempting both at Western Oregon State College.

Interestingly, the problem of trade-offs never has surfaced with students enrolled in teacher education programs at Western Oregon. Work samples are known to be required of all prospective teachers in Oregon, and both the philosophy and demands of work samples are in keeping with what prospective teachers think practicing teachers are supposed to do and accomplish.

We are not sure whether we ever will be able to resolve the many nagging dilemmas referred to in these and our critiquers' pages to the satisfaction of everyone involved, but we have moved a long way toward doing so already and believe that we will be able to move still further in the future. In this regard, it needs to be pointed out that in the large scheme of things we barely have begun the work we have laid out for ourselves. For example, after 5 years, we have been able to complete only two rounds of instrument development and refinement, and we still are missing several measures that are central to our theory of teacher effectiveness. Also, we have conducted only limited analyses of the data now available, and these have been carried out largely to determine either the confidence we can place in the Index of Pupil Growth (IPG) metric as a measure of learning gain or the extent to which our theory of teacher effectiveness appears to have explanatory power. Even more telling, because it has taken us so long to lay the foundation of our work and establish to our own satisfaction the promise it holds, we are only now beginning to engage in the kind of conversation represented here by making the work known to others.

Our slowness in all these matters has been due both to a sense of caution and to limited resources. We did not want to advertise more than we had done nor advocate more than we could defend empirically. Also, up to the time our chapter was drafted, all of our work had been supported through regular institutional (state) funds. At this point, however, we now have attracted external funds to support our work. With what has now been accomplished as a foundation, we should be able to move forward on all fronts more rapidly than we have in the past. We also are pleased that a condition of our external funding is that we network broadly with others who share our interests in connecting pupil learning to teacher work. This being the case, the discussion initiated in these pages should serve only as a beginning of discussions to come.

Note

1. With the exception of exploratory work several years ago with one school district, we have not considered TWSM applications in tenure or merit pay decisions.

References

Cowart, B. F. (1996, September). *A profession out-of-focus and the realignment of responsibility.* Paper presented at the annual meeting of the Society for Philosophy of Education, Dallas, TX.

Koziol, S. M., Minnick, J. B., & Sherman, M. A. (1996). What student teaching evaluation instruments tell us about emphases in teacher education programs. *Journal of Personnel Evaluation in Education, 10*(1), 53-74.

Linn, R. L., Baker, E. L., & Dunbar, S. B. (1991). Complex, performance-based assessment: Expectations and validation criteria. *Educational Researcher, 20*(8), 15-23.

Messick, S. (1995). Validity of psychological assessment: Validation of inferences from a person's responses and performances as scientific inquiry into score meaning. *American Psychologist, 50,* 741-749.

Resnick, L. B., & Resnick, D. P. (1996). Performance assessment and the multiple functions of educational measurement. In M. B. Kane & R. Mitchell (Eds.), *Implementing performance assessment: Promises, problems, and challenges* (pp. 23-38). Mahwah, NJ: Lawrence Erlbaum.

Shulman, L. S. (1987). Assessment for teaching: An initiative for the profession. *Phi Delta Kappan, 69*(1), 38-44.

PART III

The Dallas Value-Added
Accountability System

CHAPTER 7

In the Beginning

Luvern L. Cunningham

This is a story of capacity building. It covers a 30-year trek down a sometimes smooth, often rocky road of internal and external work leading to unusual institutional competence.

A Bit of History

The investment in research and development within the Dallas Independent School District (DISD) in Texas began a long time ago, dating back to the superintendency of Nolan Estes in the late 1960s and 1970s. Estes assumed leadership of the DISD during interesting times. He came to the Dallas head job from an important administrative position within the old U.S. Office of Education, before it became a Cabinet-level department. Prior to that, he had been successful as a suburban district superintendent in St. Louis, Missouri. There he earned a national reputation for experimentation through the widely disseminated descriptions of Valley Wind Elementary School. Arriving from Washington, D.C., he brought to the DISD respect for research and development (R&D) and a belief that educational decisions of merit could be made only if there were a sound database within which to anchor them. His federal experience stood him in good stead; he was able to view educational development from a national perspective and brought his knowledge of the federal system with him to Dallas. He knew where to tap federal pockets and was able to garner generous amounts of federal money to invest in the development of the largest, and most effective, R&D unit in the country.

Estes' tenure coincided with the social and racial tumult of the late 1960s and 1970s. Dallas was filled with racial and ethnic tensions, leading to a school desegregation lawsuit. That litigation, beginning in 1971, continued through the 1970s, 1980s, and early 1990s, reaching a federal district court declaration of unitary status in the summer of 1994. The institutional research capability that was developing within the DISD became a central force in the development of desegregation initiatives and the assessment of their effectiveness. The DISD research strength earned the respect of the court as its staff was drawn into the review and analysis of the work of the court-ordered external monitoring unit headed by a special master. This monitoring body conducted studies of the implementation of desegregation remedy plans, passing those appraisals, including recommendations, along to the court. The court in turn required the defendant DISD to submit its analysis of the submissions of the monitoring unit to the court. The point is that the existence of the court-ordered desegregation remedies and the need to perform professional reviews of the special master's work gave the DISD research department important work to do, contributing markedly to the department's development. Quality was superior, and the Board of Education and superintendents depended on the department to supply information essential to implementation of the remedy plans and to assess the work of the court's assessor.

The strident voices of accountability began to appear in the 1970s. Estes was positioning the DISD to be responsive to those voices, and the most effective way in which to do so was through the use of assessment data.

Key to the effectiveness of current evaluation initiatives within the DISD is the long-term leadership of William Webster. He came to the DISD in 1967 and headed an R&D unit that employed, at one time, 40 Ph.D. specialists in evaluation. Webster and his colleagues were (and are) leaders in evaluation, working with specialists in universities, regional laboratories, and other large districts across the country. Over nearly three decades, a remarkable assessment capacity has emerged in Dallas. That capacity includes conceptualization, measurement, and dissemination competence. It includes an ability to address short- and long-term assessment needs. It involves local and statewide leadership and often involves (sometimes reluctant) participation in political work at the state level. Webster's files are stuffed with data of all kinds, most of it analyzed, reported, and entered into arenas of decision making.

Note should be taken of modifications in the management side of Webster's efforts, especially in purpose and focus. Whereas in days gone by there were large numbers of specialists on the payroll and considerable freedom for research staff to select individual research projects (much like within a university research setting) and pursue them with vigor, now freedom is restricted with the sharply reduced resources, and the focus of research and assessment has shifted to targeted work. Many R&D departments in large districts have been decimated by budget reductions; some have little capability left, certainly not enough to produce work equivalent to that of the DISD. As this chapter was being written, here in Ohio the large urban districts have lost their internal R&D capacities almost without exception and are unable to provide essential management information for decision making, let alone the presentation of system performance data that can be used for judging performance by local citizens and public officials at all levels. It is a paradox. At a time when calls for accountability are coming from all quarters, our large districts across the country, with few exceptions, are unable to provide even minimum levels of data to keep stakeholders at all levels informed.

Value Added in Dallas

For a period of 15 months in the early 1990s, I served as a state commissioner-appointed monitor of the DISD, focusing essentially on the work of the school board and superintendent. This responsibility allowed me to view the school district and its leadership and management from a reasonably objective perspective, including the performance of management functions in areas such as assessment. A requirement of monitors serving the Texas Education Agency (the state department) is to report periodically to the state on local district policy and managerial activities in those districts where monitors are placed. This positioning at the nexus of state-local relationship and responsibility is a remarkable vantage point from which to witness the ebb and flow of accountability, among other things. It was during this period, too, that I participated with Dan Stufflebeam and Peggy Siegel in an analysis of the Texas Education Agency's statewide accountability system. The point of this is to say that the remodeling and strengthening of the Texas state accountability system was aided remarkably by the work of Webster in Dallas. Simultaneously, the evolution of new capacities in Dallas was occurring, enabling the DISD to respond to a flood of mandates flowing from the Texas General Assembly, the governor's office, the Southern Regional Education Board, the Texas State Board of Education, the commissioner, and others in the administrative arms of the Texas Education Agency from about 1989 to early 1996.

Few leaders in education or politics who call for reform have any idea about the massiveness of change required of individuals and institutions when, in this instance, a statewide accountability system is introduced and implementation begins. And the same holds for a large district the size of the DISD. The complexity grows further when the concept of state mandate comes face to face with local control. Fortunately in Texas, some leaders recognized in the early 1990s that some new ground in state-local relationships had to be plowed, new ways of working had to be found, and new partnerships had to be forged with the recognition of interdependency as the key to accomplishing the task.

Over the years in many states, Texas among them, there has been a history of legislative initiatives about items in education. Bills are introduced helter-skelter by legislators young and old without much investigation of need or impact. These bills often pass through the rough and tumble of the legislative process and move on to the administrative side of the house for implementation. State department of education personnel, usually dealing from positions of political weakness, are unable to head off such legislation—much of it often bad—and are then faced with implementing something of questionable professional merit that competes with earlier legislation of questionable merit passed in previous sessions—probably, maybe hopefully, not yet up and running. These conditions produce instability, wasteful use of resources, and confusion in the public mind. As education professionals and as citizens, we are naive in the extreme about what it takes to conceive an important reform, mobilize support for its legitimation, and work through the invocation stage on the way to satisfactory implementation of the reform.

The Dallas Value-Added Accountability System captures an enormous amount of growth in conceptualization and integration of information needs within a common framework of understanding, factoring in state accountability requirements within everyday assessment efforts at the local jurisdiction (school district) and, at the same time, incorporating managerial responses to effectiveness and ineffectiveness data at the teacher and school levels. The controlling philosophy of continuous improvement is, and has been, central to Dallas's history. This belief "keeps people at the table." There is so much individual and institutional learning that must take place, and assessment yields both positive and negative consequences, both good news and bad news, and both winners and losers—at least for the short term. It is hard to keep people pumped up and on board, especially when such severe amounts of learning have to occur to keep pace with change and deal with ever-escalating amounts of complexity.

Commitment to participation is emphasized in Dallas. This means the participation of school board members, parents, teachers, administrators, other employees, and community leaders in all aspects and phases of assessment and interpretation of data. Acquiring a workable understanding of "hierarchical linear modeling," for example, is an achievement for laypersons and professionals alike. Seemingly endless meetings are required. Job has to be the consultant on patience. Producing reports and meeting deadlines always are part of the environment. Maintaining communication within the collegial assessment community and responding to a seemingly endless series of requests to prepare professional papers, deliver lectures, make speeches, and participate on panels are the price of success.

The commitment to input is worth noting. The early historic unfolding of evaluation or assessment, however termed, was pretty much circumscribed by professional interest, and its theoretical and measurement tools were the product of thought within the professional family of thinkers such as Ralph Tyler from one perspective and persons such as Eric Lindquist and Benjamin Bloom from another. There was not a lot of "Let's take this to the parents" type of activity. There was not a whole lot of "Let's invite teachers or administrators to help us figure things out" either. Much work was of a highly technical nature, leading to an increasingly specialized literature—exciting to some, boring to others. In hindsight, the development of specialization probably was essential, and it occurred in quite a different time. Now society's expectations are different. Teachers and their organizations are different, and increasingly parental interests are different. "Technology for the common person" has dramatically impacted on private, occupational, and institutional lives and living. The historic isolation and insulation of assessment theoreticians and craftpersons is crumbling. It is a new ball game, and Dallas's experience with participation at the classroom, building, district, and state levels is worthy of study and analysis in its own right.

Responding to input acquired through participation is difficult in most circumstances. But it is especially tricky where change is expected and the changes must occur in the behaviors of professionals (most likely teachers and administrators) and laypersons (most likely parents, politicians, and public officials). We are dealing with educational professionals and laypersons at the nexus of interinstitutional responsibility, for example, schools and families. Thus what Dallas has learned, and is learning, is of some importance interprofessionally, interinstitutionally, and intergovernmentally.

CHAPTER 8

The Dallas Value-Added Accountability System

WILLIAM J. WEBSTER
ROBERT L. MENDRO

A public school system, perhaps more than any other institution, is faced with the need to determine, fairly, which schools and school personnel are effective. An urban public school system contains sufficient diversity to make such a task very difficult. The Dallas Public Schools have felt the need for a fair method for determining effectiveness for several decades. Since 1992, as an outgrowth of a decade's work, the district has determined effective schools using a fair and equitable value-added accountability system. The system recently has been expanded to include the identification of effective teachers and to shape teacher evaluation for the district.

In 1984, the Dallas Public Schools began an effective school ranking system using multiple regression to develop longitudinal student growth curves on norm-referenced tests and to determine effectiveness by the degree to which schools exceeded their students' predicted growth (Webster & Olson, 1988). The system remained in effect for several years but was abandoned when a new state accountability system was mandated. In 1990, the Board of Education established the Commission for Educational Excellence, which, after extensive study, recommended the development of an accountability system that was fair, was based on variables in addition to norm-referenced test data (while retaining an array of test scores as the primary measure of effectiveness), could be extended downward to include measures of teacher effectiveness, and used similar methodology to the 1984 system. The current accountability system, using a combination of multiple regression and hierarchical linear modeling, is an outgrowth of the commission's report.

The accountability system is multifaceted, tying together district and campus improvement planning, principal and teacher evaluation, and school and teacher effectiveness. As such, all district elements directly related to student learning, from teaching in the classroom to campus instructional leadership to district curriculum and instruction and staff development programs, are directly related to improvement on the same set of variables. At the district level, the system sets and measures progress on absolute continuous achievement goals. Internally, at the campus and classroom levels, relative effectiveness is identified, rewarded, and used as a model for improvement. Ineffectiveness is targeted for analysis, assistance, and, if all else fails over repeated attempts, change of personnel. The entire system is focused on continuous improvement (Chapter 22). (For a discussion of the accountability system, see Webster & Mendro, 1995.)

Identifying Effective Schools

Effectiveness and Fairness

School effectiveness must be defined fairly and must be measured in terms of relevant goals. In the public schools, fairness presents a formidable technical problem. The Dallas Public Schools accountability system controls for preexisting student differences in ethnicity, gender, language proficiency, and socioeconomic status (hereafter termed *fairness variables*) as well as prior achievement levels. Additionally, the hierarchical linear model (HLM) employed controls for school-level variables including mobility, crowding, percentage minority, and socioeconomic status (Chapter 22). The political context, however, adds a dimension in which fairness not only must be controlled but also must be capable of being shown to be controlled.

The definition of effectiveness, in turn, must be collectively and cooperatively arrived at by all stakeholders in the system. In the Dallas system, this need is met by an Accountability Task Force. This group, composed of parents, teachers, principals, and community and business representatives, serves as the final authority concerning variable selection and weighting, formulating the rules of the accountability system and the performance awards associated with it as well as hearing appeals of system decisions. Whereas the technical demands of the system narrow the necessary tools that can be used to determine effectiveness, the Accountability Task Force makes the decisions about defining the content of the system and seeing that it is implemented fairly.

No matter what is said about the goals of education, the public defines effectiveness foremost in terms of how a school's students score on tests. The Dallas system includes a variety of important educational variables including criterion- and norm-referenced test scores, student attendance rates, dropout rates, student retention rates, student enrollment in honors courses and advanced diploma plans, graduation rates, and percentages of students taking college entrance tests. The ultimate measures, however, come from test results. A school with improving achievement results is held to be on the right track. Only then do the other variables come into play. No one perceives a school with falling test scores to be effective. For this reason, the Accountability Task Force weights test scores more heavily than it does other variables.

The outcome variables included in the Dallas system as of 1995 are defined in Table 8.1. Student-level variables consist of a number of individual test measures and individual attendance. School-level variables are determined across students for the appropriate population or subpopulation. The weights included in Table 8.1 are the relative weights assigned to each variable by the Accountability Task Force, which approves the variables and assigns weights to them each year.

Fairness also is defined in terms of holding a school accountable only for students who were enrolled in the school long enough for the school to impact their education as well as for all students eligible for the testing programs. In the first instance, only students who are continuously enrolled in a school are used in the analyses. A continuously enrolled student is defined as a student who enrolls in the school by the end of the first 6 weeks of school and remains in the school until the end of the school year. In the second instance, a school is required to test at least 95% of its eligible student population. Therefore, a school cannot gain an advantage by withholding students from testing.

TABLE 8.1. Weighting of Criterion Measures by the Accountability Task Force

Elementary Criteria		Middle School Criteria		High School Criteria	
Criterion	Weight	Criterion	Weight	Criterion	Weight
ITBS— Reading	4/Grade	ITBS— Reading	4/Grade	TAP— Reading Grade 9	6
ITBS— Mathematics	4/Grade	ITBS— Mathematics	4/Grade	TAP— Mathematics Grade 9	6
TAAS— Reading	5/Grade	TAAS— Reading	5/Grade	TAAS— Reading Grade 10	12
TAAS— Mathematics	4/Grade	TAAS— Mathematics	4/Grade	TAAS— Mathematics Grade 10	12
TAAS— Writing Grade 4	5	TAAS— Writing Grade 8	5	TAAS— Writing Grade 10	12
Attendance	1/Grade	TAAS— Science Grade 8	1	ACP— Language	2/Grade
Promotion rate	1/School	TAAS— Social studies Grade 8	1	ACP— Mathematics	2/Grade
		Attendance	1/Grade	ACP— Science	2/Grade
		Promotion rate	1/School	ACP— Social studies	2/Grade
		Dropout rate	1/School	ACP— Reading improvement Grade 9	2
		Percentage in honors courses	4/School	ACP— Honors/ advanced	3/School
				ACP— Foreign language	2/School
				SAT— Verbal Grade 12	2

TABLE 8.1. Continued

Elementary Criteria		Middle School Criteria		High School Criteria	
Criterion	Weight	Criterion	Weight	Criterion	Weight
				SAT— Mathematics Grade 12	2
				PSAT— Verbal	1/School
				PSAT— Mathematics	1/School
				Graduation rate	5/School
				Percentage taking SAT	5/School
				Percentage taking PSAT	3/School
				Percentage in honors courses	4/School
				Percentage in advanced diploma plan Grade 9	3/School
				Percentage in advanced diploma plan Grade 10	2/School

NOTE: ITBS = Iowa Tests of Basic Skills; TAAS = Texas Assessment of Academic Skills, a state-mandated criterion-referenced test; ACP = Assessment of Course Performance, a series of approximately 150 end-of-course criterion-referenced tests.

The Statistical Models

Student outcome variables are analyzed with a two-stage model. The first stage employs multiple regression to control the effects of the fairness variables; the second state, a two-level HLM, controls the effects of prior achievement or attendance and the influence of variables aggregated across the campus. School-level outcome variables are analyzed with a simple multiple regression model using 2 prior years of data for a school on each variable.

The two-stage model for student-level outcomes is used for two reasons. First, by regressing against the fairness variables and their interactions, leveling of existing differences associated with the fairness variables is demonstrated by computing subgroup and marginal means at the end of the first stage. The political advantages of this simple calculation cannot be overemphasized. (No one trusts statistical manipulations unless he or she can see their effects demonstrated; it is not enough to say one has controlled for the fairness variables.) Second, the HLM used in the second stage cannot control the complex set of fairness variables. Mathematically, the school data matrices are not invertable if all variables are entered in the HLM model. However, if fairness variables are removed in the first stage, then HLM proves to be quite robust (Mendro, Webster, Bembry, & Orsak, 1995; Webster, Mendro, Bembry, & Orsak, 1995).

The first stage of the student-level analysis regresses a combination ethnicity/language proficiency variable (four levels: black, Hispanic, limited-English proficient, and other), gender (two levels), free-lunch status (two levels), the first- and second-level interactions of these first three variables, census income, census poverty, and census college attendance (each defined at the census-block level) against each outcome and predictor achievement or attendance variable. The equations are given by the standard multiple regression equations in Equation 1. An outcome or predictor achievement or attendance variable is represented by the Y_i, and the fairness variables and interactions are represented by the X_j's. To control for homoscedasticity of residuals and for mean residuals departing from the regression line, the predictor space is divided into 256 equal intervals after the regression line is determined, and residuals are standardized to a mean of 0 and a standard deviation of 1. After the regression stage, it requires simple calculation to show that the residuals for the 16 possible subgroups formed by the crossing of the ethnicity/language, gender, and free-lunch variables have been equalized.

Linear Regression Equations

$$Y_i = \beta_0 + \beta_1 X_1 + \ldots + \beta_j X_j + r_i, \tag{1}$$

where $r_i \sim s\ N(0, \sigma^2)$.

Residuals from the first stage are then used in the HLM in the second stage of the student analysis. The general equations for the hierarchical analysis are given in Equation 2. Here the Y_{ij} are residuals of student outcome variables from the first stage, the X_{ij} are residuals of prior achievement or attendance variables from the first stage, and the gammas represent school-level variables including mobility, crowdedness, percentage minority, percentage black, percentage Hispanic, percentage on free-lunch program, and average census variables for each school. The HLM equations are solved using empirical Bayes estimation.

Hierarchical Linear Model Equations

$$\text{Level 1:} \quad Y_{ij} = \beta_{0j} + \beta_{1j}X_{1ij} + \ldots + \beta_{kj}X_{kij} + r_{ij} \tag{2}$$
$$\text{Level 2:} \quad \beta_{0j} = \gamma_{00} + \gamma_{01}W_j + u_{0j}$$
$$\beta_{1j} = \gamma_{10} + \gamma_{11}W_j + u_{1j}$$
$$\beta_{kj} = \gamma_{k0} + \gamma_{k1}W_j + u_{kj},$$

where $r_{ij} \sim$s $N(0, \sigma^2)$ and $u_{kj} \sim$s $N(0, \tau_{k0})$ for all k.

Two types of residuals are then used in the accountability system. The first is an empirical Bayes residual for each school that is used as the measure of a school's effectiveness after fairness variables and prior values of outcomes are controlled. The empirical Bayes residuals also have the advantage of incorporating shrinkage into their estimates. The residuals assign more weight to school estimates based on larger samples and assign less weight to estimates based on smaller samples.

The second type is individual student residuals obtained by solving the HLM equations back to the residual components. These student residuals are used as the basis of the teacher effectiveness indexes, which in turn form the basis of the teacher evaluation system (although preliminary efforts to use the student residuals have encountered some problems, which are discussed later in the section on technical issues).

As noted, effectiveness on school-level outcome variables (e.g., dropout rates) is computed using simple multiple regression. Outcome values of the school variables are predicted using the values for the previous 2 years of the variables with schools as the unit of analysis. The standard equations represented in Equation 1 are used with the Y_i representing a school value on the outcome variable and the two X_i's representing the values of the variables for the previous 2 years. Residuals from the regression then become the effectiveness scores on the school variables.

School Effectiveness, Performance Awards, and Penalties

The intent of the Commission for Educational Excellence in establishing school and teacher indexes was the use of indexes to reward effective schools and to provide extensive help and resources to train or retrain the staff of ineffective schools. In light of this, the Dallas Public Schools awarded $2.4 million to effective school staff each of the years from 1992 to 1994 and increased the amount to $3 million for 1995. Ineffective schools have had increased attention ranging from additional resources to replacing administrators to restructuring the schools.

Prior to 1995, approximately 20% of the staff in the district received performance awards. Awards went to the top schools in each of the grade categories K-3, 4-6, K-6, 7-8, and 9-12 with the moneys prorated by the proportion of total staff in each category. The awards were set at $1,000 for each professional staff member and $500 for each support staff member in each winning school. Part-time personnel evaluated by campus administrators received prorated awards. For 1995, the district provided the staff of any school that exceeded prediction with an award in a two-tier system in which the top tier received a full award ($1,000/$500) and the second tier received a smaller award ($480/$240). Schools had to meet improvement thresholds to receive awards; that is, their students had to grow at least the growth rate of the national norm group (Dallas Public Schools, 1994). Given the achievement improvements noted in preliminary analyses of 1995 tests in the system, it was expected that approximately 50% of all district staff in schools would receive awards under the tier system.

No awards were planned for top teachers outside of the effective schools. The intent of the performance awards made at the school level was to encourage cooperation and assistance within a school building. The Accountability Task Force rejected any plan in which a teacher might be encouraged to withhold information or assistance from a fellow teacher in a school. Research on effective and ineffective schools in the district has supported this position to the extent that effective schools were observed to have higher senses of community and teamwork than did their ineffective counterparts (Bearden, Bembry, & Babu, 1995).

Although no formal plans existed at first for increased levels of assistance and scrutiny of ineffective schools, plans were generated each year as a result of increased interest in these schools on the part of the Board of Education. Each year, the degree of assistance and the formality of a structure to provide such assistance have increased.

Identifying Effective Teachers

As planned by the Commission for Educational Excellence and the Board of Education, identifying students above and below prediction for the measurement of school effectiveness has implied the ability to sort information within a school and thereby identify effective teachers in that school. In 1994-1995, the Dallas Public Schools prepared its first set of Teacher Effectiveness Indexes for teachers at the elementary and middle school levels. These indexes were produced for internal school planning purposes only. The trial of teacher indexes led the board to order the district to prepare and implement a system of teacher evaluation based on the indexes. That system is described in the next section.

The Teacher Effectiveness Indexes were prepared from the effectiveness data resulting from the School Effectiveness Indexes program. Teachers of core courses relevant to the test data available (e.g., reading test data for students of teachers of language arts or social studies test data for students of teachers of social studies) were matched to the students to whom they had given grades, and the School Effectiveness Indexes student residual data were computed for each teacher. The effectiveness data all had been standardized to a mean of 50 and a standard deviation of 10 across the district, and this made interpretation of the indexes relatively easy. Teachers with mean performance above 50 were above the district mean. Standard errors of the mean ranged from 2 to 3 for most class sizes, implying that a mean Teacher Effectiveness Index in the range of 2 to 3 points above or below 50 identified significantly higher or lower student testing gains.

The actual computations of indexes immediately highlighted the strengths and weaknesses of the indexes system. In terms of strengths, indexes immensely simplified the fair attribution of effect to teachers, principals had an easily interpretable guide to the relative effectiveness of staff, and test data were readily comprehensible in terms of progress of students. Among the weaknesses of the initial system were that not all teachers had indexes, not all teachers with high indexes were necessarily ideal teachers, attribution of effect in situations where several teachers instructed students in an area was impossible, not all principals were able to use indexes to guide their efforts to work with staff, and errors in grade assignment and in the student database were rapidly highlighted by the indexes.

Given the aforementioned strengths and weaknesses, Teacher Effectiveness Indexes generally performed as they were designed and expected to perform. A fair measure of relative achievement was attributable to most teachers with indexes. The design of indexes with a T-score scale implying a set district mean across indexes facilitated interpretation. As anticipated from the beginning, the indexes had to be used with caution. Not all important outcomes of education are measured by tests (although many more are than the detractors of testing imagine). Indexes had to be placed in a school context and evaluated with the same degree of perception as all other data about a classroom and a teacher. Once they were, they provided a valuable source of information in estimating an individual teacher's ability to influence student learning outcomes.

Despite several hours of training, many principals were unable to make effective use of the indexes. This was partly due to an initial design that provided too much information and did not simplify it sufficiently. Indexes for 1995 eliminated unnecessary information and provided, for each class, the index; the school index on the same variable; a listing of the students on whom the index is based; and the pretest, posttest, and effectiveness scores for each student. For those who deal better with pictures, graphs showing student progress also were included. Additionally, training on the use and interpretation of the indexes was expanded.

The main fact affecting a principal's use of Teacher Effectiveness Indexes is that the indexes do not include, nor were they intended to include, formal diagnostic information about either the students or a teacher. Although they may contain clues—indeed sometimes strong clues—to this information in some instances, the connection is not formally there. The Teacher Effectiveness Indexes provide an indicator that, for nearly all teachers and students, reliably implies that the teacher is effective or ineffective in promulgating achievement gains with those students. From there, it generally requires focused inquiry on the part of the principal or some degree of self-directed examination on the part of the teacher to determine why effectiveness is present or absent. The degree to which a principal or a teacher can focus the inquiry or, in some instances, the degree to which resources are available to help a principal or teacher do so is directly related to the utility of the indexes.

Technical Issues

Because the School Effectiveness Indexes are based on a two-level HLM analysis, it is logical to assume that Teacher Effectiveness Indexes might lend themselves to a three-level HLM analysis. In this analysis, student data would comprise the first level and be nested in classrooms matched to teachers at the second level, which in turn would be nested in schools at the third level. (In this analysis, the school effects would have to be added back into the teacher effect or else nesting of teachers within schools would determine teacher effectiveness relative to the school as opposed to the district, which is what was intended.) Although the two-level HLM analysis showed itself to be both robust and an improvement on single-level multiple regression methods when used with residual scores (Mendro et al., 1995; Webster et al., 1995), current research on three-level HLM analyses for use in Teacher Effectiveness Indexes has not shown the method to be practical or, in many instances, computable on the scale required in this system.

Preliminary investigations indicate that when conditioning variables are introduced at the second and third levels, the HLM analysis is not able to analyze all classroom-level data arrays, and some schools and teachers must be dropped from the analysis. Research into the utility of the three-level model, compared to a two-level model, in a context where second- and third-level conditioning variables are not used is ongoing. The most promising option seems to be using a two-level HLM for the Teacher Effectiveness Indexes in which student residual scores from a fairness analysis form the first level and classrooms form the second level.

Until the two-level (student nested in classroom) HLM investigations for Teacher Effectiveness Indexes are complete, the intention was to use student residuals from the two-level School Effectiveness

Index analyses (student nested in school) for the teacher Indexes. The next technical issue was encountered in using these student residuals in program evaluation and teacher indexes. The residuals from the HLM analysis are not homoscedastic and do not have identical means as assumed in the model. The residuals show a small correlation (most often ranging between .12 and .17) between the initial pretest scores and the residuals. (In the previous multiple regression model, residuals were standardized after the second stage as they are in the first stage.) Research is being conducted to determine how to best standardize these residuals before using them in analyses.

A third technical issue is that of appropriate sample size. The initial Teacher Effectiveness Indexes, which were not intended as a component of teacher evaluation, were computed whenever six or more students were assigned to a classroom with a minimum of six students being used to mask individual student identities. Because the indexes originally were intended as information for both the principal and the teacher, and because the principal received information about appropriate size for making interpretations, this arrangement was sufficient. Although the teacher evaluation system will make an operational definition about sufficient sample size for an index, the issue of how large a sample is needed for valid interpretation still is an important one with no readily available answers. One safeguard, however, is to design the system in a manner that requires observations over more than 1 year. A second is to apply a shrinkage estimate that weights each index by the degree of associated uncertainty that is being applied (personal communication, W. L. Sanders, June 29, 1995). The third option solves the problem directly. If the two-level HLM model (students nested in teachers) is employed, then shrinkage will be built in through the use of the model.

Using Teacher Effectiveness Indexes
in Teacher Evaluation

The Dallas Public Schools is in the midst of constructing a teacher evaluation system based on the Teacher Effectiveness Indexes that was field tested on the entire district in the 1995-1996 school year. The Board of Education approved a framework for the system that was used as the basis of the elements included in the field trial (Dallas Public Schools, 1995; Webster, 1995). A committee of teachers, teacher organization representatives, principals, community members, administrators, and parents, denominated the Teacher Evaluation Task Force, has been assembled and has assigned subcommittees to develop the instruments and procedures necessary to construct a system from the framework. Again, attention has been paid to systematically soliciting input from stakeholders.

The framework addresses the practical aspects of using indexes as a component of teacher evaluation. Many such aspects are addressed, but there are several major issues that needed to be dealt with before the framework could be constructed. The first was the issue of timing. Teacher evaluation must be completed long before indexes are available for a current year. Next was the necessity of addressing all teachers. Approximately 30% to 40% of teachers will not have indexes. As noted earlier, sufficient sample size had to be addressed. The system had to be designed to reflect reliable estimates of effectiveness. Another issue was one of meshing with other district processes already in place in that the system must complement district and school improvement planning as well as principal evaluation. Finally, the issue of concentration of resources had to be addressed. That is, because the emphasis on the entire system is continuous improvement, the teacher evaluation system had to consider the number of teachers for whom the district had sufficient resources to provide extensive help.

As indicated in the discussion of the Teacher Effectiveness Indexes, one problem in using indexes is determining which aspects of performance to improve and how to improve them once low performance is identified. Coupling that fact with the timing problem (i.e., teacher evaluation must be completed about the time most students take tests), the framework specified the use of the Teacher Effectiveness Indexes as the basis of a formative system of teacher evaluation. Teacher indexes, computed and available by mid-September of a current school year and based on the performance of the teacher's students in the previous year, would be used to determine the level and extent of a teacher's evaluation in the current year. Using the indexes to guide the following year's evaluation in an effort to discover and correct the reasons underlying the performance of ineffective teachers directly focused the system on improvement and dealt with the timing issue.

The issue of teachers without indexes had to be addressed next. First-year teachers, teachers of noncore areas, teachers of supplemental or remedial courses, and core teachers without specific measures in the Teacher Effectiveness Indexes also must be evaluated. The intent was to also tie this evaluation more closely to student performance. A second track was proposed in the framework for these teachers. Their evaluation is primarily dependent on how well they use information about student outcomes in the classroom, particularly tests, assignments, and profiles of student progress. This served to tie their evaluation to the only readily available measure of student performance for them. The focus on student outcomes was referred to as the Basic Duties of the Teacher and is based on the work of Scriven (1994). Table 8.2 summarizes the Basic Duties of the Teacher.

Part of the answer to the concern regarding sample sizes for indexes was addressed by placing teacher evaluation on a 3-year cycle. This allows for the collection of sufficient data for estimation of teacher effectiveness, for estimating the stability of the teacher's performance, for the teacher and principal to examine teacher performance, and for the teacher to make substantive adjustments in performance and show improvement. The use of shrinkage estimates is being investigated as a further safeguard.

The mesh with other district processes was built into the framework for teacher evaluation and is part of the consequences of using the School Effectiveness Index variables and outcomes as the underlying basis of district and campus improvement planning and principal evaluation. The school effectiveness process focuses on what the Accountability Task Force defines as the most important outcomes of schooling and a school's performance on them. The District Improvement Plan is required by the Board of Education to address the School Effectiveness Index outcome variables, and a school's Campus Improvement Plan must address identified weaknesses on these variables. Principals are required to focus on the same weaknesses and to focus on planned assistance for teachers with low Teacher Effectiveness Indexes. Finally, teachers, as a required part of teacher evaluation, must implement changes in their teaching behavior that will improve their students' outcomes. This singleness of focus serves to unify the three processes.

Concentration of resources was addressed by using the Teacher Effectiveness Indexes and the Basic Duties of the Teacher to divide teachers into three groups for evaluation purposes. The top tier of

TABLE 8.2. Basic Duties of the Teacher

Duty	Expectation
Profiling	Teacher shows evidence of profiling individual student and class progress by objective and evidence that instruction and individual help have been adjusted based on the profiles
Use of teacher tests	Teacher shows evidence of the use of appropriate tests, frequency of testing, feedback to students, and use of results to adjust instruction
Student portfolios	Teacher shows evidence of appropriate assignments (classwork and homework), grading of assignments, feedback to students from assignments, and use of assignments to adjust instruction
Curriculum and instructional design	Teacher shows evidence of covering all of the essential elements

teachers, approximately 40%, will receive a classroom observation based on a rescaled Texas Teacher Appraisal System in the 1st year of each cycle, and this will be the extent of their evaluation provided the observation indicates no problems and the teachers' indexes remain above average. In essence, high indexes or Basic Duties of the Teacher ratings provide their evaluation in the 2nd and 3rd years of the cycle. Thus the level of evaluation is reduced for the most effective teachers. Middle-tier teachers, approximately 50%, receive a classroom observation in each year of the cycle provided their indexes remain in the middle level. This amounts to the same level of evaluation that they currently receive. The bottom tier of teachers, approximately 10% (or 750 teachers in Dallas), receive extensive evaluation including classroom observation, Basic Duties of the Teacher, and extra assistance from staff development and curriculum and instruction personnel each of the 3 years in the cycle until such time as their students' performance improves. Additionally, supplemental evaluation instruments and processes are available to both the teachers and the principal during the cycle to use as needed.

These supplemental indicators include a formal teacher portfolio, a structured formative classroom observation, a peer review process, a student survey, a parent interview, and, where necessary, a content knowledge assessment. Thus evaluation and help are greatly increased for the least effective teachers.

The system is summarized in Table 8.3. It shows the index and nonindex groups, the three tiers, the concentration of resources, and the formative nature of the process. As expected, the system, as being designed and developed by the Teacher Evaluation Task Force within the guidelines of the framework, is and will be much more detailed and richer than the summary in Table 8.3. However, the table shows the essence of the system as it was to be field tested in 1995-1996.

Future Considerations

Several future considerations spring from the student performance-based systems defined in the preceding. This summary has not addressed changes in testing and testing policy resulting from the implementation of these systems. An important part of that policy is the analysis and detection of cheating and the more fundamental question of teaching to the test or even the yet more fundamental question of teaching only to the objectives being tested. Nor has the distinction between relative and absolute systems been addressed.

The system includes comprehensive computerized cheating analyses that are done on a classroom-by-classroom basis. Unusual increases in achievement, or outliers, are analyzed and, where deemed necessary by the Accountability Task Force, are investigated. Cases of apparent inflated test scores from previous years also are investigated. Where necessary, examination of test documents and retesting is done. If evidence of cheating exists, then schools are disqualified from the awards program, and personnel are dealt with through the district's personnel system.

The overall accountability system contains absolute goals and specifies them for campuses and the district. However, these goals are not currently empirically determined. The systems for School Effectiveness Indexes, Teacher Effectiveness Indexes, and teacher evaluation all are designed to identify relative performance. A pressing need for future development of the system is to determine

TABLE 8.3. Three-Year Teacher Evaluation Cycle

Teacher	Group	Year 1	Year 2	Year 3
Teachers of elective courses and others without indexes	Tier 1 (top 40%[a])	TAAS BDOT[b]	No additional evaluation	No additional evaluation
	Tier 2 (middle 50%[a])	TAAS BDOT	TAAS	TAAS
	Tier 3 (bottom 10%[a])	TAAS BDOT Supplemental Instruments	TAAS BDOT Supplemental Instruments	TAAS BDOT Supplemental Instruments
Teachers with indexes	Tier 1 (teacher indexes top 40%)	TAAS	Indexes	Indexes
	Tier 2 (teacher indexes middle 50%)	TAAS	TAAS	TAAS
	Tier 3 (teacher indexes bottom 10%)	TAAS BDOT Supplemental Instruments	TAAS BDOT Supplemental Instruments	TAAS BDOT Supplemental Instruments

NOTE: TAAS = Texas Assessment of Academic Skills, a state-mandated criterion-referenced test; BDOT = Basic Duties of the Teacher.

a. Percentages are determined after the first administration of BDOT and TAAS by taking all scores, ranking them, and dividing into the three groups.

b. Basic Duties of the Teacher include profiling, testing, student portfolios, and curriculum/instructional design.

whether absolute minimums of performance can be and should be empirically established. Is there a point in the future when many teachers or schools will reach acceptable absolute levels of performance so that their relative performance is immaterial? What technical problems must be overcome to identify satisfactory minimal performance? As a minimum, the most effective schools and teachers should be used to establish goals based on best practice.

The next major task in the development of this system is the establishment of meaningful criterion-referenced objectives for students and teachers. Although it always will be enlightening and useful from a training perspective to determine the most effective schools and teachers, there may come a time, if the district continues to improve, when perhaps 90% of teachers and schools will deserve recognition. When that occurs, the methodology for recognizing them must be available.

References

Bearden, D. K., Bembry, K. L., & Babu, S. (1995, April). *Effective schools: Is there a winning combination of administrators, teachers, and students?* Paper presented at the annual meeting of the American Educational Research Association, San Francisco.

Dallas Public Schools. (1994). *School Performance Improvement Awards: 1994-95.* Dallas: Author.

Dallas Public Schools. (1995). *Proposal for a comprehensive teacher evaluation system.* Dallas: Dallas Public Schools, Department of Institutional Research.

Mendro, R. L., Webster, W. J., Bembry, K. L., & Orsak, T. H. (1995, April). *An application of hierarchical linear modeling in determining school effectiveness.* Paper presented at the annual meeting of the American Educational Research Association, San Francisco.

Scriven, M. (1994). The Duties of the Teacher. *Journal of Personnel Evaluation in Education, 8,* 151-184.

Webster, W. J. (1995). The connection between personnel evaluation and school evaluation. *Studies in Educational Evaluation, 21,* 227-254.

Webster, W. J., & Mendro, R. L. (1995). Evaluation for improved school level decision-making and productivity. *Studies in Educational Evaluation, 21,* 361-399.

Webster, W. J., Mendro, R. L., Bembry, K. L., & Orsak, T. H. (1995, April). *Alternative methodologies for identifying effective schools.* Paper presented at the annual meeting of the American Educational Research Association, San Francisco.

Webster, W. J., & Olson, G. H. (1988). A quantitative procedure for the identification of effective schools. *Journal of Experimental Education, 56,* 213-219.

⤙ CHAPTER 9 ⤚

Value-Added Productivity Indicators
The Dallas System

Yeow Meng Thum
Anthony S. Bryk

Increased accountability is a major theme in public education today. A broad distrust of all public institutions; very tight local, state, and federal budgets; and a public rhetoric that decries our diminished educational productivity internationally all have combined to fuel this movement. Moreover, there is little reason to believe that the press for greater productivity from schools is likely to ease anytime soon. Accountability seems to be here to stay for the foreseeable future. How best to accomplish this, however, is far from clear.

School accountability systems evolve over time, usually in cycles of continuous negotiations over objectives, consequences, and schedules. Each new phase begins with the stakeholders' decisions regarding for what the school or the teacher can fairly be held accountable. The system must then demonstrate that the proposed analyses are clear, that effects are accurately measured and the tweaks reasonable when compared to plausible alternatives, and that the results be replicable simply because, in high-stakes evaluation, follow-up demands for timely external audits cannot be far behind. The Dallas Public Schools system no doubt has undergone several such cycles in the past two decades.

The previous chapter, by Webster and Mendro, highlights some of the numerous political and technical issues that confront efforts to develop defensible information systems to support accountability processes for public schools. The chapter shares some of the authors' accumulated experience from more than a decade-long effort in this area by the Dallas Public Schools. By virtue of this longevity, if nothing else, Dallas is a leader among urban school districts in this regard. Much of what Dallas has done or attempted to do sets the standard for other urban districts.

On the political side, the Dallas team appears quite effective in that it has established an operative system and appears to have built a stable political coalition around it. The importance of the stakeholder process that it has employed and the leadership *buy-in* that this tends to promote cannot be overstated. Although most of our remarks in this chapter focus on technical aspects of the information and analysis system that undergirds their accountability processes, political considerations are arguably at least as significant. The public has to trust that important aspects of schooling are being assessed and that the system operates fairly. Although technical procedures can provide considerable assistance in this regard, in the end this is fundamentally a community education process. Unless civic, political, and professional leaders understand and endorse the system, it cannot be sustained.

The Dallas System

Of its more salient features, standardized test scores comprise the primary outcomes measuring student learning in the Dallas system, although we expect that, once their measures are adequately established, alternative assessments also can be accommodated. At its outset, it is a clear strength of the Dallas system that proper allowances in the design of the database are made to credit a school with a student's improvement or deficit only if the student is enrolled in the school by the end of the first 6 weeks and takes the test in that school at the end of the school year. Not only is it fair that a school should not be held accountable for students it has little or no opportunity to educate, but it is critical to minimize the effects of student mobility on the evaluation. High and usually uneven student mobility typical in urban school systems can severely affect both teaching and learning with disastrous consequences for year-end assessments of those students who moved as well as those who stayed. Recent research in Chicago has found that about a quarter of the 4th grades see their average achievement levels improve considerably once mobile students are excluded from consideration (Kerbow, 1996). Equally commendable are precautions taken to prevent schools from gaining an advantage by withholding less prepared students from being tested; schools with fewer than 95% of test-eligible students are excluded from subsequent analyses (or should be scrutinized separately).

The general thrust of the analyses is to compare a student's observed test score to the prediction of how well the student can be expected to do based on his or her performance during the previous year. An estimate of the deviation from expectation, the student-level residual, is considered to be the "value added" by the teacher or, at a more aggregate level, by the school.

The advantages of a value-added approach to the measurement of change have been demonstrated in recent years (Bryk, Deabster, Easton, Luppescu, & Thum, 1995; Meyer, 1993; Sanders & Horn, 1993). Adoption of this model is a distinctive feature of the Dallas system that separates it from most other districts that focus only on annual reports of average test scores. As Meyer (1993) has forcefully demonstrated, significant school improvements can be occurring but are masked under status-based accountability systems, especially under conditions of high student mobility and other factors that depress average scores. From a purely technical perspective, the arguments seem very clear: Anything other than a value-added-based approach is simply not defensible.

The Dallas analyses control for the usual politically sensitive covariates—the so-called *fairness variables*—as well as the student's attendance, both at the level of the student and at the school level. We recognize that this is a controversial issue in many accountability systems, mainly because the aim of this analysis activity often is confused. If the purpose is to develop fair and defensible indicators of school and teacher productivity, then such statistical adjustments are quite appropriate. Clearly, certain student populations are more difficult to educate; if we are to hold all schools and teachers accountable, then we have to create a *level playing field* for making these judgments. Although the question of fairness can be difficult to deal with, it must be confronted openly.

This concern, however, in no way diminishes the importance of another, entirely different (and very important) goal: setting high and common standards of attainment for all students. For charting progress against this aim, no adjustments are appropriate, as ultimately all students are societal members who eventually will have to compete in a global economy. The general point here is that the purpose of the analysis (i.e., productivity indicators vs. charting progress against standards) dictates how the adjustment issue should be addressed. We commend Webster and Mendro in this regard and now direct the reader's attention to their analyses.

At the analytic core of the Dallas Public Schools accountability system is a two-phase analysis strategy. Analyses are performed separately for each grade using 2 years of test data at a time. We have several suggestions and also some questions regarding various details of the analysis, but first we offer a summary of how we understand the procedure. In practice, the analysis is implemented as follows.

Phase 1. Taking each student outcome or student covariate separately, multiple regression is used to remove the effects of ethnicity, gender, free-lunch status, and census proxies for student socioeconomic status (SES) from each of the variables. Reproduced here in matrix notation is another version of Webster and Mendro's Equation 1:

$$y = X\beta + r, \tag{1}$$

where $r \sim N(0, \sigma^2 I)$. Residuals from each Phase 1 regression are then forced to be homoscedastic with respect to the predictor space spanned by ethnicity, gender, and free-lunch status.

Phase 2. Standardized Phase 1 residuals of outcomes and of covariates, now represented as the random variable y_j and fixed predictors X_j, respectively, next enter into the student-level equation for each school j ($j = 1, 2, 3, \ldots, J$) of a two-level hierarchical linear model (HLM). Recall that one critical component of the covariates in X_j is the pretest score. For consistency, we again rewrite Webster and Mendro's Equation 2 as

$$y_j = X_j\beta_j + e_j; \overset{+}{2^n} \beta_j = W_j\gamma = v_j, \tag{2}$$

where $e_j \sim N(0, \sigma^2 I, T)$, 0 is of order n_j, and $v_j \sim N(0, T)$. At the school level are covariates, W_j, such as the promotion rate, dropout rate, percentage of students enrolled in honors courses, percentage taking SATs, and so on. Note that the residual parameter terms in v_j are generally correlated with variance-covariance matrix T. Finally, γ estimates the regression on school factors.

We have several reservations regarding the analysis as represented here. From a technical point of view, the two-phase analysis is neither necessary nor defensible. The types of adjustments can easily be accomplished within the standard multilevel framework.

First, even though the political rationale for homogenizing subgroup residuals by standardizing to a mean of 0 and a standard deviation of 1 may have some rationale, the practice is likely to induce unpredictable biases in teacher or school effectiveness estimates. What we can expect when we consider the test score alone is that, although the ranking of students within each subgroup is preserved, removing nonzero residual means will affect teachers and schools serving students primarily drawn from various "deviating" subgroups. It also is likely that distributional differences in subgroup residual distributions are related to the distributive effects of school organizational characteristics, in which case appropriate school-level covariates should be used to model these differences instead (Chapter 11).

Second, accepting the strategy for controlling fairness variables X as described, its results should be compared to the conventional approach for predicting a student's score, $y^{(2)}$, based on his or her pretest, $y^{(1)}$, after adjusting for the covariate set, X:

$$y^{(2)} = X^*\beta^* + \delta, \tag{3}$$

where $X^* = (y^{(1)}, X)$. When written for each school j, Equation 3 actually appears as the student-level equation in Webster and Mendro's multilevel linear model. This begs the question as to why the Phase 1 analyses (without the questionable attempt to homogenize subgroup residual distributions) could not formally represent the student model at Level 1 of a two-level HLM.

Most programs for multilevel regression assume at the outset that random effects are correlated. Thus the number of free variance-covariance terms to be estimated increases as $p(p-1)/2$ if p is the number of random effects. We surmise from Webster and Mendro's Equation 2 that they treated all Level 1 coefficients as random. Given the number of variables and first- and second-order interactions, they may well have had 20 random effects, which results in a T matrix at Level 2 with 210 unique elements! Very few school systems have that many units, so in situations like these there are simply too few degrees of freedom to specify or estimate the model. It is almost certain, therefore, that the source of many of the technical headaches referred to by Webster and Mendro is simply a model overspecification problem. If the number of random coefficients is not too large relative to the number of Level 2 units, then a two-level multilevel model should produce stable and sensible results.

In many applications in school effects research, only the intercept term is considered random because the adjustment coefficients are not of direct interest. We note that to the extent that slope heterogeneity exists for the adjustment covariates, it means that the basic parameterization of school (or teacher) effects is incorrect (Bryk & Raudenbush, 1992). We maintain that school effects can be characterized in terms of one effect (i.e., mean differences) when the analysis indicates otherwise. Thus either all coefficients should be fixed (and corresponding predictors grand mean centered) or the random slopes should be objects of study. In either case, the analysis can routinely be accommodated within the multilevel framework.

In addition, doing the analysis in two steps may result in incorrect estimates for the Level 1 adjustment coefficients. Within the multilevel model, these are pooled within group relationships, for example, how variation in SES within a school affects achievement. Under the ordinary least squares strategy used here, the adjustment coefficient is an unknown combination of the within- and between-group relations. This is not easily interpretable, and it is not clear whether it is defensible for this purpose. The approach adopted here has little to recommend itself.

No comments are offered by Webster and Mendro as to how the Level 1 variables are treated in the analysis. Bryk and Raudenbush (1992) note that centering and specification of the Level 1 coefficients are very important considerations that, unfortunately, are ignored in many analyses. In this application, the Level 1 predictors should be grand mean centered and the slope coefficients should be specified as fixed if the intent is for the intercept, β_{0j}, to be interpreted as an adjusted school mean (which is what the authors seem to imply as their intent). We also note that if grand mean centering were used, treating the slopes as random in this application would remain very problematic. In effect, each school has an adjusted mean outcome, but the adjustments are based on school-specific slopes. It is unclear to us how or why one would want to do this. At a minimum, some explicit rationale should be offered here.

In general, residuals are notoriously unreliable. Residuals from a set of residuals analysis would only further compound this problem, leading to serious questions concerning the reliability of the productivity indicators. At several points, Webster and Mendro imply that their results are reliable but provide little evidence to support this. Frankly, it is hard to conceive how this could possibly be true, at least for use at the teacher level. There is measurement error in the tests, error in the residuals from the Level 1 analysis, and further error added in the residuals from the Level 2 analysis. At a minimum, the authors should articulate a full error-in-indicators model, estimate the relevant variance components, and then examine the necessary sample sizes required to achieve a reasonably precise indicator. Again, perhaps this was done and just not presented in their chapter. Anyone considering using this approach, however, should be satisfied on this account before proceeding.

Finally, in place of Webster and Mendro's statement that *the HLM equations are solved using empirical Bayes estimation*, which appeared just before their restatement of the HLM model, several clarifications probably will be helpful. The principal parameters of a multilevel model are γ, σ^2, and $\mathbf{T}$. In all versions of the Bryk, Raudenbush, and Congdon program, γ is estimated by generalized least squares and the variance components by restricted maximum likelihood. Given these estimates, the student- and school-level residuals are empirical Bayes (Bryk & Raudenbush, 1992, p. 39), with increasing shrinkage reflecting relatively diminished reliability of individual student or school estimates.

The Case for Analyzing Gains

The strategy of predicting performance from a pretest score with covariate adjustment is a straightforward analysis of covariance. Regular users of this technique no doubt are familiar with the usual caveat regarding this approach in quasi-experimentation. In the absence of randomization, we never can be sure whether we have identified and controlled for all the relevant background variables. As a result, our choice of control variables can have a substantial impact on our inferences. Use of residuals from prior regression analyses, as in the Dallas study, does not diminish the significance of this problem, although it would be helpful for the authors to report the strength of their predictions. So long as we are uncertain about the predictions from each of the separate analyses, we have at best a weak basis for making projections of performance. By extension, it is easy to see why the approach is doubly problematic for the purposes of measuring gain. Finally, at the teacher level, the information thins and the inference becomes proportionately more tenuous.

We argue that a relatively stronger basis for measuring growth or change in performance can be based on the student's gain score, the basis of a value-added analysis shared by Bock, Wolfe, and Fisher (1996), Bryk et al. (1994), and Sanders and Horn (1993). This direct approach has the principal advantage that, for a range of intraindividual variation, the student *acts as his or her own control*. Properly adjusted, the student gain score measures the amount of learning added during the period of instruction (or schooling) between testing.

In an ongoing study to fashion a defensible indicator of a school's impact on student learning (or a school's productivity) for the purposes of assessing a school's impact on learning over time, we have to ensure that the measuring instruments are equated in the proper manner and that they have the metric necessary for modeling change and growth (i.e., measures are linear on a continuous scale). An earlier report of this research is found in Bryk, Raudenbush, and Congdon (1994). Some of the same technical issues have been discussed recently in Bock et al.'s (1996) review of the Tennessee Value-Added Assessment System.

Without going into detail, we adopt a three-level HLM that first weighs each observed student gain score by its precision. To keep the models manageable, and because gain profiles vary considerably from one grade to the next, we analyze each grade separately. At Level 2, we estimate the school gains profile for the entire study period after adjusting the student *true* gain score for changing composition of the student body over time due to neighborhood changes in ethnicity, student mobility, and system policies on bilingual testing and retention at each grade in the school over the years. It is important to note that the residual parameter terms are assumed to be uncorrelated within schools because students in a grade are observed for only 1 year. At Level 3, the residual parameter variance-covariance matrix is free to vary. Here, we may examine the components of the estimated school gains profile in relation to school-level covariates. Also under development are enhancements to the model to handle a reparameterization of coefficients at the higher levels to facilitate, for example, direct estimation of trends in the school learning indexes.

Conclusion

We have highlighted a number of technical issues that raise serious questions for us about the validity of the Dallas information and analysis system. Taken together, these uncertainties must erode one's confidence in any accountability decisions that might be made about either schools or teachers on the basis of these analyses. We simply cannot determine whether or not they are justified. On balance, there is much to commend about this work. It is more sophisticated in its recognition of a wide spectrum of technical and political problems than are most systems. Nevertheless, our examination of this system provides reasons for caution. Substantial public rhetoric today demands initiatives of this sort. In our view, it it easy to do this badly but very hard to execute such a program well. As much as Webster and Mendro have accomplished, we are still not there.

References

Bock, R. D., Wolfe, R., & Fisher, T. H. (1996). *A review and analysis of the Tennessee Value-Added Assessment System.* Nashville, TN: Comptroller of the Treasury, Office of Educational Accountability.

Bryk, A. S., Deabster, P., Easton, J. Q., Luppescu, S., & Thum, Y. M. (1995). Measuring achievement gains in the Chicago Public Schools. *Education and Urban Society, 26,* 306-319.

Bryk, A. S., & Raudenbush, S. W. (1992). *Hierarchical linear models: Applications and data analysis methods.* Newbury Park, CA: Sage.

Bryk, A. S., Raudenbush, S. W., & Congdon, R. T. (1994). *Hierarchical linear modeling with HLM/2L and HLM/3L programs.* Chicago: Scientific Software International.

Kerbow, D. W. (1996). *Pervasive student mobility: A moving target for school improvement.* Chicago: University of Chicago, Center for School Improvement.

Meyer, R. H. (1993). *Can schools be held accountable for good performance? A critique of common educational performance indicators.* Working paper, Harris Graduate School of Public Policy Studies, University of Chicago.

Sanders, W. L., & Horn, S. (1993). *An overview of the Tennessee Value-Added Assessment System.* Knoxville: University of Tennessee.

∽ CHAPTER 10 ∾

On Trial

The Dallas Value-Added Accountability System

GARY SYKES

echnical advances in the analysis of student test score data create
new opportunities for administrators and policymakers to use
such evidence for decision making in education. At the same time,
empirically based challenges to such use have emerged and require
serious consideration. This conjunction of technical advances with
educational reservations of various kinds suggests the need for a
framework that administrators and policymakers might use to judge
the overall merit of systems employing student outcome indicators
for organizational decision making.

One such framework is emerging within reconsiderations and
reconceptualizations of validity as a foundational concept of psycho-
metrics. Although the classic approaches to validity theory within
the field retain their hold on practice, raising doubts about the immi-
nent prospect of a paradigm shift, progressive social scientists are
raising fundamental questions and are beginning to explore new approaches that operate out of the American philosophical tradition of
pragmatism. The new work (see, e.g., Cronbach, 1987; Shepard,
1993) seeks to interrogate the properties and uses of measurement
from the perspective of consequences broadly construed. I argue that
administrators and policymakers, in pursuit of consequences, must

pose six questions that together constitute *a framework of account-ability for accountability systems:*

What are the consequences of the testing system for
- learning and learners?
- teaching and teachers?
- the representation of knowledge in the curriculum?
- the organization and management of the educational process?
- the school as culture and community?
- public knowledge and understanding of the educational process and its outcomes?

Such a framework might be used in a variety of ways, ranging from the conduct of formal or informal inquiry on the effects of a testing system to use within a judicial model of evaluation that puts the accountability system on trial via testimony from witnesses according to rules of evidence. From the information presented in Webster and Mendro's chapter on the Dallas Value-Added Accountability System (Chapter 8), neither advocates nor critics of the system can assess its merits because the evidence is not available. A first order of business, then, is to begin assembling relevant data on the effects of the system within a consequentialist frame for validity.

As a proxy for inquiry, I adopt the role of prosecuting attorney in challenging this system, drawing on arguments and evidence from studies of testing and of related matters in each of the areas indicated.

Learning and Learners

The central issue facing any testing system should be its effects on learners and learning. From this perspective, scrutiny of the Dallas system raises several issues. First, a testing system that emphasizes discrete items in multiple-choice format covering basic skills together with attention to criterion-referenced items in the content areas leaves out attention to complex cognitive performances and tasks. Such an assessment system does not provide adequate measures of the kinds of learning now widely regarded as the appropriate standard for U.S. schools (see, e.g., Gardner, 1991; Perkins, 1992). The kind of learning tested here does not reflect the kind of learning called for in the standards established by professional groups such as the mathematics and science communities. In Meier's (1995) phrase, the contemporary standard is to assist students in learning to use their minds well. This way of putting the central goal of education stresses student engagement with real-world problems, active construction of knowledge, and use of disciplinary knowledge for work on complex tasks. Assessments that reflect such a view of learning must parallel in their form and content the kinds of learning tasks that teachers employ in instruction. If the assessment tasks require selection of correct answers on items testing factual recall and use of basic skills on decontextualized problems, then such tasks press toward a narrow, impoverished conception of learning that comes to influence students and teachers alike.

In response, it may be argued that Dallas is using tests that are widely recognized (e.g., Iowa Test of Basic Skills [ITBS]) and/or are required by the state (e.g., Texas Assessment of Academic Skills). But a school or school district might be charged with the responsibility to supplement federal and state requirements with local assessments that reflect community and professional consensus on desirable learning. At least from the perspective of much expert professional opinion, the Dallas test batteries are of doubtful worth and arguably look to psychometric testing's past, not its future.

Regarding effects on learners, at least two views compete for attention. Some evidence suggests that regular repeated testing of students, particularly in the early elementary grades, creates considerable stress and anxiety from which many teachers seek to protect students (see, e.g., Smith, Edelsky, Draper, Rottenberg, & Cherland, 1990). Heavy doses of testing in the early elementary years can have damaging effects on young children. Likewise, other critics of testing decry the overemphasis on extrinsic motivation to learn, pointing to the social-psychological evidence that a regular diet of extrinsic rewards and sanctions undercuts intrinsic motivation to learn (for review of this evidence, see Kohn, 1993). The counterargument is that learning standards, expectations, and consequences are dangerously weak in many schools today, constituting both a cause and an effect of student disengagement from school (see Steinberg, 1996, for one such argument). Some school critics, then, argue for more rigorous tests attached to real consequences for students as a response to the general problem of students' weak motivation to learn, particularly at the high school level. The obvious question underlying this debate is the following: What effects do the Dallas test batteries and assessment system have on learners? Local studies of various kinds are needed to answer this question.

Teaching and Teachers

A small body of research has examined the impact of standardized testing on teachers and teaching, and the findings reveal a number of serious concerns. One study of elementary teachers (in Arizona), for example, used surveys, interviews, and classroom observations to uncover a representative list (see Smith, 1991b; Smith et al., 1990). Teachers reported experiencing negative emotions in response to the state-mandated ITBS and a determination to do whatever was necessary to avoid low scores. They also perceived frequent mismatches between the test and their instructional aims. Classroom observations led to the conclusions that the testing program reduced time available for instruction, narrowed curricular offerings and teaching methods, discouraged innovation, and reduced teacher capacity to use methods and materials that were not tightly linked to test content and format. In one case presented as typical,

> What we saw in one school's sixth grade was a transition, as the school year progressed toward ITBS testing in April, from laboratory, hands-on instruction in science several days a week, to less frequent science out of textbooks (choral reading from the text and answering comprehension and vocabulary questions on worksheets), to no science instruction at all in the weeks before the test, to either no science at all or science for entertainment value during the ITBS recovery phase, to science instruction precisely tailored to the questions in the district criterion-referenced tests, to no science at all. (Smith, 1991b, p. 10)

Supporting evidence from a national teacher survey reported that 60% of math and science teachers were negatively disposed to standardized tests, regarding them as narrowing and fragmenting the curriculum, limiting the nature of thinking, and forcing the pace of content coverage to prepare for the tests (Madaus, West, Harmon, Lomax, & Viator, 1992).

These two studies also examined how teachers prepared students for the tests, uncovering a range of practices that mixed the educationally defensible with the indefensible. This range includes teaching test-taking skills, teaching content covered on the test, teaching to the test format, practicing test or parallel test items, and cheating (e.g., supplying answers, coaching during the test, altering the pre-post test-taking population) (see Shepard, 1988; Smith, 1991a). This range of teaching practices renders uncertain the meaning of test scores as an indicator of what students know and can do because the scores are susceptible to teaching strategies unrelated to substantive knowledge.

Finally, the study of mathematics and science teachers reported that teachers with more than 60% minority students in their classes indicated greater pressures to increase scores, more direct test preparation strategies, and more use of standardized tests in their instruction. Based on such evidence, the investigators concluded that the adverse effects of standardized testing fall disproportionately on low-income and minority students and their teachers. Presumably this indictment would apply to many schools and classrooms in Dallas, raising questions about the equity of test impacts.

The Representation of Knowledge in the Curriculum

A third area for careful scrutiny is the congruence between the goals or aims of education and the particular means used to assess them. Across the country today, progressive educators are calling for greater attention in the curriculum to goals such as learning for conceptual understanding, the development of critical thinking skills, the capacity to apply knowledge to novel problems, and the ability to work in groups on complex learning tasks. Although public opinion continues to favor attention to basic skills, cognitive psychologists (e.g., Resnick, 1987) now argue that the basic-advanced dichotomy is misleading and that educators should engage students from the outset in complex cognitive tasks and performances through which they naturally acquire basic skills and common cultural knowledge.

Consonant with these views, the assessment of school learning is undergoing significant change. Large- and small-scale trials are pioneering new forms of performance-based assessment that more accurately reflect the new goals of learning. Rather than representing knowledge as discrete bits of information and decontextualized skills formatted within the framework of standardized, multiple-choice tests, so-called "authentic assessment" introduces complex, holistic performances that engage students in the creation of intellectual products, the solution of real-world problems, and the application of knowledge and skill to novel situations. Technical difficulties in administering and scoring the new assessments continue to make their use problematic as instruments of public policy, but they serve as strong challenges to the tests in use that do not represent the emerging views about knowledge, its acquisition, and its use. Stated most provocatively, the Dallas system relies on an outmoded set of tests reflecting obsolete conceptions of knowledge, curriculum, and the goals of education (Chapter 19).

Finally, close analysis of test and textbook content, particularly in mathematics and science, reveals serious mismatches between contemporary content standards—as put forth by the National Council for the Teachers of Mathematics (NCTM), the American Association for the Advancement of Science (AAAS), and others—and what is covered in the school curriculum. The most common tests, including the ITBS used in Dallas, feature an overwhelming emphasis on low-level conceptual knowledge and low-level thinking (see Madaus et al., 1992).

The Organization and Management of the Educational Process

The Dallas accountability system reflects a bureaucratic conception of organization and management that allocates planning and design to the central office and implementation of central directives to subordinate workers in schools. Control is primarily centralized in the hands of managers who design the system, even if design involves limited forms of worker participation. The aim of such a system is to standardize production processes, to impose uniform quality control procedures on work, and to control worker behavior through the manipulation of rewards, incentives, and sanctions (Chapter 11).

Competing conceptions of organization and management have gained considerable currency in recent years. These emphasize the devolution of authority to local schools, the exercise of greater school-community control and/or the empowerment of teachers as professional workers capable of greater involvement in school decision making, and the diffusion of leadership to teams and multiple role players within the school community. As Rowan (1992), among others, has argued, the jury is still out on whether organizational and managerial forms characterized as "mechanical" versus "organic" are more effective in schools, but the dominant tendency in the Dallas system is clear. The mechanical form of organization, relying on classic bureaucratic principles of central command and control, is present in Dallas. The commitment strategy, also characterized as organic, relies on the creation of professional community within organizations and the lateral spread of knowledge through networks and other forms to enhance worker competence through development and involvement. It is difficult to envision what place such an approach has in Dallas. Depending on teachers' entering orientations to instruction, many would feel alienated by the Dallas system because they were not consulted in its development and because it does not represent their deepest aspirations and intentions for students.

Management experts today regard schools as hybrid organizations requiring a mix of centralized-decentralized, top down-bottom up, public-professional controls—a combination of commitment and control strategies, in Rowan's (1992) terms. Getting this mix right is a source of continuing ferment in education, but most large urban systems continue to feature the classic bureaucratic form despite its many critics (e.g., Darling-Hammond, 1997). The Dallas accountability system reflects a highly traditional and, some would say, outmoded form of organization, and so it is open to challenge on these grounds as well.

The School as Culture and Community

Recent study of schools has emphasized ethos or culture as an important element in school functioning and outcomes (see, e.g., Newmann & Associates, 1996; Rutter, Maughan, Mortimore, Ouston, &

Smith, 1979). The beliefs and norms shared among a school's faculty about standards, students, teaching, learning, and working together create a community that supports learning more or less well. In particular, shared beliefs and expectations about the value and importance of learning, the prospect that all students are capable, and the value placed on faculty collaboration and continuous improvement through professional development, inquiry, dialogue, and responsible innovation contribute to the quality of student learning (see Louis, Kruse, & Associates, 1995; McLaughlin & Talbert, 1993; Newmann & Associates, 1996). Joint work on curriculum, assessment, study of children's learning, and other core matters both produces and is produced by strong professional cultures. Collegial work in turn leads to enhanced student achievement.

Joint faculty engagement with assessment may be particularly important as a professional task because such work relates directly to the heart of the school's mission. Although the Dallas system appears to have the virtue of allocating group rather than individual rewards for the production of student achievement, it does not much encourage teacher involvement in assessment as a central professional task. Teachers administer standardized assessments that supply little diagnostic feedback on learning, create few opportunities to examine student work products, or bring teachers together to translate shared learning goals into assessments of their own devising. Where professional community in schools is strong, teachers are engaged more directly in complex, qualitative forms of assessment tied to curriculum planning, study of student learning, and provision of more personalized forms of education. Although the Dallas system does not discourage such work, it does not particularly encourage it. Instead, the system directs attention to the production of standardized, systemwide outputs on a series of quantitative measures. Such assessment is unlikely to contribute positively to the formation of professional cultures within schools, although considerable school-to-school variation will be likely within the district.

Public Knowledge and Understanding of the Educational Process and Its Outcomes

Whether the Dallas system enhances public knowledge and understanding of education depends on what is valued. At least some critics of the schools argue that standardized tests contribute to public misunderstanding of what students know and can do. Judged against the ambitious aims of education projected in many of the new content standards, most of the tests in use constitute very weak indications. On the other hand, standardized tests have such a powerful hold on the public mind that they are difficult to replace with more sophisticated qualitative assessments that better represent the new standard of learning to use one's mind well. Norm- and criterion-referenced tests whose results may be communicated in numerically simple forms enjoy widespread use today but arguably do not serve as good indicators of the learning agenda that many educational experts argue we must pursue. Such experts are beginning to recognize the importance of persuading the public to revalue what it wants from schools, to seek not only higher but also different standards that project qualities of learning, knowing, and acting absent in our current testing practice. Depending, then, on one's view of the necessary learning agenda ahead, assessment systems that use traditional forms of testing are part of the problem. They perpetuate a status quo in need of transformation.

Conclusion

This commentary has posed a set of challenges to the Dallas accountability system. The arguments and observations constitute an indictment warranting greater scrutiny. Speaking as the prosecuting attorney before a grand jury, I believe the potential defects and shortcomings of the Dallas system require a jury trial that brings both expert and lay opinion to bear, based on impartial study of the system in operation. The evidence of testing's effects from other studies is sufficiently damning to call the Dallas system to account.

References

Cronbach, L. J. (1987). Five perspectives on test validation. In H. Wainer & H. Braun (Eds.), *Test validity* (pp. 3-17). Hillsdale, NJ: Lawrence Erlbaum.

Darling-Hammond, L. (1997). *The right to learn.* San Francisco: Jossey-Bass.

Gardner, H. (1991). *The unschooled mind: How children think and how schools should teach.* New York: Basic Books.

Kohn, A. (1993). *Punished by rewards: The trouble with gold stars, incentive plans, A's, praise, and other bribes.* Boston: Houghton Mifflin.

Louis, K. S., Kruse, S. D., & Associates. (1995). *Professionalism and community: Perspectives on reforming urban schools.* Thousand Oaks, CA: Corwin.

Madaus, G., West, M., Harmon, M., Lomax, R., & Viator, K. (1992). *The influence of testing on teaching math and science in Grades 4-12.* Boston: Boston College, Center for the Study of Testing, Evaluation, and Educational Policy.

McLaughlin, M., & Talbert, J. (1993). *Contexts that matter for teaching and learning.* Stanford, CA: Stanford University, Center for Research on the Context of Secondary School Teaching.

Meier, D. (1995). *The power of their ideas: Lessons for America from a small school in Harlem.* Boston: Beacon.

Newmann, F., & Associates. (1996). *Authentic Achievement.* San Francisco: Jossey-Bass.

Perkins, D. (1992). *Smart schools: Better thinking and learning for every child.* New York: Free Press.

Resnick, L. (1987). *Education and learning to think.* Washington, DC: National Academy Press.

Rowan, B. (1992). Commitment and control: Alternative strategies for the organizational design of schools. In C. Cazden (Ed.), *Review of research in education* (Vol. 16, pp. 353-389). Washington, DC: American Educational Research Association.

Rutter, M., Maughan, B., Mortimore, P., Ouston, J., with Smith, A. (1979). *Fifteen thousand hours: Secondary schools and their effects on children.* Cambridge, MA: Harvard University Press.

Shepard, L. A. (1988). *Inflated test score gains: Is it old norms or teaching to the test?* Boulder: University of Colorado, School of Education.

Shepard, L. A. (1993). Evaluating test validity. In L. Darling-Hammond (Ed.), *Review of research in education* (Vol. 19, pp. 405-450). Washington, DC: American Educational Research Association.

Smith, M. L. (1991a). Meanings of test preparation. *American Educational Research Journal, 28,* 521-542.

Smith, M. L. (1991b). Put to the test: The effects of external testing on teachers. *Educational Researcher, 20*(5), 8-11.

Smith, M. L., Edelsky, C., Draper, K., Rottenberg, C., & Cherland, M. (1990). *The role of testing in elementary schools.* Los Angeles: University of California, Los Angeles, Center for Research on Educational Standards and Student Tests, Graduate School of Education.

Steinberg, L. (1996). *Beyond the classroom: Why school reform has failed and what parents need to do.* New York: Simon & Schuster.

CHAPTER 11

Little Practical Difference and Pie in the Sky

A Response to Thum and Bryk and a Rejoinder to Sykes

WILLIAM J. WEBSTER
ROBERT L. MENDRO
TIMOTHY ORSAK
DASH WEERASINGHE
KAREN BEMBRY

This response addresses the primary methodological issues discussed by Thum and Bryk (Chapter 9) with a point-by-point approach, provides a general response to Sykes (Chapter 10), and gives an update of the Dallas Teacher Evaluation System since the original Chapter 8 was prepared. It would be useful, however, to address globally the issues brought up by the respondents before launching into specific remarks. In regard to Thum and Bryk, based on the hundreds of analyses and dozens of systematic research studies conducted in the Dallas Public Schools over the past decade involving 200 schools, at least 6,000 teachers, and at least 300,000 students, there is no one best way in which to estimate teacher and school effects (Olson & Webster, 1986; Webster, Mendro, & Almaguer, 1993;

Webster, Mendro, Bembry, & Orsak, 1995; Webster & Olson, 1988). Rather, carefully thought out prediction models, whether they are conducted in one or two stages, are ordinary least squares regression models using appropriate interactions or hierarchical linear models, or treat predictor variables as fixed or random, produce practically identical results. (Because gain models measure a different outcome, we cannot comment on them until we have more thoroughly analyzed the outcomes and their relation to the raw data. If anything attracts our attention to the gain model, then it is Bereiter's [1963] suggestion that gain scores may not have the seemingly straightforward intrinsic meaning imputed to them when subjected to careful inspection.)

There are some exceptions to this rule. For example, consider models in which only school-level data are available because student-level data have been aggregated to the school level and models in which the only student assessment data available are the outcome measure, which is then regressed against classifying variables to produce results. Both are seriously biased with respect to the initial achievement levels of students or the classificatory variables that are related to their outcomes.

Once the information from typically used classificatory variables and their interactions—from pretest measures (for a single year or many years in a longitudinal model) and from school- or classroom-level variables—have been used in a prediction model, there is very little systematic information left. From a practical standpoint, there is no significant variation left that can be accounted for, and resulting estimates of overall effects are nearly identical to those from another model using the same information. The point is that our experience with the data has shown that there is only so much systematic variation in these data and that a carefully thought out and explicated model will produce results virtually identical to those from another such model.

Of course, this is a simplification. We would not be using a hierarchical linear model for our own school and teacher effectiveness analyses if we did not believe, on the basis of extensive investigations summarized in our published results, that the multilevel approach offered a way in which to obtain estimates of effects that were minutely improved over estimates from other models. However, the basic characteristics of all of the models are similar. The correlations of resulting estimates of effectiveness at the school level and of effectiveness components at the student level with the variables controlled in the model all are acceptably low or practically zero, and the intercorrelation of the effectiveness estimates is quite high.

Considering Sykes (Chapter 10), 25 years of experience in operating testing systems—15 years in developing curriculum-referenced testing programs and 10 years in devising and implementing fair and accurate accountability systems—has shown the impracticality of "authentic" or performance tests in large-scale accountability programs. This is not to say that performance assessments have no place. We firmly believe that they should be used as an integral part of the curriculum. It is simply in large-scale accountability testing that these measures have yet to show practical applicability, especially when compared to commercially available or carefully constructed local assessment instruments (Webster, 1991; Webster & Schuhmacher, 1973).

There certainly are drawbacks to any real accountability system. Implementing systems of school and teacher evaluation, assessing school effectiveness, or making any attempt to assign accountability to individuals or organizations will tempt a small percentage of individuals to indulge in unethical behavior to beat the system. However, this is not limited to testing systems. Systems of teacher evaluation rating teacher performance in a small number of visits have produced cheating and distortion on a scale equal to or exceeding any done with testing systems. This lamentable conclusion in no way justifies giving up on accountability systems.

A more serious concern is the damage done to the curriculum by those who limit it to what they perceive will be covered on a test instrument. We feel that there is a very direct answer to this concern. Assessments must cover a sufficient portion of the curriculum and assess higher order skills with enough thoroughness that this broad array of skills and abilities is taught to meet the assessments. If assessments are sufficiently broad and deep, then there is nothing wrong with teaching to the assessment.

There are no magic answers to these concerns to be found in performance assessment systems or a yet-to-be-devised system of "real" outcomes and "authentic" attributes. A small percentage of misguided individuals still will be inclined to cheat on these measures if they perceive real rewards or penalties attached to them (not to mention a small percentage of parents and students who are inclined to cheat in producing products for extended assessments). The curriculum still will suffer from those who perceive the necessity of limiting it to the outcome tasks (not to mention the limitation to the curriculum that comes from the necessarily small number of tasks that can be assessed in practical applications of these systems). Finally, the reliability and, consequently, the validity of these systems still are not established for use in large-scale accountability.

Specific Concerns With Thum and Bryk

Outcome Variables

A number of outcome variables (promotion rate, dropout rate, etc.) have been classified as school covariates. The school covariates are listed in the text in the description of the hierarchical linear model (HLM) analysis and are further explicated in the following text. The variables listed in Table 8.1 all are outcome variables weighted and used in determining school effectiveness. The broad array of outcome variables used in the Dallas system is the result of many hours of discussion about the purposes of education by the Accountability Task Force, which oversees the system. The task force is discussed in more detail subsequently.

Two-Phase Analysis

A complaint is registered against the homogenizing of residuals in the predictor space on the grounds that it is "likely to induce unpredictable biases in teacher or school effectiveness estimates" (p. 104) because teachers and schools might primarily serve students drawn from one or a few of the subgroups. The homogenization of the individual predictor space responses is done exactly to address this concern. If a school has a concentration of students from one of these groups, then the homogenization is performed to ensure that it would have no particular advantage or disadvantage. Thorough examination of our data sets for the past 5 years has shown that there are small perturbations in the means of the residuals and that the variances of the residuals at the lower end of the distribution tend to be larger than those at the upper end. It also has shown that our concerns are largely groundless. Students from any one school do not cluster in any of the particular intervals in the regression space.

However, to ensure that these perturbations do not add a bias, they are standardized.

We have found from experience with the data sets that the use of these corrections is largely for our own peace of mind. The practical effect is virtually nil in terms of the school effectiveness outcomes. Analyses with the two-stage model and with the one-stage HLM model produce virtually identical effect outcomes with correlations of outcomes above .978. Careful analysis of the data shows that students are distributed across the outcome space so completely that there is a wide variety of student ability across schools as well as in each school and classroom. (District policy prohibits homogeneous grouping except for temporary purposes such as reading groups within a reading class. The data bear out the relatively thorough implementation of this policy.) However, if this were not the case, then the homogenization would guarantee that no school or teacher gained an advantage from the mean differences within each adjustment grouping. The comments regarding the reliability of residuals would be of concern except for the fact that correlations between the results produced by one-phase HLM models and those produced by the two-phase model are very high.

This brings up an issue regarding the use of the effectiveness data. If we were attempting to research the relationships in the data to show the degree or nature of the interactions in the data set, then we would not use the smoothing technique because of its grievous damage to accurate probability estimation. Because we are limiting our analysis to a descriptive situation, there is leeway in the analysis to adjust our data without concern for inferential uses.

Regarding the two-phase analysis, we agree that as a regression analysis it can be done in one step. However, by using two phases, the output of the first phase includes an analysis of mean residuals showing that the fairness subgroups have been equalized and that the playing field has been leveled. At the direction of the Accountability Task Force (which is described in more detail later in the response to Sykes), the two-phase analysis was specifically retained because, in the task force's opinion, it offered proof to critics that for every analysis in the system, student inequities had been adjusted within all fairness groups. The continual need to use this output, particularly when the system has come under more formal challenges, has demonstrated the political insight of the task force in desiring to retain the two-phase analysis. If the analysis cannot be demonstrated as fair, the degree of community buy-in to the process definitely falters.

Fixed or Random Slopes

The choice of fixed or random slopes depends, in our view, on the nature of the sources of variation in the slopes. The slopes are modeled using a number of school parameters at the second level. These include, as mentioned in Chapter 8, percentage of minority students, percentage black, percentage low income, percentage mobility, and the like. To the extent that slopes vary as a result of these factors, their use adjusts the differences. We choose a random model to control for the effects of possible interactions of concomitant variables in specific school settings. If we had evidence of an interaction of school effect with these variables, then we would use the fixed model because using the random model would mask these effects. Other analyses of the data that we have conducted regarding slopes within subgroups do not lead us to suspect an interaction of the slopes with instructional effect. However, our analyses of fixed and random results show that any effects due to these factors and the possibility of interactions both are very remote. Correlations of school effects from fixed and random slope models are above .985.

Variable Treatment

In our analyses, we grand mean center all variables at Level 1. Also, regarding our misstatement of the HLM solution, our statement should have read, "The HLM equations are solved and empirical Bayes residuals used for school effects." A more explicit statement of the model can be obtained from the authors.

Response to Issues Raised by Sykes

The Sykes critique (Chapter 10) demonstrates straightforwardly why the public is losing confidence in public education. If one follows his argument to its logical conclusion, then no one can be held accountable for anything. To indulge in a diatribe against standardized testing without presenting a meaningful alternative is of little value. "Authentic assessment" is, because of generally low reliability when employed in accountability systems, neither authentic nor assessment. The Dallas system does in fact include some authentic assessment in that the Texas Assessment of Academic Skills includes a writing sample that is used as one of the outcome measures in the system. It is, of course, the least reliable measure imposed on the district by the state.

The district's Assessments of Course Performance (ACP), final examinations in each high school core course, originally were designed by master teachers at the behest of the central bureaucratic organization to include performance sections. The plan was to include these parts of the ACP in the accountability system as outcomes and to weight them by their reliability. Negative reaction from the field in terms of too much time spent testing for too little information received, as well as from the Board of Education in terms of the costs of this portion of the testing, led to the demise of this part of the plan.

This does not imply that performance assessments have no place. Schools are encouraged to develop or adopt expanded measures of student performance and supplied help in the process as well as to develop student portfolios. The teacher evaluation system includes these data, when schools and teachers choose, as part of the needs assessment on the teacher evaluation instrument. However, because of expense in time and money as well as the unreliability of results, authentic assessments are viewed as curriculum measures and instructional tools rather than as large-scale assessment measures and accountability tools.

Whereas the authors are familiar with most of the literature related to authentic assessments and, in particular, to their use in large-scale accountability systems, Sykes's understatement that "technical difficulties in administering and scoring the new assessments continue to make their use problematic as instruments of public policy" (p. 115) says it all. It is not practical in terms of time, money, or information received to include authentic assessments as part of a large-scale accountability system. The only reason the Dallas system includes a writing sample is because the state of Texas mandates it and pays for the scoring. Standardized tests, either commercially available or locally developed at the behest of bureaucrats, are not outmoded and still provide accurate, reliable, and efficient measures of student achievement. The norm-referenced tests used in Dallas, the survey forms of the Iowa Tests of Basic Skills that include primarily higher order skill-based items, provide adequate estimates of students' abilities to read and compute. The curriculum-based measures, whether the local measures in the Assessment of Course Performance or the state measures in the multiple-choice portions of the Texas Assessment of Academic Skills, provide accurate measures of the elements of the curriculum (Chapter 10).

Sykes's contention that the Dallas accountability system reflects a "bureaucratic conception of organization and management that allocates planning and design to the central office and implementation of central directives to subordinate workers in the schools" (p. 115) is wrong. The Dallas accountability system was suggested by a citizens task force after a comprehensive review of the state of accountability across the country. This task force, consisting of parents, community members, and statisticians from outside education, did not recommend that authentic assessments be included in the accountability system for exactly the reasons Sykes mentions, cited earlier. Furthermore, the system was designed and continues to be implemented under the auspices of an Accountability Task Force that includes teachers, parents, administrators, and community members. The teacher evaluation system was designed and continues under the direction of a Teacher Evaluation Task Force that includes 63 members, the majority of whom are teachers. The major teacher organizations have participated in the development of the system, and the most prominent among them has publicly endorsed it (Chapter 10).

To say more than this would give Sykes's suggestions more value than they deserve. To close, we draw on Sykes's analogy to the judicial system. A grand jury, considering the Dallas system in light of Sykes's charges and prosecution, would be bound to no-bill the system. To extend the analogy a bit further, a civil suit on the same charges would run a strong chance of being declared frivolous litigation.

Update on the Dallas Teacher Evaluation System

Throughout the 1995-1996 school year, the Dallas Public Schools developed and field tested a new teacher evaluation system. As noted, central to this development was the Teacher Evaluation Task

Force, whose members include teachers from each of the 10 geographic areas of the city, parents, principals, community members, and representatives from teacher organizations as well as a representative from an administrator organization. Based on input received from these various constituents, from the field test that was conducted throughout the school district, and from one of the teacher organizations, the following adjustments to the system have been made.

The emphasis on continuous student improvement remains the focus of the teacher evaluation system. Student achievement data drive the teacher evaluation system, just as they drive the principal evaluation process, the campus improvement plan, and the district improvement plan. The alignment of all accountability systems districtwide has been retained. However, how the system would use Effectiveness Indexes for the teachers has been redefined.

The initial framework for the teacher evaluation system included a composite Teacher Effectiveness Index for each teacher who administered an achievement test or end-of-course examination. This composite score was used to assign each teacher to one of three tiers. Tier 1 was determined to be the top 40% of teachers across the district, Tier 2 the next 50%, and Tier 3 the bottom 10%. The initial purpose for establishing tiers was to focus the finite resources of the district where they were most needed, presumably in support of the bottom 10% of the teachers. However, the tier system was not well received, and it resulted in negative feelings from teachers that interfered with the ultimate purpose of the system: continuous student improvement. The tier system was voted out by the task force, and both the composite score for each teacher and the tier designation were dropped from the Effectiveness Indexes format. Also, the recommendation that the name be changed from Teacher Effectiveness Indexes to Classroom Effectiveness Indexes was accepted. While leaving the indexes unchanged, the name change made the process less intimidating to school staff. Now, Classroom Effectiveness Indexes summarize student residual data computed for each standardized test a teacher administers aggregated by variable or class and used strictly for the purpose of diagnosing student growth or lack thereof.

Classroom Effectiveness Indexes are one way in which to diagnose the needs of students in the revised teacher evaluation system. The process has been expanded to incorporate other forms of needs assessment as well. Each teacher submits an Instructional Improvement Plan that consists of three sections: a Needs section, a Concepts/Content/Strategies section, and a Final Evaluation section. The first section, Needs, requires the teacher to list identified needs for his or her students. These needs take two forms: needs of the teacher's students from the previous year as identified in the Classroom Effectiveness Indexes and needs of current students as identified from other available sources. Other data sources may include student profiles, portfolios, teacher-made tests, diagnostic skills analyses, and performance information. If a teacher does not have Classroom Effectiveness Indexes, then he or she uses the alternative forms of assessment to diagnose current students. Thus, although the system still includes teachers with indexes and teachers without indexes, this distinction no longer divides teachers into two different groups for evaluation; it simply indicates the potential sources of data available to a teacher for his or her needs analysis.

Each teacher, whether or not he or she has Classroom Effectiveness Indexes, lists identified needs in the first section. Instructional practices designed to meet those needs are listed in the Concepts/Content/Strategies section, and documentation that will indicate the instructional practices have been accomplished is listed in the third column. The successful completion of the Instructional Improvement Plan results in a successful evaluation for the year. All teachers will follow the same process for evaluation each year, yet the extent of the evaluation will fluctuate in response to the identified needs of the students. A form for an Instructional Improvement Plan is included.

The Teacher Evaluation Task Force will continue to refine the system. The ultimate test of the system will be whether or not student achievement and performance continue to improve.

References

Bereiter, C. (1963). Some persisting dilemmas in the measurement of change. In C. W. Harris (Ed.), *Problems in measuring change* (pp. 3-20). Madison: University of Wisconsin Press.

Olson, G. H., & Webster, W. J. (1986, April). *Measuring school effectiveness: A three-year study.* Paper presented at the annual meeting of the American Educational Research Association, San Francisco.

Webster, W. J. (1991). An analysis of available student achievement data in the Dallas Independent School District. In *Executive summaries of evaluation reports* (pp. 1-12). Dallas, TX: Dallas Independent School District.

Webster, W. J., Mendro, R. L., & Almaguer, T. O. (1993, April). *Effectiveness indices: The major component of an equitable accountability system.* Paper presented at the annual meeting of the American Educational Research Association, Atlanta, GA.

Webster, W. J., Mendro, R. L., Bembry, K. L., & Orsak, T. H. (1995, April). *Alternative methodologies for identifying effective schools.* Paper presented at the annual meeting of the American Educational Research Association, San Francisco.

Webster, W. J., & Olson, G. H. (1988). A quantitative procedure for the identification of effective schools. *Journal of Experimental Education, 56,* 213-219.

Webster, W. J., & Schuhmacher, C. C. (1973). A unified strategy for systemwide research and evaluation. *Educational Technology, 13*(5), 68-72.

PART IV

The Tennessee Value-Added
Assessment System

The Impetus for the Tennessee Value-Added Accountability System

PATRICIA E. CEPERLEY

KIP REEL

The Tennessee Value-Added Assesment System (TVAAS) is the first accountability system of its type to be adopted statewide. TVAAS applies a new yardstick to school performance, a yardstick that is lauded by some and questioned by others. The system compares each student's achievement to that of the previous year instead of comparing student achievement to national norms. The result is a measure of student gain or progress that is statistically attributable to the school district, school, and teacher (Sanders & Horn, 1994).

Value-added assessment was the "heart" (Davis, 1991, p. B2) of a comprehensive education reform package passed in 1992 by Tennessee, a state more likely to be known for its lack of support than for its leadership in education reform (Alexander, 1990). The state was thrust into education reform by a lawsuit that challenged the state's school funding system. The court found that, because per-pupil spending in wealthy urban districts was twice that in poor rural districts, school funding was inequitable and thus unconstitutional (*Tennessee Small School Systems v. McWherter,* 1993).

Tennessee has no income tax and relies primarily on a state sales tax to fund education. In the past, the burden to fund schools fell on local government, which also relied primarily on sales taxes that were levied locally. So long as the state's economy was dominated by evenly dispersed small community-based businesses, sales tax revenues were spread equitably across the state. But when large shopping malls and Wal-Mart stores emerged on the scene, the distribution of sales tax revenues changed dramatically—and so did the wealth of individual school systems (W. Qualls, personal communication, March 29, 1995). Revenues dropped and budgets were squeezed. Some schools discontinued bus service and others ran out of essential school supplies. Superintendents of small rural districts first sought relief from the legislature but were unsuccessful. So, as a last resort, 66 of them formed a coalition to sue the state (Associated Press, 1990).

Seeking a more equitable funding system, Tennessee policymakers wanted to avoid redistributing existing resources—what they called a "Robin Hood" strategy. They preferred to resolve the funding dilemma by raising taxes and then providing greater annual funding increases to the poorer districts until equity was achieved. Increasing taxes was popular among educator groups as well as local city and county politicians, but it was not popular among the general public, who remembered that earlier education tax increases had been diverted to other causes.

To raise taxes, legislators needed the support of business. In return for that support, business interests, led by the Tennessee Business Roundtable, demanded accountability. First, business wanted accountability for results at the district level; all superintendents would have to be appointed by elected boards instead of by the public. Business argued that school systems needed a single point of accountability; however, in districts that elected superintendents as well as board members, no one could be held accountable. Business also wanted accountability for results at the school building level; building principals should be required to execute performance contracts and then be held accountable if they failed to achieve the agreed-on results. And, finally, business wanted accountability for results at the classroom level—concrete evidence that dropout rates, promotion rates, proficiency test passage rates, and student achievement were improving from year to year (Tennessee Business Roundtable, 1994).

Early drafts of the Education Improvement Act (1992) had all the accountability components desired by business except a way to link student progress to the classroom. As one legislator put it, "What we want to know is who's teaching and who's not" (quoted in Davis, 1991, p. B2). The search for an answer to that question led legislators to the value-added assessment model, which was based on studies by University of Tennessee statisticians McLean and Sanders (1984). They first tested the model in Knox County, where they concluded that (a) schools and teachers differed in their effect on student learning, (b) school and teacher effects seemed to be consistent across time, (c) teacher effects were not influenced by the location of the school, (d) teacher effects found statistically were highly correlated with subjective reports of supervisors, and (e) student gains were not correlated with previous achievement levels (Sanders & Horn, 1994, p. 300). Subsequently, they found similar results in nearby Blount County and Chattanooga City schools. Together, these studies convinced Sanders and Horn that this new methodology successfully measured "the influence that school systems, schools, and teachers have on indicators of student learning" (p. 301).

Sanders and Horn's (1994) model appeared to be just what legislators had been looking for. Sanders was invited to Nashville, where he spoke with the governor and testified before house and senate education committees. His testimony was so convincing that within a week of hearing Sanders' testimony about the model, both houses of the legislature amended their respective versions of the education reform bill. The wording of the amendments was based largely on a paper that Sanders had prepared for the state officials; even the bibliography was included in the legislation. Specifically, the legislation defined TVAAS as

> a statistical system . . . which uses measures of student learning to enable the estimation of teacher, school, and school statistical distributions . . . to account for differences in prior student attainment, such that the impact which teacher, school and school district have on the educational progress of students may be estimated on a student attainment constant basis. (Education Improvement Act, 1992, pp. 14-18)

The legislature also set performance standards for districts and schools. Using data from the norm-referenced items on the Tennessee Comprehensive Assessment Program (TCAP), all districts and all schools within districts were expected to demonstrate a mean gain for each academic subject within each grade greater than or equal to the national gain. Failing that, districts and schools were required to show progress toward that goal. Those that failed to show progress could be placed on probation. Also implied in the law was the expectation that teachers would show a similar effect on student progress. Beginning in 1995, data collected on teacher effects was to be one of five items used in teacher evaluation. Concerned, Tennessee Education Association (TEA) officials prepared 33 amendments, including some that diminished the effects of value-added assessment on teacher evaluation. TEA leaders successfully argued to keep teachers' records closed to the public and to exclude from accountability calculations of scores of students who (a) did not attend school for at least 150 days and/or (b) were in special education (W. Copley, personal communication, March 30, 1995). Despite the amendments, TVAAS raised the stakes for Tennessee educators, and TCAP test results would affect administrators and teachers as well as children.

References

Alexander, K. (1990). *Review of public school finance in the Appalachia Educational Laboratory states.* Charleston, WV: Appalachia Educational Laboratory.

Associated Press. (1990, January 26). Hearing date set for school funding suit. *The Tennessean,* p. B4.

Davis, D. (1991, April 18). Committee votes to add amendment onto reform bill. *Nashville Banner,* p. B2.

Education Improvement Act, 9 Ten Stat. Ann. §§49-1-603-608 (1990 Supp. 1992).

McLean, R. A., & Sanders, W. L. (1984). *Objective component of teacher evaluation: A feasibility study* (Working Paper No. 199). Knoxville: University of Tennessee, College of Business Administration.

Sanders, W. L., & Horn, S. P. (1994). The Tennessee Value-Added Assessment System (TVAAS): Mixed-model methodology in educational assessment. *Journal of Personnel in Education, 8,* 299-311.

Tennessee Business Roundtable. (1994). *Promises to keep.* Nashville, TN: Author.

Tennessee Small School Systems v. McWherter, 851 S.W.2d 139, 151 (Tenn. 1993).

CHAPTER 13

The Tennessee Value-Added Assessment System

A Quantitative, Outcomes-Based Approach to Educational Assessment

WILLIAM L. SANDERS

ARNOLD M. SAXTON

SANDRA P. HORN

The Tennessee Value-Added Assessment System (TVAAS) is the process by which the effects of schools, school systems, and teachers on the academic growth of students in Grades 3 through 8 in science, math, social studies, language arts, and reading are estimated in Tennessee. TVAAS uses mixed-model methodology to solve many of the statistical problems that traditionally have been cited as impediments to the use of achievement data in an assessment program. This process enables a repeated-measures, multivariate response analysis allowing the inclusion of all of the information available for each student regardless of the degree of missing information.

The statistical models used in TVAAS are not restrictive as to the indicator variables that can be employed in the process. Rather, any variables linear in their metrics, highly correlated with curricular objectives, and possessing appropriate measurement sensitivities could be used.

Presently, the raw data for TVAAS are the scaled scores from the norm-referenced portion of the Tennessee Comprehensive Assessment Program (TCAP). All Tennessee students in Grades 2 through 8 take the TCAP yearly. These scaled scores in the five subjects listed earlier are included within the record for each child (up to 5 years) along with information on where the child attends school and which teacher(s) he or she had for each grade or subject. Each new year's data are merged with those of previous years to give the most complete record possible. Currently, the TVAAS database contains more than 4 million records. Later, end-of-course tests will be developed and implemented for all academic courses for high school students and then will be included into TVAAS (Chapter 24).

By taking advantage of the longitudinal aspect of the data, each student serves as his or her own "control." In other words, each child can be thought of as a "blocking factor" that enables the estimation of school system, school, and teacher effects free of the socioeconomic confoundings that historically have rendered unfair any attempt to compare districts and schools based on the inappropriate comparison of group means. The unfairness of these simple comparisons has led some educational researchers to propose a methodology that would eliminate these biases by including a number of covariables into an analysis to adjust for socioeconomic differences. However, this approach immediately creates another huge problem. It is a hopeless impossibility for any school system to have all the data for each child in appropriate form to filter all of these confounding influences via these more traditional statistical approaches. Pilot studies revealed, and subsequent research confirmed, that the statistical mixed-model theory and methodology on which TVAAS is based alleviates many of the problems associated in the past with the use of student data in educational assessment (McLean & Sanders, 1984).

Background and Reporting of Tennessee Value-Added Assessment System Findings

In 1990, when the Tennessee legislature undertook to rewrite the laws governing education in Tennessee, accountability was high on its list of priorities. A great deal of new money was slated to be allocated to the schools through the new funding formula, and, as in almost all such cases, legislators wanted to ensure that the money was being spent wisely. To this end, the legislature adopted TVAAS as part of the statewide program for assessing academic efficacy embodied in the Education Improvement Act (EIA) of 1992.

Under the law, TVAAS is to provide unbiased estimates of the effects of schools, school systems, and teachers on the academic growth of students and to distinguish between these effects and those of outside influences. Furthermore, provisions are made within the law and within the TVAAS model to ensure fairness. These provisions include basing assessment on at least 3 years of data and enabling distinction between the effective and the ineffective while providing broad, inclusive statistical parameters for the definition of success. Schools, school systems, and teachers cannot be assessed solely on the basis of TVAAS. The EIA also provides for the annual production and distribution of reports based on TVAAS findings to those assessed as well as to appropriate administrators and, in the case of school system and school reports, to the public (Chapter 23).

Reports of TVAAS findings are provided annually for all school systems and schools in Tennessee. Currently, information is available for Grades 3 through 8 in five subject areas: reading, math, language arts, science, and social studies. Development of subject-specific high school tests currently is underway, but high school testing will not be fully implemented until 1999. TVAAS reports include information on student gains for each subject and grade for the 3 most recent years as well as the 3-year average gains. The cumulative average gain is the primary indicator by which success is measured.

The primary purpose TVAAS serves in the EIA is to provide information for summative evaluation regarding how effective a school, system, or teacher has been in leading students to achieve normal academic gains over a 3-year period. Certainly, these data can be used in this fashion. However, the real value of TVAAS lies in its ability to serve as a data source for formative evaluation purposes (Chapter 22).

The information supplied in TVAAS reports has been found to be invaluable by many school administrators involved in curricular planning, program evaluation, and developing strategies to meet the needs of students with differing academic attributes and abilities. In addition to the formal annual reports, for diagnostic purposes, individual schools are provided reports on the gains of their students for each subject and grade grouped by achievement levels. TVAAS reports allow school systems to pinpoint grade or subject problems and successes and to direct efforts and resources accordingly. School reports, for example, may inform principals not only about how effective the 4th-grade math program is in regard to enhancing student academic gains but also whether it is equally effective in encouraging such growth in both its high-achieving and low-achieving students. When the teacher reports were issued for the first time in 1996, similar information was available on the classroom level.

Efforts to Inform Groups About the Tennessee Value-Added Assessment System and Its Use

Since its adoption in the EIA, extensive efforts have been undertaken to increase understanding of TVAAS in the educational community. The first publication from the TVAAS office (now the University of Tennessee Value-Added Research and Assessment Center [UT-VARAC]) was a booklet addressed to teachers detailing the history and development of TVAAS and answering questions teachers had expressed as concerns (Sanders & Horn, n.d.). Thousands of copies were distributed throughout the state, some by request and some in the course of numerous workshops and presentations for teachers, administrators, state Department of Education and state Board of Education personnel, and the media. Subsequently, the director and staff of UT-VARAC have produced papers about TVAAS and about educational findings that have resulted from examination of TVAAS data that have been published in several venues including refereed journals and educational newspapers and newsletters (e.g., Sanders & Horn, 1994, 1995; Sanders et al., 1994). Additionally, more than 100 video presentations have been distributed throughout the state. However, the best spokespersons for TVAAS have been the educators who have used the TVAAS reports to inform educational practice in their schools and systems.

Since the first reports were distributed, the number of educators who enthusiastically support TVAAS has been growing steadily. In the beginning, the support came from educators who recognized in the reports strengths and weaknesses they had suspected in their school systems but who had no hard data to support their suspicions. These local administrators used the TVAAS reports to guide curricular reform in their schools. As word of their successes spread, other administrators, both on the system and school levels, began to look more closely at the information TVAAS offered about the success of their programs and to use the data for school improvement. Teachers also began using TVAAS data, even before TVAAS teacher reports were issued, utilzing a simplified method of determining their students' gains to assess their own performance. A few school systems generated this simplified data for their teachers, and UT-VARAC published instructions for teachers who wished to produce this "rough and dirty" estimate of their students' gains for themselves. However, beginning in the fall of 1996, all Tennessee teachers for whom data were available received individualized TVAAS teacher reports proving them detailed information on their effectiveness as evidenced by the academic progress of their students.

In addition to the analysis and reporting of the effects of educational entities, research initiatives are a priority for TVAAS. The enormous, longitudinally merged database, at present comprised of more than 4 million records, is a unique resource for research into educational issues. Research is a natural outgrowth of the UT-VARAC goal to provide educators with information for the improvement of educational practice. To this end, UT-VARAC has undertaken several research initiatives, both in-house and in collaboration with outside researchers.

An example of the important findings that already have resulted from the examination of information available from the TVAAS database is what has been termed the "building change phenomenon." Briefly, TVAAS data have shown that when students transfer to the lowest grade in a receiving school, their gains are severely retarded in the succeeding year. For many children, such building change occurs when they leave primary school, leave middle school, and once again when they enter high school, and so the likelihood of a collective impairment to their overall academic progress is very likely and cumulatively can be most severe (Sanders et al., 1994). UT-VARAC is actively seeking serious researchers who are interested in this and other questions that can be identified through TVAAS. It is hoped that, through research and through the information TVAAS provides to educators throughout Tennessee, a better understanding of how to sustain academic growth will lead to a better future for all students.

The Tennessee Value-Added Assessment System Statistical Methodology

A Description of Some of the Properties of the Tennessee Value-Added Assessment System

The advantages of increased precision offered through longitudinal analysis has long been recognized. Raudenbush and Bryk (1988) stated in their concluding remarks,

> Such time-series data strengthen attempts to base causal inferences in nonexperimental research. Moreover, time-series data make growth rather than status the outcome, and short-run effects of schools are more likely to influence growth rates than status. Hence, the longitudinal perspective is a hopeful one; the substantial effects of schooling that have eluded researchers using one or two time points are likely to appear when multiple time points are available and analyzed sensibly. (p. 469)

Two points are alluded to in this quote: gain and efficiency. Longitudinal analysis allows differences among individual students to be controlled (blocking), yielding more precise estimates of other factors that influence academic gain of populations of students. By blocking for each student, many of the exogenous influences most often cited as influencing academic progress—educational attainment of parents, socioeconomic level, race, and so on—could be partitioned without having direct measures of each one. But the use of a longitudinal analysis introduces the severe problem of missing records.

Students miss tests, move from district to district, and move into and out of the state, creating an enormity of fractured records. Traditional statistical approaches to longitudinal analyses are not appropriate for most educational assessment applications because student records range from sparse to complete, especially when testing is conducted on a large scale over time. A variety of methods have been developed and employed, with varying degrees of success, to overcome the problem presented by incomplete records so that conventional statistical methods and software could be used. These include various schemes for imputation of missing data. However, even if reasonable imputational procedures are used, the practical result is that the number of exogenous variables and student records that can be included often is restricted due to the limitations of these statistical approaches. This is perhaps one reason why many states and districts that collect data annually as Tennessee does either do not employ a longitudinal approach to analysis or restrict it to two adjacent testing periods.

The statistical methodology undergirding TVAAS (to be presented in detail subsequently) is built on Henderson's mixed-model equations. These equations, and the modifications to them, enable the use of all test information for each student regardless of how sparse or complete. Furthermore, if it is found that additional concomitant variables are needed to ensure fairness, then these variables may be included into the mixed-model equations. Solutions of these equations furnish unbiased estimates of the influences of districts, schools, and teachers on the rate of academic progress of populations of students without imputation for missing data or elimination of fractured records, providing important advantages over more traditional assessment models.

Perhaps the most significant of these advantages is that estimates of the influence of systems, schools, and teachers on the academic gain of student populations may be obtained without *direct* measures of gain for each student. Instead, these estimates of gain can be obtained with considerable precision from the solution vector of the mixed-model equations because covariances among all test scores for each student are included.

In addition to a solution to the fractured record problem and the advantage of including all the available data, the mixed-model approach provides other important statistical advantages. TVAAS is designed to provide rigorous protection against the severe misclassification of a school's, system's, or teacher's influence on student gain. For instance, in the teacher model, by considering "teacher effects" as a random class, each teacher's effect on the gain of the population of his or her students is a shrinkage estimate. The consequence of this approach is that all teachers are assumed to be the average of their school system until the weight of the data pulls their specific estimates away from their school system's mean. A very important consequence is that it is nearly impossible for individual teachers with small quantities of student data to have estimates measurably different from their system mean.

In summary, the following statistical claims are made concerning the TVAAS process.

- Individual student records are incorporated into the model as statistical blocks, thereby partitioning exogenous influences on test performance.
- All available data are used, and no imputation for missing data is required.
- Longitudinal analysis over years improves the efficiency of the estimates of the model parameters.
- Additionally, repeated measures across subjects provide similar benefits.
- Educational influences on gain can be estimated from a model that uses scores, not gains.
- Shrinkage estimates of teacher effects provide protection against fortuitous misclassification of individuals.
- The "layered model" (presented later) improves the efficiency of the estimate of teacher effects.

The application of the mixed-model process to student data produces a rigorous methodology that supports these claims. The process is presented in detail in the next section.

Statistical Models and Encoding of the Tennessee Value-Added Assessment System

In this section, the specific models used in the TVAAS process are presented with examples of the encoding of data. To understand how the TVAAS models are fitted to student data, a general understanding of Henderson's mixed-model equations and the properties of a solution to these equations is necessary.

General Form of Henderson's Mixed-Model Equations

The general form of Henderson's mixed-model is

$$y = XB + ZU + e,$$

where y in the TVAAS context is the $m \times 1$ observation vector representing all of the scale scores for individual students for all academic subjects tested over all grades, X is a known $m \times p$ incidence matrix that allows the inclusion of any fixed effects (including "regressors," if needed), B is an unknown $p \times 1$ fixed vector to be estimated from the data, Z is a known $m \times q$ incidence matrix that allows for the inclusion of random effects, U is an unobservable $q \times 1$ random vector representing the realized values of the random effects to be estimated from the data, and e is a nonobservable $m \times 1$ random vector variable representing unaccountable random variation. (For extensive discussions of this methodology, see Harville, 1976; Henderson, 1973, 1975, 1984; McLean, Sanders, & Stroup, 1991; and Sanders, 1989.)

Both U and e have null means and variance

$$\text{Var}\begin{bmatrix} U \\ e \end{bmatrix} = \begin{bmatrix} G & 0 \\ 0 & R \end{bmatrix}.$$

R is the $m \times m$ variance-covariance matrix that reflects the correlation among student scores residual to the specific model being fitted to the data. G is the $q \times q$ variance-covariance matrix that reflects the correlation among the random effects. If (U, e) are normally distributed, the joint density of (y, U) is maximized for variations in B and U by the solution to the following equations:

$$\begin{bmatrix} X'R^{-1}X & X'R^{-1}Z \\ Z'R^{-1}X & Z'R^{-1}Z+G^{-1} \end{bmatrix} \begin{bmatrix} b \\ u \end{bmatrix} = \begin{bmatrix} X'R^{-1}y \\ Z'R^{-1}y \end{bmatrix}.$$

Let a generalized inverse of the coefficient matrix be

$$\begin{bmatrix} X'R^{-1}X & X'R^{-1}Z \\ Z'R^{-1}X & Z'R^{-1}Z+G^{-1} \end{bmatrix} = \begin{bmatrix} C_{11} & C_{12} \\ C_{21} & C_{22} \end{bmatrix} = C.$$

If G and R are known, then some of the properties of a solution of these equations are as follows.

1. $K'b$ is the best linear unbiased estimator (BLUE) of the set of estimable linear functions, $K'B$, of the fixed effects.
2. u is the best linear unbiased predictor (BLUP) of U.
   a. $E(U \mid u) = u$.
   b. $\text{Var}(u - U) = C_{22}$.
   c. u is unique regardless of the rank of the coefficient matrix.

3. a. $K'b + M'u$ is the BLUP of $K'B + M'U$ provided $K'B$ is estimable.

   b. $\text{Var}(K'b + M'u - K'B - M'U) = (K'M')C(K'M')'$.

4. With G and R known, the solution is equivalent to generalized least squares. If u and e are multivariate normal, then the solution is maximum likelihood.

5. If G and R are not known, then as an estimated G and R approach the true G and R, the solution approaches the maximum likelihood solution.

6. If u and e are not multivariate normal, then the solution to the mixed-model equation still provides the maximum correlation between U and u.

Tennessee Value-Added Assessment System Models

In TVAAS, three different model equations are used. Separate models for system, school, and teacher have been deemed appropriate.

$$\text{System Model: } y_{iklmn} = \mu_{iklm} + e_{iklmn},$$

where y_{iklmn} represents a test score in the mth subject for the nth student, and this student was in the ith school system, k^{th} year, and l^{th} grade; μ_{iklm} is the fixed system mean score for all students in the ith school system, k^{th} year, l^{th} grade, and m^{th} subject; and e_{iklmn} represents the random deviation of the test score for the nth student from the school system mean.

The covariance structure of the e_{iklmn}, assuming scores are sorted by student, is block diagonal, each student having a covariance block (referred to as "little R"). This block is unstructured, meaning all covariances can be numerically different.

In Table 13.1, the patterns in the R matrix (the master R) for cohorts of students with complete data histories over 5 years are presented. Each "x" indicates a different covariance parameter; as can be seen, there are 120 possible variance-covariance parameters to be estimated per cohort. The zeros in the lower corner are due to the restriction that only 5 years of data will be used, thus making it impossible (without skipping a grade) for one student's record to span from 2nd to either 7th or 8th grade. The three overlapping squares denote three possible cohorts of students.

School Model: $y_{ioklmn} = \mu_{ioklm} + e_{ioklmn}$,

where y_{ioklmn} represents a test score in the mth subject for the nth student, and this student was in the ith school system, o^{th} school, k^{th} year, and l^{th} grade; and μ_{ioklm} is the fixed school mean score for all students in the ith school system, o^{th} school, k^{th} year, l^{th} grade, and m^{th} subject; and e_{ioklmn} represents the random deviation of the test score for the nth student from the school mean.

The covariance structure of the e_{ioklmn} is exactly the same as that for the system model; of course, the actual estimates will differ.

Teacher Model: $y_{ijklmn} = \mu_{ijklm} = \sum_{p=1}^{N_{mk}} c_{m(ijkl)_p} \times t_{m(ijkl)_p} + e_{ijklmn}$,

where y_{ijklmn} represents a test score in the mth subject for the nth student, and this student had the jth teacher in the ith school system, k^{th} year, and l^{th} grade; μ_{ijklm} is the fixed system mean score for all students in the ith system, k^{th} year, l^{th} grade, and m^{th} subject; t_{ijklm} is the random effect of teacher j who taught the nth student in the ith system, k^{th} year, l^{th} grade, and m^{th} subject; c_{ijklm} is the fractional contribution of teacher j to this score; and e_{ijklmn} represents the random deviation of the test score for the nth student from the system mean. The pattern of the covariance structure for the e_{ijklmn} is the same as that for school or system models.

The summation over the teacher effects creates a "layered" model in which the score in subject m in the current year k is attributed to the current and all previous teachers that student n had. The index p tracks the student across years, accounting for changes in system, year, and grade, and also allows for multiple teachers in 1 year. The limit N_{mk} is the total number of teachers the student had through year k in subject m.

Historically, classification variables in a linear model context that have their own probability distribution have been referred to as random. By considering the effects of teachers to comprise a random class, the distribution of this class contributes information to improve the estimation of a specific teacher effect. This contribution is included in the modeling through the G matrix, which contains the variances and covariances among the teacher effects, t_{ijklm}. In TVAAS, all off-diagonal covariances in the G matrix are set to zero, even

TABLE 13.1. General Form of the Variance-Covariance Structure Over Subjects and Grades for the *R* Matrix

		2			3			4			5			6			7			8		
		R	L	M	R	L	M	R	L	M	R	L	M	R	L	M	R	L	M	R	L	M
2	R	×																				
2	L	×	×																			
2	M	×	×	×																		
3	R	×	×	×	×																	
3	L	×	×	×	×	×																
3	M	×	×	×	×	×	×															
4	R	×	×	×	×	×	×	×														
4	L	×	×	×	×	×	×	×	×													
4	M	×	×	×	×	×	×	×	×	×												
5	R	×	×	×	×	×	×	×	×	×	×											
5	L	×	×	×	×	×	×	×	×	×	×	×										
5	M	×	×	×	×	×	×	×	×	×	×	×	×									
6	R	×	×	×	×	×	×	×	×	×	×	×	×	×								
6	L	×	×	×	×	×	×	×	×	×	×	×	×	×	×							
6	M	×	×	×	×	×	×	×	×	×	×	×	×	×	×	×						
7	R	0	0	0	×	×	×	×	×	×	×	×	×	×	×	×	×					
7	L	0	0	0	×	×	×	×	×	×	×	×	×	×	×	×	×	×				
7	M	0	0	0	×	×	×	×	×	×	×	×	×	×	×	×	×	×	×			
8	R	0	0	0	0	0	0	×	×	×	×	×	×	×	×	×	×	×	×	×		
8	L	0	0	0	0	0	0	×	×	×	×	×	×	×	×	×	×	×	×	×	×	
8	M	0	0	0	0	0	0	×	×	×	×	×	×	×	×	×	×	×	×	×	×	×

NOTE: R = reading; L = language arts; M = math.

though there is correlation among the teacher effects over subjects and years. This was chosen to protect teachers that emphasize subjects differently or change their teaching emphasis from year to year. Thus the G matrix is diagonal and unstructured, allowing teacher variance components to differ over years, grades, and subjects.

Discussion of the Encoding Examples

Tables 13.2, 13.3, 13.4, and 13.5 are illustrations meant to conceptually describe the encoding of the X and Z matrices and the estimation of teacher gains via estimable functions. The illustrations refer to the teacher model because of its complexity in comparison to the school and system models, although comparisons can be made across models if care is taken to retain the distinctions.

To keep the illustrations simple, the tables are limited to three grades, three students, two teachers per grade, and three subjects over 3 years. In actuality, TVAAS provides data on five subjects for all teachers, schools, and systems based on the scores of all Tennessee students in Grades 2 through 8 (Grades 3 through 8 are reported) who have taken the TCAP in the past 5 years.

Encoding the Fixed Effects

As mentioned previously, one of the most powerful advantages of TVAAS is that all available information for each student can be included in the process without either imputing data or eliminating fractured records. Consider the hypothetical example presented in Table 13.2. Observe that the encoding for Tommy's data into the X matrix (the fixed part that allows the estimation of the subject * grade means) represents a student who had complete information for each grade and subject. In both the $X'(R^{-1})X$ and the $Z'(R^{-1})Z$ parts of the mixed-model equations, the "little R"—that part of the master R matrix that matches the specific records for this specific student—is inverted. It is the inversion of this "little R" that supplies the differential weighting to individual student records. This results in the fact that students with more complete information provide heavier weights to the estimates. Observe that Susan did not have a 4th-grade language arts score; therefore, the "little R" for her records is an 8×8 matrix, whereas Tommy's is a 9×9 matrix. Thus Susan's records will contribute less weight to the estimation process than will Tommy's.

TABLE 13.2. A Hypothetical Example of the Encoding of the X Matrix for Three Students Within One Cohort

Grade	Subject	Student	2nd Grade			3rd Grade			4th Grade		
			M	R	L	M	R	L	M	R	L
2	M	Tommy	1	0	0	0	0	0	0	0	0
	R		0	1	0	0	0	0	0	0	0
	L		0	0	1	0	0	0	0	0	0
3	M	Tommy	0	0	0	1	0	0	0	0	0
	R		0	0	0	0	1	0	0	0	0
	L		0	0	0	0	0	1	0	0	0
4	M	Tommy	0	0	0	0	0	0	1	0	0
	R		0	0	0	0	0	0	0	1	0
	L		0	0	0	0	0	0	0	0	1
2	M	Susan	1	0	0	0	0	0	0	0	0
	R		0	1	0	0	0	0	0	0	0
	L		0	0	1	0	0	0	0	0	0
3	M	Susan	0	0	0	1	0	0	0	0	0
	R		0	0	0	0	1	0	0	0	0
	L		0	0	0	0	0	1	0	0	0
4	M	Susan	0	0	0	0	0	0	1	0	0
	R		0	0	0	0	0	0	0	1	0
	L		0	0	0	0	0	0	0	0	1

2	M	Eric	1	0	0	0	0	0	0	0	0	0	0	0	0
	R		0	1	0	0	0	0	0	0	0	0	0	0	0
	L		0	0	1	0	1	0	0	0	0	0	0	0	0
3	M	Eric	0	0	0	0	0	1	0	0	0	0	0	0	0
	R		0	0	0	0	0	0	1	0	1	0	0	0	0
	L		0	0	0	0	0	0	0	0	0	1	0	0	0
4	M	Eric	0	0	0	0	0	0	0	0	0	0	1	1	0
	R		0	0	0	0	0	0	0	0	0	0	0	1	0
	L		0	0	0	0	0	0	0	0	0	0	0	0	1

NOTE: M = math; R = reading; L = language arts.

Encoding the Random Effects

In Table 13.3, the encoding for the Z matrix for this hypothetical example is presented. The Z matrix is the incidence matrix for the random effects portion of the mixed-model equations. Observe that Tommy was taught in the 2nd grade for all subjects by Teacher A. Also, observe that Tommy was taught all subjects by Teacher C in the 3rd grade and by Teacher E in the 4th grade. Susan, on the other hand, received instruction in math and language arts in the 2nd grade from Teacher A and reading instruction from Teacher B. She was instructed in reading and language arts by Teacher C in the 3rd grade, but her math teacher is unknown. In the 4th grade, Susan had Teacher E for reading and Teacher F for math, but no language arts record is included because Susan had no language arts score. In the 2nd grade, Eric was instructed in math by Teacher A, in reading by Teacher B, and in language arts in equal parts by Teachers A and B. In the 3rd grade, his teacher for all subjects was Teacher D, whereas in 4th grade he had two teachers in varying proportions for math and language but received all of his reading instruction from Teacher E.

The TVAAS teacher model allows for the accommodation of team teaching, departmentalization, and other such structuring of instruction by encoding the Z matrix as described in the preceding. In all of these cases, note that information regarding previous teachers is included in the coding for subsequent years. In other words, the 2nd grade teacher is included in the 3rd-grade equations, and both are included in the 4th-grade equations.

Estimates from the solution vector resulting from this method of coding provide TVAAS with distinct advantages. This approach, unique to TVAAS and referred to as a layered model, recognizes that achievement as measured at any point in time, say 4th grade, is a function of a student's base of knowledge and/or potential, the effect of the current teacher, and the retained influences of previous teachers. However, just as the height of the bottom layer of a cake decreases with the addition of each subsequent layer, the influence of previous teachers on the present score would be expected to decrease. Because all data for each student over time are included, and because the R matrix reflects not only correlation among subjects but correlation over time, all data are given the appropriate weights.

This approach to the modeling captures more information and enables all teacher effects to be estimated with greater precision than if traditional encoding of the incidence matrix were used. This is especially helpful when the teacher effects are expressed as gains, as will be presented later.

One of the properties of a solution to the mixed-model equations is that the part of the solution vector for the teacher * year * grade * subject provides the BLUP, a shrinkage estimate of the teacher effects for each subject * grade * year combination. The use of a shrinkage estimate for the teacher effects is another advantage of TVAAS in that protection against a fortuitous misclassification of an individual is greatly enhanced. All teachers' estimates are assumed to be the mean of their school system until the preponderance of the data pulls the estimates away from the system mean. This is particularly important for teachers for whom there are only small amounts of student data. Without the BLUP, such teachers could unfairly appear either below or above the mean on the basis of a small quantity of data.

Because the magnitude of shrinkage is a function of the quantity of the data, the magnitude of the teacher variance component for the system (included in the equations via the G matrix), and the variance-covariance structure within the *R* matrix, there will be cases of certain subject * grade combinations in some systems for which all teachers will have the same estimate (the system average). This will be true as the teacher variance component approaches zero.

Referring again to Table 13.2, which depicts the encoding of the *X* matrix, we can see that Susan has scores for all three 3rd-grade tests. However, in Table 13.3, which shows the encoding of the *Z* matrix, observe that no teacher is indicated for math for Susan. We know that Susan took the test, but we do not have any information as to who her teacher was for 3rd-grade math. This is not an infrequent reality because the information could have been improperly read from the data forms or could be unavailable for many other reasons. This record contributes to the estimates of the means that will be used in the conversion to teacher gains but, of course, will not be in the estimation for any specific teacher. This is an example of how TVAAS uses all available information and does not require the elimination of any record due to incompleteness.

TABLE 13.3. A Hypothetical Example of the Encoding of the Z Matrix

| | | | 2nd Grade | | | | | | 3rd Grade | | | | | | 4th Grade | | | | | |
| | | | A | | | B | | | C | | | D | | | E | | | F | | |
Grade	Subject	Student	M	R	L	M	R	L	M	R	L	M	R	L	M	R	L	M	R	L
2	M	Tommy	1	0	0	0	0	0	0	0	0	0	0	0	0	0	0	0	0	0
	R		0	1	0	0	0	0	0	0	0	0	0	0	0	0	0	0	0	0
	L		0	0	1	0	0	0	0	0	0	0	0	0	0	0	0	0	0	0
3	M	Tommy	1	0	0	0	0	0	1	0	0	0	0	0	0	0	0	0	0	0
	R		0	1	0	0	0	0	0	1	0	0	0	0	0	0	0	0	0	0
	L		0	0	1	0	0	0	0	0	1	0	0	0	0	0	0	0	0	0
4	M	Tommy	1	0	0	0	0	0	1	0	0	0	0	0	1	0	0	0	0	0
	R		0	1	0	0	0	0	0	1	0	0	0	0	0	1	0	0	0	0
	L		0	0	1	0	0	0	0	0	1	0	0	0	0	0	1	0	0	0

Subject	Measure	C1	C2	C3	C4	C5	C6	C7	C8	C9	C10	C11	C12	C13	C14	C15	C16	C17	C18
2 Susan	M	0	0	0	0	0	0	0	0	0	0	0	0	0	0	0	0	0	1
	R	0	0	0	0	0	0	0	0	0	0	0	0	0	1	0	0	0	0
	L	0	0	0	0	0	0	0	0	0	0	0	0	0	0	0	1	0	0
3 Susan	M	0	0	0	0	0	0	0	0	0	0	0	0	0	0	0	0	0	1
	R	0	0	0	0	0	0	0	0	0	0	1	0	0	1	0	0	0	0
	L	0	0	0	0	0	0	0	0	0	1	0	0	0	0	0	1	0	0
4 Susan	M	0	1	1	0	0	0	0	0	0	0	0	0	0	0	0	0	0	1
	R	0	0	0	0	1	0	0	0	0	0	1	0	0	1	0	0	0	0
	L	0	0	0	0	0	0	0	0	0	0	0	0	0	0	0	0	0	0
2 Eric	M	0	0	0	0	0	0	0	0	0	0	0	0	0	0	0	0	0	1
	R	0	0	0	0	0	0	0	0	0	0	0	0	0	1	0	0	0	0
	L	0	0	0	0	0	0	0	0	0	0	0	0	0	0	0	.5	0	0
3 Eric	M	0	0	0	0	0	0	0	0	1	0	0	0	0	0	0	0	0	1
	R	0	0	0	0	0	0	0	1	0	0	1	0	0	1	0	0	0	0
	L	0	0	0	0	0	0	1	0	0	0	0	0	0	0	0	.5	0	0
4 Eric	M	0	0	.2	0	0	.8	0	0	1	0	0	0	0	0	0	0	0	1
	R	0	0	0	0	1	0	0	1	0	0	0	0	0	1	0	0	0	0
	L	.5	0	0	.5	0	0	1	0	0	0	0	0	.5	0	0	.5	0	0

NOTE: M = math; R = reading; L = language arts.

Conversion of Elements From the Solution Vector
of the Mixed-Model Equations Into Estimates of
Teacher Influence on Mean Gain of Students

In Table 13.4 for this hypothetical example, the solution to the mixed-model equations, the standard error of each element of the solution, and a set of estimable functions corresponding to the teacher * grade * subject combinations are presented. (For a definition and detailed description of estimable functions, see Searle, 1971.)

Another advantage of TVAAS, as mentioned previously, is that the influence of teachers on student gains can be estimated without having *gain* as the metric for the response variables. This is accomplished via estimable functions of the solution vector. Property 3a of the mixed-model equations, $K'b + M'u$ is the BLUP of $K'B + M'U$, is a property that is exploited. Assume that the 2nd-grade mean (the BLUE from the mixed-model solution vector) for the previous year is subtracted from the 3rd-grade mean (also the BLUE) for the current year; then the resulting difference is the BLUE for the gain for a specific cohort of students for that system. Now the u's, which are the BLUPs (the shrinkage estimates for a specific teacher * grade * subject), are direct measures of the teacher deviation from the system mean. Thus estimable functions that add the teacher effect to the system gain translate the teacher effect into a measurement of gain. Also, the standard error for each teacher's estimated mean gain is readily available from Property 3b of the mixed-model equations.

From Table 13.4, to estimate the reading gain for Teacher C, estimable Function 1 would be multiplied by the solution vector to obtain $(-1) * 662.9 + (1) * 688.1 + (1) * 1.6 = 26.8$. The BLUEs for the 2nd- and 3rd-grade means, 662.9 and 688.1, are obtained directly from the "b part" of the solution vector, and the BLUP for the teacher effect comes from the "u part" of the solution vector. Once a solution vector of the mixed-model equations is obtained, much flexibility in application is available without having to recompute a solution, which is very computing-intense for large school systems. In addition to gains, other statistics of interest can be generated merely by defining estimable functions suitable for the purpose. For example, if the need arises, an "index" combining the performance over several subjects can easily be constructed merely by defining estimable functions suitable for the purpose.

The Tennessee EIA specifies that the individual teacher reports will be based on a 3-year average for each subject. The appropriate estimable function for the 3-year average is easily obtained by averaging the individual functions for each teacher for the 3-year period, element by element. The application of the resulting function produces the appropriate 3-year estimate and its corresponding standard error.

Presented in Table 13.5 are the gains and standard errors of each of the 11 estimable functions defined in Table 13.4. Observe that Teacher F has no estimated gain in reading. When a teacher does not instruct in a tested subject, no estimate is calculated for that particular teacher in that subject area.

Observe also the magnitude of the standard errors of the estimated mean gains given for this example. This example contains only one cohort of students. In reality, it has been observed that if a teacher has taught 20-25 students per year over 3 years, then the standard error for estimated gain from metrics presently used in TVAAS will be approximately 3.0. This level of sensitivity is most adequate to distinguish over the wide range of effectiveness that often is observed.

Computing Requirements

One of the major obstacles to the creation of a statewide longitudinally merged database is that the identifying information for each record can vary over years. Students' names change, social security numbers may be wrongly encoded, birthdates may be inconsistently reported, and mark sense readers may fail to read accurately. These and other errors have been detected in the raw data provided for TVAAS. Thus a major software effort to ensure that each student's record is accurately merged with previous records has been necessary. A system has been developed that produces approximately a 90% merge rate. This system does not require any information external to the raw data. Of course, the unmerged 10% is retained in the database and considered as single records, which are a legitimate possibility. Presently, more than 4 million merged records reside in the master database.

TABLE 13.4. Estimation of Teacher Gains via Estimable Functions of the Solution Vector From the Mixed-Model Equations

						3rd-Grade Teacher						4th-Grade Teacher				
						C			D			E			F	
						R	L	M	R	L	M	R	L	M	L	M
Year	Grade	Teacher	Subject	b	SE				Estimable Function Number							
						1	2	3	4	5	6	7	8	9		
1993	2		R	662.9	7.4	−1									1	1
1993	2		L	699.7	6.1		−1								1	0
1993	2		M	650.3	7.0			−1							1	1
1993	3		R	700.1	6.7				−1							
1993	3		L	702.5	6.3					−1						
1993	3		M	692.1	6.2						−1					
1993	4		R	712.4	7.0	All zeros						−1				
1993	4		L	722.2	8.0								−1		−1	
1993	4		M	700.5	5.0									−1		−1
1994	2		R	657.3	8.1							All zeros				
1994	2		L	683.2	6.5											
1994	2		M	632.1	11.8											

Elements of K: All zeros

158

1994	3		R	688.1	8.3	1			1							
1994	3		L	701.7	7.8		1			1						
1994	3		M	695.6	7.4			1			1					
1994	4		R	719.1	7.3							1				
1994	4		L	715.8	6.1								1		1	
1994	4		M	717.7	8.1									1		1

Submatrices Dealing With ***Random Effects***

Year	*Grade*	*Teacher*	*Subject*	u	*SE*	*1*	*2*	*3*	*4*	*5*	*6*	*7*	*8*	*9*	*0*	*1*
													Elements of *M*:			
1994	3	C	R	1.6	8.0	1										
1994	3	C	L	–1.2	5.8		1							All zeros		
1994	3	C	M	1.7	4.8			1								
1994	3	D	R	–14.3	8.3				1							
1994	3	D	L	1.3	5.9					1						
1994	3	D	M	–2.3	4.9						1					
1994	4	E	R	3.4	5.1			All zeros				1				
1994	4	E	L	1.5	3.8								1			
1994	4	E	M	5.9	7.9									1		
1994	4	F	L	–1.4	5.6										1	
1994	4	F	M	–1.6	4.1											1

NOTE: R = reading; L = language arts; M = math.

TABLE 13.5. Estimated Teacher Gains and Standard Errors Using Estimable Functions

Grade	Teacher		Reading	Language Arts	Math
3	C	Gain	26.8	0.8	47.0
		SE	7.3	5.9	7.3
		Estimable function	(1)	(2)	(3)
	D	Gain	10.9	3.3	43.0
		SE	8.0	6.3	7.5
		Estimable function	(4)	(5)	(6)
4	E	Gain	22.4	14.8	31.5
		SE	5.6	4.7	5.3
		Estimable function	(7)	(8)	(9)
	F	Gain		11.9	24.0
		SE		5.7	7.6
		Estimable function		(10)	(11)

Obviously, the computing requirements for TVAAS are enormous. Even though the records for each student in Tennessee are merged over all systems in the state, the fitting of the three models (system, school, and teacher) is done separately for each system, with the exception of the counties that contain multiple systems. In those cases, all the data within a county are processed with one set of equations. Even with these processing strategies, the number of mixed-model equations is huge. Considering Shelby County and Memphis City, one of the largest systems in the United States, the number of equations to be solved for the teacher model is in excess of 15,000. These equations have to be solved not just once but rather many, many times. The variance components for the G and R matrices are estimated with a derivative-free restricted maximum likelihood algorithm (Patterson & Thompson, 1971). This is an iterative process and requires many iterations, each necessitating a solution to the complete set of mixed-model equations. Software to accommodate a mixed-model application of this size has been developed by UT-VARAC. At present, all processing for TVAAS is accomplished on a UNIX workstation with 1 gigabyte of physical memory and 13 gigabytes of hard disk storage.

Conclusion

TVAAS is a dynamic process that offers several advantages over traditional models of educational assessment. Among these is the ability to use all information that contributes to the measurement of academic progress of populations of students. The data can derive from any of a wide variety of indicator variables; the only requirements are that they provide linear metrics, are strongly related to defined curricular objectives, and possess appropriate sensitivities. Thus the TVAAS process is flexible and adaptable to accommodate many different assessment instruments.

TVAAS offers conservative estimates of teacher effects due to the shrinkage estimation contained in the teacher model. The inclusion of the shrinkage estimate ensures that a preponderance of evidence to the contrary is required to differentiate a teacher's effect from that of the school system mean, thereby guaranteeing that teachers are fairly treated. Furthermore, the longitudinal aspects of all three models protect schools and systems as well as teachers against short-term fluctuations while also providing enhanced precision.

The expectation of the EIA is that each system and school will work toward providing instruction that will enable its students to achieve academic gains equal to or greater than the national norm gain in each subject every year. This goal is attainable by all Tennessee schools, causing some to voice concerns that the standards for success have been set too low. On the contrary, if all schools sustain appropriate gains for all students, then education will have improved for all students without demanding unreasonable improvements from those excellent programs currently in place. Presently, the gains for students in many Tennessee school systems already are at desirable levels. The problem in Grades K-12 throughout Tennessee is that there is enormous variability among systems, schools within systems, and teaching effectiveness within systems. The goal of TVAAS is to shrink this variability by providing educators with information that will provide direction for improving student academic gain, enabling students to receive more equal opportunity regardless of where they go to school.

References

Harville, D. A. (1976). Extension of the Gauss-Markov theorem to include the estimation of random effects. *Annals of Statistics, 4,* 384-395.

Henderson, C. R. (1973). Sire evaluation and genetic trends. In *Proceedings of the Animal Breeding and Genetic Symposium in honor of Dr. Jay L. Lush* (pp. 10-41). Champaign, IL: American Society of Animal Science and American Dairy Science Association.

Henderson, C. R. (1975). Best linear unbiased estimation and prediction under a selection model. *Biometrics, 31,* 423-447.

Henderson, C. R. (1984). *Applications of linear models in animal breeding.* Guelph, Ontario: University of Guelph.

McLean, R. A., & Sanders, W. L. (1984). *Objective component of teacher evaluation: A feasibility study* (Working Paper No. 199). Knoxville: University of Tennessee, College of Business Administration.

McLean, R. A., Sanders, W. L., & Stroup, W. W. (1991). A unified approach to mixed linear models. *American Statistician, 45,* 54-64.

Patterson, H. D., & Thompson, R. (1971). Recovery of interblock information when block sizes are unequal. *Biometrika, 58,* 545-554.

Raudenbush, S. W., & Bryk, A. S. (1988). Methodological advances in analyzing the effects of schools and classrooms on student learning. *Review of Research in Education, 15,* 423-479.

Sanders, W. L. (1989). A multivariate mixed model. In *Applications of mixed models in agriculture and related disciplines* (Southern Cooperative Series Bulletin No. 343, pp. 138-144). Baton Rouge: Louisiana Agricultural Experiment Station.

Sanders, W. L., & Horn, S. P. (n.d.). *An overview of the Tennessee Value-Added Assessment System (TVAAS) with answers to frequently asked questions.* Knoxville: University of Tennessee.

Sanders, W. L., & Horn, S. P. (1994). The Tennessee Value-Added Assessment System (TVAAS): Mixed model methodology in educational assessment. *Journal of Personnel Evaluation in Education, 8*(1), 299-311.

Sanders, W. L., & Horn, S. P. (1995). Educational assessment reassessed: The usefulness of standardized and alternative measures of student achievement as indicators for the assessment of educational outcomes. *Educational Policy Analysis Archives, 3*(6).

Sanders, W. L., Saxton, A. M., Schneider, J. F., Dearden, B. L., Wright, S. P., & Horn, S. P. (1994). Effects of building change on indicators of student academic growth. *Evaluation Perspectives, 4*(1), 3, 7.

Searle, S. R. (1971). *Linear models.* New York: John Wiley.

CHAPTER 14

The Tennessee Value-Added Assessment System

A Challenge to Familiar Assessment Methods

RICHARD B. DARLINGTON

School principals and superintendents often are derided as overpaid bureaucrats who do little to advance important educational goals. Sanders and his colleagues have data suggesting that this negative characterization does apply to some but that, even in schools serving some of the poorest American neighborhoods, there are teachers, principals, and superintendents who are genuine heroes who use talent, empathy, and dawn-to-dusk hard work to produce important and long-lasting gains in student achievement. Sanders has convinced me that these people can be identified, and they should certainly be honored, rewarded, and emulated.

Of course, claims like this must be examined critically, and the critical eye must be cast first at the tools on which these claims are based. The tool considered here is the Tennessee Value-Added Assessment System (TVAAS), which was developed and is being applied at the University of Tennessee Value-Added Research and Assessment Center (UT-VARAC), directed by Sanders. TVAAS is a major new way in which to evaluate teachers, schools, and school systems through the achievement gains of their students. In trying to evaluate TVAAS, two principal questions must be considered:

1. Can any such system work well enough to make it worth-while?
2. How does TVAAS compare to the more widely understood regression method?

My answer to the first question is positive. My answer to the second is that I have not ruled out the possibility of combining the advantages of the regression and TVAAS methods. However, unless or until that proves possible, it does seem to me that TVAAS is superior. I say that as an "advocate" of regression who has been extolling its advantages and uses in print for some 30 years.

I now consider these two questions in turn.

Is a Reasonably Objective Teaching Evaluation System Even Possible?

Several factors can be cited against the very possibility of a reasonably objective sytem for evaluating teachers through student achievement: classroom effects, cohort effects, and vindictive or exploitive school officials.

Classroom effects are chance events affecting an entire classroom. A class may include a few troublemakers who lower class achievement by disrupting the class all year, a class may include a popular student who destroys initiative by being openly bored without being overtly disruptive, or a class may simply be on the hot side of the building. Cohort effects are chance events affecting all classes of an individual teacher in a given year, such as the teacher's illness or divorce. Vindictive school officials can affect the achievement gains of a teacher's pupils by regularly assigning the teacher to a classroom that is too hot, too cold, or too noisy or by assigning disruptive students to that teacher. When I mention *exploitive* school officials, I am thinking of a teacher I knew who was routinely assigned the worst discipline cases because he could handle them far better than could other teachers. Perhaps because of these assignments, he "burned out" and retired very early.

Two points convince me that these factors do not prevent a reasonably accurate system for teacher evaluation. First, Sanders and his colleagues considered classroom and cohort effects at the very beginning of the TVAAS project and were able to show a reasonable consistency in teacher evaluations from year to year. They now have far more data on that point, and it continues to support a claim of year-to-year consistency. I avoid including the data here both for reasons of space and because new data come in rapidly enough so that publication lags would make any figures given here obsolete by the time they appeared. School officials wanting more information should contact UT-VARAC directly.

Second, all these concerns can be allayed by remembering that under TVAAS, the officials are themselves being evaluated by the achievement gains of their students. The officials thus have every incentive to evaluate and compensate teachers fairly, lest arbitrary and unfair practices damage teacher morale and thus student achievement. Fair evaluations mean not just the avoidance of unfair and expoitive practices but also the active consideration of factors such as individual classroom and cohort effects (e.g., too-hot classrooms, a teacher's divorce) in making the final decisions about the evaluation and compensation of individual teachers.

Can the Tennessee Value-Added Assessment System Outperform Regression?

A complex statistical system clearly is needed to help make these evaluations. There are two major candidates: regression and mixed models (the TVAAS approach). Both systems assume that reasonable decisions have been made about what achievement tests and norms should be used, which students should be tested, and how students should be motivated to try to do well. These questions certainly are important, but they are outside the purview of this chapter. I start by briefly sketching the competing approaches.

In the regression approach, one collects all the data one can about each student that might usefully predict that student's score on an end-of-year achievement test. These data certainly will include the student's test scores in previous years and might include personal factors such as IQ test scores, English as the student's second language, attendance, field trip absences from class, socioeconomic status as measured by eligibility for special lunch programs, discipline problems, and whether the mother and father report the same address. One then uses the regression method to combine all these data to predict each student's score on the achievement test. Then the difference between a classroom's average predicted score and the actual average score is attributed to the teacher. The average of such teacher effects within a school gives a "school effect," and the average of such school effects within a district gives a "district effect."

The regression approach uses statistical formulas that are beyond the understanding of the average teacher or school board member but are reasonably well understood by virtually every educational statistician teaching in a school of education or department of psychology as well as by a large proportion of school superintendents and psychology Ph.D.s. The methods are easily applied on a typical desktop computer using software that costs $1,000 or less.

For the purposes considered here, the major limitation of the regression method is its inelegant handling of missing data. If a child has missing data on even one of the "predictor variables" used in the regression, then that child typically is left out of the analysis. There are methods for trying to estimate the missing data, but these introduce distortions and are generally unsatisfactory. Therefore, if even 5% of the students are missing data on each predictor variable, then it may well turn out that half or more of the students are missing data on at least one variable, so that the data of less than half the students actually will be used in the assessment process. Knowing this, the people designing the process must make difficult decisions about which variables to include in the analysis. Including each variable might add some predictive power; however, if it has much missing data, then its inclusion lowers the sample size.

The problem of missing data applies not just to attendance and the other variables listed earlier but also to previous achievement test scores. Ideally, one would like to use the achievement test results not just from last year but also from all previous years. But this compounds the missing data problem; children are sick the day of the test, children move in from out of state, or the evaluation program may not have the time or funds to determine whether the James Dock now in 4th grade in Nashville is the same child as Jimmy Ray Dock-Smith in 2nd grade 2 years ago in Chattanooga.

The mixed-model approach used by TVAAS goes on the theory that *less is more*. At least in its present form, it uses only achievement test data, ignoring IQ scores, attendance, and the other personal factors listed earlier. The defenders of the mixed-model approach argue that these personal factors often are constant across a child's school career, and so they all get incorporated into the child's previous achievement record. That ignores the fact that Johnny was happy for 3 years but is now unhappy because his father lost his job and his parents are divorcing. The frequency and importance of such changes is unknown (Chapter 16).

The mixed-model approach is far more complex and less well known than is regression. It is familiar to many statisticians studying plant and animal breeding and other agricultural applications, but it is little known to the human behavior statisticians who teach in schools of education and departments of psychology. Although computer programs for regression are available from dozens of vendors and appear even in the ubiquitous spreadsheet packages, there is just one widely available computer program for mixed models: PROC MIXED from SAS.

It seems likely that mixed models gradually will become better known to behavioral statisticans. These people often are thrilled when they learn of PROC MIXED and its ability to handle problems that are otherwise intractable. However, PROC MIXED has many limitations, and the central contribution of UT-VARAC has been to write what I presume is the world's most powerful program for mixed-model analysis—a program that compares to PROC MIXED much as a Ferrari compares to a Yugo.

Although any analytic method wants all the data it can get, one might say that TVAAS does not "overreact" to missing data. If we are missing 1 year of Johnny's past test data, then we are missing just that 1 year, whereas the regression approach would discard all of Johnny's data. TVAAS does not attempt to "fill in" the missing data; rather, it is capable of solving the necessary equations using whatever data it has.

TVAAS automatically employs a regression-to-the-mean logic that avoids making unwarranted attributions about individual teachers or schools based on little data. If a teacher taught math to only 15 children and all of them did very well, then the teacher will get some credit but less credit than a teacher who taught 50 children who did equally well. This desirable feature is not an automatic part of a regression approach, although it can be added by an extra formula. Therefore, provided the extra formula is used, I do not think there is a large difference between TVAAS and regression in this respect.

Conclusions

In comparing TVAAS to regression, I conclude that it depends on the data available. In an ideal school system, with little missing data and with readily available measures of IQ, attendance, and the other personal factors listed earlier, I would bet on regression to outperform TVAAS in measuring the effects of individual teachers. However, three points should be considered.

1. In the real world, the personal factors used in regression analysis are either unmeasured or not readily available to an analyst at a central location.

2. In the real world, there often will be substantial missing data on even the most central predictor variables—the achievement test scores from prior years. This will handicap regression relative to TVAAS.

3. In the real world, classroom and cohort effects always will be large enough so that a certain amount of subjective judgment always will be useful in evaluating individual teachers. Therefore, the real purpose of an evaluation system is to let principals and superintendents know that they too are being evaluated in terms of the student progress in their schools and school systems. Once they know that, they will use a reasonable combination of objective data and subjective impressions to make the best possible evaluations of individual teachers. If the most important evaluations are then at the level of the school or school system, then these are large enough aggregates so that the personal factors average out. The important goal is then to make the best possible use of past achievement test data, and I am convinced that TVAAS does that.

There are at least a few heroes out there in the public schools. We should support those such as Sanders, Saxton, and Horn who are doing their best to identify and reward them.

CHAPTER 15

Assessment Requires Incentives to Add Value

A Review of the Tennessee Value-Added Assessment System

HERBERT J. WALBERG

SUSAN J. PAIK

The Tennessee Value-Added Assessment System (TVAAS) is a state-of-the-art, results-based teacher assessment system. Yet, like similar systems, it seems driven by technicalities and lacks adequate incentives for educational improvement. Its designers may be intimidated by expected resistance to rigorous personnel evaluation by the education establishment, especially administrators and teachers' unions. Such reticence is a reason why the most productive country on earth has the least productive school system. U.S. achievement test scores in foreign languages, mathematics, and science have long lagged behind those of many industrialized countries.

AUTHORS' NOTE: We thank Jason Millman and W. James Popham for suggestions, not all of which we had the resources, time, and space to incorporate into the present chapter.

The Policy Context of
Personnel Assessment Policy

What is less well known is that even in reading, American students ranked last in progress made between the ages of 9 and 14 years among 18 participating countries surveyed by the Organization for Economic Cooperation and Development (OECD, 1995, p. 208). With the worst outcomes, the United States also managed to spend the most on public elementary and secondary schools, $6,010 per student, among 20 reporting OECD countries. Given such inefficiency, we should expect citizens, legislators, parents, and educators to be clamoring for prompt, wide-scale, tough-minded evaluation. Because of international competition, heads have rolled in American industries. Even government bureaucracy is being downsized, reinvented, and incentivised. Why not education?

The United States surely has administrative staffers to carry out teacher evaluation; it spends 25.1% of the public school budget on administration, more than twice the average of other countries surveyed by the OECD. School boards and administrators have shirked their responsibilities, and state legislators are taking the initiative.

In productive industries, people's jobs and salaries and their firms' survival depend on the results they attain. However, a panel of eminent education economists ranging from liberal to free-market views concluded that the major reason for the failing American school system is the lack of incentives; the pervasive examples are the near absence of teacher merit pay systems and rare dismissals in public education (Hanushek, 1994).

In assessing employee performance, firms make adjustments for "value-added performance" and field conditions (e.g., sales gains may be harder in Mississippi than in Connecticut because of income differences). Firms, however, can hardly survive international competition by waiting for the perfect system agreeable to all employees. Indeed, making it temporarily harder on themselves as producers, firms have greatly benefited consumers, the economy, and themselves by improving quality, reducing costs, and eliminating organizational parts that contribute little to customer satisfaction.

The United States has maintained the highest level of manufacturing and service productivity in the world mainly because of competition, incentives, and a consumer focus. To avoid ill preparing young people and to escape the drag of inefficient education on the economy, assessment and significant incentives and sanctions for education results are in order today rather than in the year 2000.

Evaluation and Standards of Personnel Assessment

Having considered the policy context of teacher assessment, let us turn to assessment standards. Despite the timidity of results-based teacher assessment, TVAAS deserves accolades for being, like democracies, the least bad of systems. Its designers are serious, careful (if not too careful) professionals who have taken pains to get the technical details right; they express the usual academic cautions about further trials and eventually putting some teeth into the system. To us, however, teeth would mean clear and appropriately enacted probation and dismissal policies as well as individually based merit pay. Aggregate TVASS data for schools and districts might be employed for administrator assessment. Additional criteria such as ratings of teachers by students and parents, graduation rates, and employment of graduates might be considered for assessment, although much can be said for parsimony and priority in art, science, and evaluation.

Particularly strong points of TVAAS are the analysis of several years of data on teachers and an apparent system robustness despite ubiquitous missing data problems in longitudinal records. Still, it might be argued that using the most recent year would avoid many missing data problems and be psychologically wiser. Why should a current assessment and a merit raise be based on old results?

Our intention in this review of TVAAS is to evaluate the assessment system by the criteria set forth by the Joint Committee on Standards for Educational Evaluation (Stufflebeam, 1988). The joint committee's leaders were able to achieve a consensus of authorities on the standards for judging the adequacy of personnel evaluation. If the adolescent field of evaluation is to be taken seriously by economics, psychology, and its other senior academic siblings, then evaluators will have to achieve consensus on such standards and judge their colleagues' work accordingly.

Before turning to our review, it should be said that the standards themselves should bear brief and initial evaluation. In our exploratory exercise evaluating TVAAS, some standards seemed redundant. Others required guesstimates because the materials initially provided to us lacked direct evidence. Our concern with system outcomes (i.e., learning) lacked emphasis in the list of standards. Perhaps the standards are insufficiently well known to serve as general guidelines for the planning, conduct, and evaluation of evaluations. Perhaps they are too numerous and unwieldy, although it would seem that wide-scale adoption would upgrade the quality of evaluation.

Application of the Standards

Table 15.1 shows the 21 joint committee standards in four general categories: propriety, utility, feasibility, and accuracy. The five propriety standards concern legal, ethical, and participant welfare. The five utility standards concern information needs of intended users through factual information, timeliness, and influence. The three feasibility standards concern practicality, political viability, and cost-effectiveness. The eight accuracy standards concern technical aspects and linking detailed information for the most accurate assessment.

In Table 15.1, an "x" in the "SM" column indicates that a standard was addressed and probably met. To make a confident assessment of the fulfillment of each standard would require firsthand on-site evidence from multiple sources. In several cases, therefore, we used an "x?" to stress the tentativeness of our indication that the standard was met.

Table 15.1 shows that a few standards were only partially addressed. With respect to propriety, for example, it was not clear whether formal agreements were negotiated and signed by the parties, nor was it clear whether financial matters were discussed. One of the five utility standards also was only partially addressed in terms of its impact on its audience and teachers. Obviously because TVAAS still is in its developmental stage, not much archived documentation beyond the anecdotal seems available on some points.

With respect to feasibility, cost-effectiveness was not addressed. What is the cost of the evaluation relative to a typical teacher's salary? Costs for development and for each teacher and typical schools and districts would be useful to know. Other states or school systems might want to adopt the system, and presumably the per-unit costs would decline in a scaled-up version.

Finally, with respect to accuracy, some qualitative information is provided. It generally concerns the enthusiasm of educators for the system. It is not clear, however, how the anecdotal material was gathered, whether it is representative, and so on.

Still, as indicated in Table 15.1, 19 of the 21 standards were addressed, and specific references in TVAAS documents usually can be cited as information sources. We find this impressive documentation from reports that made no claims for comprehensiveness or conformity to the joint committee standards. Our guess is that the authors could meet all the standards, and they may wish to enlarge their documentation in further writings.

If we had the mission and resources for a thorough "meta-evaluation" (evaluation of the evaluation), then we would conduct third-party interviews, seek further documentation, and look for multiple sources of converging evidence to make our conclusions less tentative. For a still more definitive evaluation, we would look not to process and procedural standards but rather to outcomes, that is, learning trends over time in schools, districts, and the state. Contrasts of districts using and not using the system also might be helpful in sorting out effectiveness issues. Also, districts and schools employing various incentive and dismissal schemes might be analyzed.

Conclusion

From the information before us, it appears that Sanders and his colleagues have developed an assessment system that is exemplary in its longitudinal, statistical approach. In terms of indicators, the system might be extended or supplemented in several ways we have suggested. Even the best assessments, however, lack the capacity to improve education unless they incorporate probation and dismissal policies and compensation plans based in substantial part on individual merit.

TABLE 15.1. TVAAS Conformity to Personnel Evaluation Standards

Standards	Definition	SM	PM	NM	NA	Comment	Archives Documentation
Proprietary	Standards considered legal, ethical, and in the welfare of all participants					Four of five standards apparently met	
P1. Service orientation	The evaluation should be designed to assist and serve the needs of targeted participants	x				Measurable differences and consistency exist in teacher effects	Sanders and Horn (1994, p. 300)
P2. Formal evaluation	Obligations should be contracted on paper for adherence of all negotiations				x		
P3 Conflict of interest	Honesty is encouraged to overcome any compromise in the process or results	x?					
P4. Access to personnel evaluation reports	All persons involved should have accessibility to reports and should have the right to be protected	x				All reports are public except for individual teacher effects	Sanders and Horn (1994, p. 299)
P5. Inter-actions with evaluatees	Evaluations should respect all rights and assess an accurate record of strengths and weaknesses	x?					

Utility	Standards that ensure an evaluation will serve the information needs of intended users			Four of five standards apparently met (one partially)	
U1. Constructive orientation	Evaluations should be encouraging through constructive assessment	x?		Working Paper No. 199 (McLean & Sanders, 1984) includes most information concerning standards	McLean and Sanders (1984)
U2. Defined uses	Uses and intended uses should be identified so that the evaluation can address appropriate questions	x			McLean and Sanders (1984)
U3. Evaluator credibility	Conductors should be trustworthy and competent to perform the evaluation	x		Working paper on Knox County formed a credible foundation for TVAAS	McLean and Sanders (1984)
U4. Functional reporting	Reports should be clear, timely, accurate, and germane for practical purposes	x		April 1, 1993 statewide report; July 1, 1994 first report to public; July 1, 1995 report on teacher effects	Sanders and Horn (1994, p. 309)
U5. Follow-up and impact	Evaluations should encourage stakeholders to continual use and referral of assessment through necessary follow-ups		x	Some evidence of continual use of the first report exists; 1995 is yet to be determined	Sanders and Horn (1994)

continued

Standards	Definition	SM	PM	NM	NA	Comment	Archives Documentation
Feasibility	Standards that ensure that an evaluation will be diplomatic and do-able					Three of three standards apparently met	
F1. Practical procedures	Procedures should be practical to minimize distractions	x?					
F2. Political viability	The evaluation is used to serve all persons involved and should be sensitive to their needs	x?					
F3. Fiscal viability	Adequate time and resources should be provided for evaluation activities	x?					
Accuracy	Standards to reveal adequate and detailed information about the program					Eight of eight standards apparently met	
A1. Defined role	The role, responsibilities, performance, objectives, and needed qualifications of the evaluatee should be clearly defined	x					McLean and Sanders (1984)

A2. Work environment	The context in which the evaluatee works should be identified to determine influencing factors affecting the situation	x	McLean and Sanders (1984)
A3. Document of procedures	Actual procedures, in relation to intended procedures, should be recorded for proper assessment	x	McLean and Sanders (1984)
A4. Valid measurement	A well-developed information system should conclude a valid interpretation	x	McLean and Sanders (1984)
A5. Reliable measurement	A well-developed information system should conclude a reliable interpretation	x?	McLean and Sanders (1984)
A6. Systematic data control	All information should be systematically processed and corrected	x?	McLean and Sanders (1984)
A7. Bias control	The evaluation should provide safeguards against bias	x?	McLean and Sanders (1984)
A8. Monitoring evaluation systems	Periodic and systematic reviews should be made for appropriate revisions	x	McLean and Sanders (1984)

NOTE: SM = standards addressed and met; PM = standards addressed and partially met; NM = standards addressed and not met; NA = standards not addressed; x = standards addressed; ? = apparently; TVAAS = Tennessee Value-Added Assessment System.

References

Hanushek, E. A. (1994). *Making schools work: Improving performance and controlling costs.* Washington, DC: Brookings Institution.

McLean, R. A., & Sanders, W. L. (1984). *Objective component of teacher evaluation: A feasibility study* (Working Paper No. 199). Knoxville: University of Tennessee, College of Business Administration.

Organization for Economic and Cooperative Development. (1995). *Education at a glance: OECD indicators.* Paris: Author.

Sanders, W. L., & Horn, S. P. (1994). The Tennessee Value-Added Assessment System (TVAAS): Mixed methodology in educational assessment. *Journal of Personnel Evaluation in Education, 8,* 299-311.

Stufflebeam, D. L. (1988). *Personnel evaluation standards: How to assess systems for evaluating educators.* Newbury Park, CA: Sage.

CHAPTER 16

Response to the Reviewers

WILLIAM L. SANDERS

ARNOLD M. SAXTON

SANDRA P. HORN

First, we gratefully acknowledge the time and consideration that obviously were given to the composition of the reviews of the chapter describing the Tennessee Value-Added Assessment System (TVAAS) (Chapter 13). The following comments on these reviews are attempts to answer questions raised therein and to offer further clarification on a few salient points.

Darlington's (Chapter 14) major conclusions recognize the methodological advantages of TVAAS. From overly simplistic attempts to measure the effects of teachers on the academic growth of student populations (i.e., simple traditional analysis of covariance) to the complexity of TVAAS, there exists a continuum of sophistication of models and methods. The teacher effectiveness estimates resulting from the use of any of a variety of approaches, simple or complex, may prove to be highly correlated for any set of data. However, given the same quantity and quality of data, TVAAS estimates are superior in that TVAAS can afford more protection against the spurious misclassification of individual teachers by incorporating all of the available data in a multivariate, longitudinal model.

Darlington expresses some reservations about the elimination of personal factors from the model because it "ignores the fact that

Johnny was happy for 3 years but is now unhappy because his father lost his job and his parents are divorcing" (p. 167). Exogenous variables have not been included in the TVAAS models, not because of restrictions in the methodology but rather because our research has demonstrated that the school, system, and teacher effects can be fairly estimated by this process without the inclusion of data pertaining to these variables.

TVAAS incorporates at least 3 years of data for at least three cohorts of students in each of its analyses. Whereas Johnny may in fact be experiencing problems, it is just as likely that his classmate, Susan, is experiencing an upswing of fortune. Furthermore, Johnny's own academic history serves as a "blocking factor," and deviations in his pattern of achievement, aggregated with those of his classmates, influence the estimation of educational effects, not only in future analyses but also in the estimation of those effects in previous years. Therefore, the personal fortunes of an individual student have little influence on the estimation of educational effects.

Walberg and Paik (Chapter 15) express a distinct educational perspective in their review. It is one of a vast array of perspectives regarding the purposes to which educational assessment should be applied. Regardless of one's position on the philosophical spectrum, few, if any, would disagree with the assertion that sustained academic growth for students of all ability and achievement levels is the primary goal of formal education. It is our contention that reliable measurement of accelerators or impediments of sustained academic growth of student populations is essential for achieving this goal, and it is for this reason that TVAAS was developed.

Policy and educational emphases differ greatly from school to school, from system to system, from state to state, and sometimes even from classroom to classroom. However, the need for measurement that can reliably and validly assess the effects of educational efforts does not vary. TVAAS has proven to be an important source of the information that educators and educational policymakers need to effectively improve educational programs and practices. We applaud Walberg and Paik's appeal to the Standards for Personnel Evaluation and are pleased at their conclusion that TVAAS meets or partially meets 19 of the 21 standards.

TVAAS is only part of the educational assessment program in place in Tennessee. School success factors also include graduation rate, promotion rate, dropout rate, and attendance in addition to measures of student outcomes as assessed by TVAAS. Teachers and administrators are locally evaluated through performance assessment and dialogues. A new state model for local evaluation, now in the pilot stage, will allow teachers to be evaluated through a variety of means including cognitive coaching, teacher-devised professional improvement plans, and cooperative teaching-related projects as well as classroom observation. Teachers and administrators also may choose to be evaluated for Tennessee's version of merit pay, the Career Ladder. TVAAS provides information unavailable from any of these other assessment options—unbiased estimates of the effects of schools, teachers, and school systems on the academic growth of students. It is, therefore, an essential part of the comprehensive Tennessee educational assessment plan. The TVAAS reports are a unique resource supporting Tennessee's efforts to provide the best education possible for its children.

It is gratifying to read the positive responses of our reviewers. TVAAS is a complex system, and complexity sometimes generates suspicion, but the complexity for which TVAAS often has been called to task is necessary to ensure fairness. With the development of appropriate software and the rapid evolution of computing power and speed, the ability to conduct TVAAS assessments is within the grasp of more and more educational entities, and complexity becomes less and less a limiting factor. It is our hope that as educational assessment and policy theorists begin to delve more deeply into this admittedly new approach to the use of scaled achievement data, they will discover, as did our reviewers, that TVAAS is a methodology that is statistically rigorous, fair, reliable, and valid on which decisions about educational practice can be firmly based. We trust that the information presented in this book will provide a starting point for those who seek answers to the questions posed by education in the 21st century and that, as understanding increases, TVAAS methodology will enlighten their efforts.

PART V

The Kentucky Instructional Results Information System

Historical Background
The Kentucky School Accountability Index

DORIS REDFIELD

ROGER PANKRATZ

In November 1985, the Council for Better Education (CBE), a non-profit corporation consisting of 66 school districts, 7 boards of education, and 22 students, sued the Commonwealth of Kentucky for not providing an equitable and efficient system of education. In October 1988, Judge Ray Corns of the Franklin County Circuit Court ruled in favor of the CBE and named seven capacities necessary for an adequate education: (a) communication skills necessary to function in a complex and changing civilization; (b) knowledge to make economic, social, and political choices; (c) understanding of government processes; (d) knowledge of one's own mental and physical wellness; (e) grounding in the arts to appreciate one's own cultural and historical heritage; (f) sufficient preparation to intelligently choose and pursue a life's work; and (g) skills to compete favorably with students in other states.

Corn's ruling was appealed to the Kentucky Supreme Court; on June 8, 1989, the state's high court upheld Corn's earlier decision and declared Kentucky's system of "common" schools unconstitutional. The Kentucky Supreme Court further directed the general assembly to establish a new system of common schools and set minimal compliance standards.

Governor Wilkenson's Council on
School Performance Standards

Independent of the actions of the courts, Governor Wallace Wilkenson issued an executive order in February 1989 that established a 12-member Council on School Performance Standards (CSPS) consisting of business executives, educators, and state-appointed officials. The CSPS was charged with (a) determining what all students should know and be able to do and (b) providing a foundation for a school improvement program based on incentives for high performance.

In the spring and summer of 1989, the CSPS and its executive director, Roger Pankratz, conducted statewide focus groups and telephone interviews, convened task forces, and employed national consultants to produce a report with four major recommendations:

1. Adopt six common learning goals for all students: (a) use and apply communication and math skills; (b) apply core concepts and principles from mathematics, the sciences, the arts, the humanities, social studies, and practical living studies to situations and problems similar to what a student will encounter in life; (c) develop the ability to become a self-sufficient individual; (d) develop the ability to become a responsible member of a family, work group, or community; (e) develop the ability to think and solve problems; and (f) develop the ability to connect and integrate knowledge and experiences.

2. Launch a major effort to assess student performance beyond what can be measured by paper-and-pencil tests.

3. Encourage and support innovative efforts by local schools to adopt new professional roles, new organizational structures, and institutional strategies to promote achievement of the six learning goals.

4. Establish two intensive, long-range development efforts to support the learning goals: (a) a 6- to 10-year program to develop new assessment measures for the goals and (b) a program to provide incentives and assistance for curriculum reform in local schools.

The council's report, *Preparing Kentucky Youth for the Next Century: What Students Should Know and Be Able to Do and How Learning Should Be Assessed,* was presented to the curriculum committee of Kentucky's Legislative Task Force for Education Reform in September 1989. The council's four recommendations became a foundation for the legislative task force's subsequent report to the Kentucky General Assembly.

The Kentucky Reform Act of 1990

In response, House Bill 940, known as the Kentucky Education Reform Act (KERA), was passed by the Kentucky Legislature on March 29, 1990. KERA put into law all the state statutes recreating the common schools and significantly revised statewide structures and processes in curriculum, school governance, and school finance. It also created a new Department of Education (KDE), replaced the elected state superintendent of schools with an appointed commissioner, and established a statewide school accountability system based on student performance and a system of rewards, sanctions, and assistance. In addition, the 1990 Kentucky General Assembly passed a $1.4 billion tax package in support of KERA. Thus the courts, governor, and general assembly were united in this historic effort to improve Grades K-12 education in the commonwealth.

Specific to the new performance assessment and school accountability system, KERA mandated the following:

- Schools shall require a high level of performance on the six learning goals.
- Schools shall increase attendance rates, reduce dropout and retention rates, reduce physical and mental barriers to learning, and increase students' successful transition to post-high school experiences.
- The CSPS shall frame the six school goals named in the law in measurable terms.
- The State Board for Elementary and Secondary Education shall create and implement a statewide, primarily performance-based assessment program.

- Based on the standards set for each goal, all schools shall be held accountable for the proportion of successful students.

In addition, KERA called for the establishment of a committee of national testing experts to design the statewide school assessment and accountability system. The group of experts was charged with designing the system, *not* with developing or implementing the actual assessment measures.

The Design of the School Assessment and Accountability System

A five-member design team was named in the fall of 1990: Pascal ("Pat") Forgione, state superintendent of public instruction from Delaware; Edward ("Skip") Kifer, professor at the University of Kentucky; Jason Millman, professor at Cornell University; Doris Redfield, chief of assessment with the Virginia Department of Education; and Grant Wiggins, president and program director at the Center on Learning, Assessment, and School Structure. Redfield chaired the team, which accomplished its charge by providing a general design for a statewide assessment and accountability system in the form of a request for proposals (RFP). The team's recommended design, crafted to meet the requirements of KERA as well as criteria of sound psychometric practice, resulted in the following recommended framework for the Kentucky system:

- *Accountability assessments*, linked to Kentucky's valued outcomes, form the basis of school-level rewards and sanctions. Accountability assessment is mandatory and restricted to Grades 4, 8, and 12.
- *Continuous assessments*, also linked to Kentucky's valued outcomes, have the purpose of informing instructional process and mirroring accountability activities. Although continuous assessment was conceived as voluntary, it was to be highly encouraged. The continuous assessments include both formal and informal aspects.
- *Informal* aspects of the continuous assessments were envisioned as ongoing, day-to-day assessments used by class-

room teachers to improve learning and instruction. These assessments also would be linked to Kentucky's valued outcomes and hence to the accountability and more formal continuous assessments. In addition to contractor-developed tasks, informal continuous assessments could include items emanating from teachers themselves, the KDE, or other sources as instructionally useful.

- In addition to *cognitive* outcomes (i.e., knowledge and skills in academic content areas), the system must reflect the *noncognitive* goals of KERA (e.g., attendance and dropout information).

- The team recommended that the system be comprised of a balance of assessment types: (a) *scheduled performance tasks* that can be administered across the state at a given time, with student responses sent to the contractor for scoring; (b) *portfolios* that can be administered prior to a cutoff date but at a time determined by the teacher or school administrator, scored by school staff, and subject to audit managed by the contractor; and (c) *scheduled restricted-response items* that are referenced to the valued outcomes in five academic content areas, administered across the state at a given time, and submitted to the scoring contractor for objective scoring.

The Kentucky Instructional Results Information System

The RFP based on the design team's recommendations and specifying the requirements of the school assessment and accountability system was released in March 1991. Seven vendors submitted proposals and bids to the KDE. In July 1991, Advanced Systems for Measurement in Education was awarded a 5-year contract to develop, implement, and administer the system.

In the spring of 1992, assessments were administered to all 4th-, 8th-, and 12th-grade students and included writing portfolios, on-demand performance tasks, open-ended questions, and multiple-choice items. These assessment results provided the "baseline" for student performance in each school statewide. In the spring of 1995, approximately $25.5 million in cash rewards was distributed to more than 480 Kentucky schools and 42 districts declared successful based on improvements of their schools' accountability indexes.

Although multiple-choice items were administered in 1992, 1993, and 1994, they never were counted as part of the School Accountability Index. In the fall of 1994, the state board voted to discontinue the administration of multiple-choice items as part of the system.

Independent Evaluations of the Kentucky Instructional Results Information System

In 1995, two reports of independent evaluations of the Kentucky Instructional Results Information System (KIRIS) were released. In February, the Kentucky Institute for Education Research (KIER) released a study conducted by the Evaluation Center at Western Michigan University, the study being requested by the state board. In June, another study was released that had been commissioned by the state's Office of Education Accountability (OEA) and conducted by a national panel of experts under the leadership of Ronald Hamilton at the University of Massachusetts. These studies are discussed further in Chapters 20 and 19, respectively.

Results of both studies agreed that although significant progress has been made in Kentucky toward the development and implementation of a primarily performance-based assessment system, considerable work still is needed for the system to fulfill the purposes intended by the law, especially with regard to measurement for high-stakes decisions. Both study teams also said that it was a mistake to eliminate multiple-choice items from KIRIS and that much more technical information and cautions about the interpretation and use of test results should be provided to schools, parents, and the public.

The response of the KDE to the reports has been to accept the findings as an opportunity to improve KIRIS. The one exception concerns the use of writing portfolios. The KDE's position is that the instructional value of the writing portfolios outweighs any problems of validity and reliability and that portfolios should be retained as part of the system.

Based on the OEA report, the Legislative Oversight Committee resolved to continue support for the development of the system and to use the report's recommendations to help achieve the purposes of KERA.

CHAPTER 18

Kentucky's Accountability and Assessment Systems

NEAL KINGSTON

ED REIDY

The previous chapter described the genesis of the Kentucky Education Reform Act (KERA). This chapter describes the undergirding philosophy and critical features of the Kentucky accountability and assessment systems, which are parts of that act. Readers interested in the statistical and psychometric characteristics of the programs should see the *KIRIS Accountability Cycle I Technical Manual* (Kentucky Department of Education, 1995).

Philosophy Behind the Kentucky Accountability Model

The primary goal of Kentucky's school-based accountability system is to motivate educators and the public to dramatically improve student learning. This goal is paramount and takes precedence over the strategies and tactics associated with the accountability system. Kentucky will achieve this goal to the extent the accountability system accomplishes four things (Chapter 22):

- focuses teachers and students on high academic standards;
- motivates educators—using a system of rewards, assistance, and sanctions—to work long, hard, and smart;
- provides models and assistance for teachers to increase the power of their instruction; and
- draws public attention to and increases demand for quality in education, greatly magnifying any direct effects of the system.

The testing program used as the major component of accountability decisions demonstrates the preeminence of the overall goal. The Kentucky Instructional Results Information System (KIRIS) is a series of tests that are intended to (a) model good instructional practice, (b) assess school progress in educating *all* students, and (c) provide parents and teachers with useful information about individual student achievement.

These purposes for KIRIS are not the end in themselves; rather, they are the tactics we chose to help us accomplish our goal of increased student learning. These tactics have changed over time and will continue to do so as needed. So, for the first 3 years of the assessment program, individually reliable student scores were not a priority. Later, when it became clear that the public credibility (and thus the political viability) of the school scores was based on the credibility of the individual student scores, their priority was elevated.

Balancing Policy, Technical, and Instructional Considerations

Policy, technical, and instructional considerations all must be balanced. For example, Kentucky assesses students with severe educational impairment[1] using alternative portfolios. The entries for these portfolios are based on the students' individualized educational plans. Technical (psychometric) considerations would deter one from treating alternative portfolio scores as comparable with other test scores. Both the constructs measured and the difficulty levels of the alternative and regular assessments are dramatically different.

Two alternatives to treating such scores equivalently might be (a) requiring all students to take the regular assessments or (b) exempting schools from being accountable for the education of severely impaired students. The policy implications of these two alternatives were unacceptable. The first alternative would provide incentives for schools to discourage such students from attending. That is, it would be in each school's interest to avoid mainstreaming special education students, regardless of the best educational interests of the children. The second alternative would reward schools that neglected their most educationally needy students because the schools would benefit from diverting to other students resources from students for which they were not held accountable.

Evolution as a Model of School Change

Cosmic rays, strong chemicals, and other factors lead to genetic mutations. Some of those mutations are useful, and the resulting individuals successfully fill an ecological niche. Some mutations are not successful, and those individuals either die or do not reproduce. They are crowded out of the ecological niche.

If an accountability system shakes up schools and allows those schools the opportunity to change, then it will lead to mutations: new and different local programs. Some of those programs will be successful in their particular niches (communities). These programs will grow and spread in similar niches. Other programs will not be successful; they will be crowded out and die. This dying out will only occur if no external bureaucracy provides life support to nonfit programs. Thus school councils with significant responsibility for local decisions are a critical component of Kentucky's educational improvement efforts.

Anecdotal evidence suggests that this evolutionary process is occurring in many schools. Kentucky schools are trying various types of programs such as cross-disciplinary instruction, block scheduling, year-round schooling (including an innovative 4-day-week program in one urban school), multi-age grouping, and business involvement in teaching. Teachers are blending elements of traditional and less traditional instructional approaches as best meets their needs. On the other hand, as might be expected with 35,000 teachers in 1,400 different schools, many teachers are confused and floundering. Taking responsibility and using authority after having never had either is difficult intellectually and emotionally.

Ready, Fire, Aim

In his lectures and seminars, business consultant and author Tom Peters claims that if one takes the time to ready, aim, and fire, then one is doomed to failure. Instead, one should fire and then adjust his or her aim. That is, to be successful, businesses must make constant changes and adjustments—so many changes and adjustments that if they took the time to aim precisely (i.e., to research a problem to death), they would be noncompetitive and unsuccessful.

In this spirit, the test component of the accountability system was designed to be dramatically and controversially different from any previous testing program; Kentucky would start the program in 1991-1992 and substantially improve it every year through the end of 1995-1996. The test administered in 1996-1997 would be the first to fully meet the goals of the legislature and the Kentucky Board of Education. A more typical approach would have been to spend 2 to 10 years on research and development before first administering the test. However, critical flaws in the Kentucky education system identified by the judicial, executive, and legislative branches of Kentucky's government made such an approach seem akin to designing a 10-year research program to decide how to best save a child who already was drowning in the river (Chapter 21).[2]

Overview of the Kentucky
Accountability Program

The Kentucky accountability system has several key features:

- Accountability is school based, with all certified staff sharing in consequences.
- Schools are responsible for the success of all students.
- Schools are judged on progress against their own baseline scores, thus taking into account demographic differences in student bodies.
- Accountability scores are based on a primarily performance-based test of academic achievement and on other indicators (attendance, dropout rate, retention, successful transition to adult life).

- Schools receive substantial financial rewards for exceeding accountability goals, with distribution of rewards decided by certified staff.
- The state provides assistance by supplying an educational consultant and planning monies if scores decline.
- The "school in crisis" provision scheduled for 1997 would lead to state takeovers of administration of schools that show significant score declines.

At the same time that the state is holding schools accountable, it has empowered educators and parents by establishing school councils that are responsible for making personnel, curriculum, and management decisions for the school. The tension between the state-mandated accountability program and the local empowerment is expected to allow—or, more to the point, to force—schools to break the mold and develop programs that have a significant chance of meeting the needs of their students *much better*. Furthermore, empowerment allows site-based councils to quickly decide whether educational programs should be continued, modified, or replaced.

Of course, empowerment usually is not enough. Resources and training must be available. To this end, the Department of Education has increased funding for professional development to about $500 per teacher per year. In addition, the state sponsors numerous regional meetings and training programs, and it produces public television broadcasts, manuals, brochures, and the like.

Accountability Is School Based

If accountability rested solely on the shoulders of students, then schools would have positive incentive to meet only the needs of those students with whom it is easiest to work and whose parents are most likely to complain if their children do not get the lion's share of the schools' resources. If the level of accountability were the individual teacher, then there would be incentive for schools to become more concerned about which teachers get the better prepared students than about teaching all students. Furthermore, there would be little incentive for teachers to work together. If the unit of accountability were the district, then there would be little opportunity for all staff to work together because physical distance and competing school-level activities would make it difficult for staff to get together regularly. Thus Kentucky normally uses the school as the account-ability unit. Exceptions are being planned for new schools that were established partway through the accountability cycle and for very small schools.

Schools Are Responsible for the Success of All Students

With very few exceptions (less than 1%), all students are tested and count toward school accountability decisions. If any student did not count, then schools would have incentive to pay less attention to that student. This requirement that schools be responsible for the success of all students has led to a highly controversial decision. Per-formance of one cohort of students in the baseline years is used to set the improvement goal applied to a different cohort of students. Edu-cators rightly recognize that a more accurate assessment of school effect could be made with a longitudinal design—looking at the im-provement of the same students over time. However, this improved reliability would come at a great cost in validity; that is, schools would be responsible only for the improvement of those students who stayed in the same school. Many of Kentucky's schools have within-year transient rates of 20% or more. Even if all students were tested in all subjects every year (at a much higher cost than the cur-rent system), many students would be lost in the cracks of the sys-tem. However, Kentucky is looking into hybrid (longitudinal cohort) models that take advantage of the strengths of each model while minimizing their disadvantages.

Schools Are Judged on Progress Against Their Baseline Scores

The Kentucky Accountability Program was designed to be more fair and equitable than most previous programs used to make judg-ments about schools.[3] Traditional programs have compared schools on resources (e.g., number of library books) or on academic success (e.g., test scores) without regard to any history of inequities in school funding or the financial means of the local community and parents. KERA changed this by judging schools' progress toward state-set goals that were based on individual schools' initial academic scores and thus eliminated many potential sources of inequity (Chapter 22).

Baseline accountability scores are computed based on three considerations: (a) the percentage of students in each performance category (novice, apprentice, proficient, distinguished), (b) policy-based weights for each category (0, 40, 100, and 140 points, respectively), and (c) the noncognitive data. The ultimate goal for all schools is 100 points—on average, all students reaching the proficient level. The improvement goal for the accountability cycle is a 10% reduction of the gap between the baseline and the ultimate goal. If a school had a baseline index of 40, then it would need to close the gap $(100 - 40 = 60)$ by 10% (10% of 60 = 6) and thus would have an improvement goal of 46 (40 + 6).

Primarily Performance-Based Test of Academic Achievement and Other Indicators

Two sets of specifications have been used to develop KIRIS tests. A subset of the 57 academic expectations that explicate four of Kentucky's six learner goals forms one set of specifications.[4] In addition, over the past 2 years, educational and political concerns have converged regarding specification of the content basis for the assessment program.[5] This has led to increased specificity of a content base that, starting in 1996-1997, is assessed using multiple-choice and other machine-scoreable item types and that will form the context for open-response questions that will be used to assess application and process. Based on the academic expectations and content frameworks, Kentucky's assessment program targets knowledge and understanding of content, large concepts, and themes; the connecting of ideas; and the application of knowledge, skills, and reasoning to solve problems.

Item types. KERA mandated that the assessment program be "primarily performance based." In 1990, no state had such an assessment program; therefore, implementing the program by duplicating the work of others was not possible. The results of efforts conducted on smaller scales were used to guide the development of the program, but all such work needed refinement before it could be implemented on a statewide scale. Although the program was by statute required to begin in the 1991-1992 school year, it was not until the end of 1995-1996 that the legislated requirements for the assessment program had to be met.

Portfolios. Kentucky writing and mathematics portfolios are compilations of five to seven best pieces of student work per portfolio. Starting in 1996-1997 (grades in which portfolios were developed were different in earlier years), all students in Grades 4, 7, and 12 are required to produce a writing portfolio, and all students in Grades 5, 8, and 12 are required to produce a mathematics portfolio (with minor exceptions as stipulated by the Kentucky Department of Education). Students produce pieces for inclusion in these portfolios throughout the school year as part of the classroom instructional process. The mathematics portfolio requires five to seven best pieces that show an understanding of the core concepts with a variety of types of work and mathematical tools. The writing portfolio has specific requirements for each grade level that include a variety of types of work and content area requirements. Both the mathematics and writing portfolios require a table of contents and a letter to the reviewer reflecting on each student's work.

In the fall of each year, students are provided with brochures that contain information about requirements, standards, and development issues. Teachers receive teacher handbooks and training to help them work with students to develop portfolios.

Kentucky classroom teachers score the completed portfolios. To prepare for scoring, teachers receive the Holistic Scoring Guides, benchmarks, and training portfolios for mathematics and/or writing. In addition, teachers receive training in standards and scoring procedures.

An alternate portfolio has been instituted for students with severe disabilities likely to prevent them from obtaining high school diplomas.

Surveys have shown almost all educators in the state believe that portfolios have had the greatest impact on classroom activities of any portion of the assessment program.

Performance events. From 1993 through 1996, a typical performance event included a period of group work on a task in a particular subject, followed by individual written work on the same or a related task. Because performance events are highly memorable and few in number, they have proved difficult to equate in a cost-effective manner. Starting in 1996-1997, performance events have been temporarily removed from the assessment program while solutions to the equating issue are developed.

Open-response questions. As part of the on-demand portion of the test, open-response questions are administered in reading, mathematics, science, social studies, arts and humanities, and practical living/vocational studies. Each open-response question is written so that students should be able to complete their answers in 10 to 20 minutes. Students also respond to a writing prompt, which typically requires about 90 minutes of work.

Open-response questions were included because they produce reliable scores and reflect KERA's educational direction. First, they require students to apply skills and generate answers. Second, they emphasize student communication skills and thus encourage teachers to use more powerful instructional practices than they used previously—ones that require communication skills integrated with other aspects of problem solving.

Multiple-choice questions. Starting in 1996-1997, multiple-choice questions are used to assess student knowledge and understanding of state-defined core content in each discipline.[6] Despite their efficiency and ability to indirectly measure students' ability to solve problems, multiple-choice questions do not closely model powerful instructional practices and so will not be used to measure problem-solving abilities.

Grade placement of tests. Originally, accountability testing was only in Grades 4, 8, and 12. To help teachers share responsibility for school accountability, starting in 1996-1997 tests are spread out over Grades 4, 5, 7, 8, 11, and 12.

Performance standards. Given the language of KERA, it was clear from the beginning of the project that some form of standard setting would be necessary. KERA calls for determining the "proportion of successful students" in a school; this phrase alone provides a mandate for standard setting. Without standards, one could not make a judgment about whether a student is successful.

Technically speaking, determining the proportion of successful students calls for one performance standard to be set. Those performing above the standard are successful, whereas those performing below are not. However, with a single standard set at the high level called for by KERA, many students (at least currently) would find the standard so high that they could not expect to achieve it even with considerable effort. This would have a negative effect on the effort that students put into their schoolwork and the assessment.

It was clear, therefore, that more than one standard was necessary; keeping standards to a reasonable number also was important. Too many standards produce at least two negative consequences. First, the difference between students performing at different standards is trivial, and so classification can become quite arbitrary. Second, it is important that everyone involved in reviewing and interpreting reports, including parents, understands the standards. A large number of standards cannot be effectively communicated to diverse audiences.

The use of four levels of success remains controversial. Four levels produce less differentiation among students than many teachers find desirable. Many teachers recount having students who had been classified as novices, worked long and hard, improved considerably, but the following year were still classified as novices. This is discouraging. To address this issue,[7] we are indicating student placement on an underlying score scale that will allow students to be classified with low, intermediate, and high ratings within the novice and apprentice performance categories for the on-demand tests.

Noncognitive data. Besides the assessment data collected through on-demand testing, performance events, and portfolios, KERA called for the accountability system to include certain noncognitive indicators of school success: attendance (included for all grades), retention (included for all grades), dropout rate (included for middle and high schools only), transition to adult life (included for high school only), and reduction of physical and mental barriers to learning (currently being studied for future use).

As with the cognitive areas, an advisory committee was created to ensure the input of Kentucky educators in the design of this component of the accountability system. Using the criteria called for by KERA as its foundation, the committee guided the development of the definitions of each variable and made suggestions for alterations in the system for future years. For example, a subcommittee currently is exploring definitions and procedures for collecting data pertaining to the reduction of physical and mental health barriers to learning, one of the indicators stipulated in KERA.

Substantial Financial Rewards

The financial rewards program, as anticipated, has drawn great public attention to school results. From the inception of the accountability program, and with increasing frequency and fervor as the first reward dissemination approached in the spring of 1995, newspapers have written many articles on school results, school programs associated with those results, and school decisions regarding how reward monies would be used.

The legislature allocated 1.75% of the 1993-1994 total salary of certified public school staff as a maximum amount to be disbursed as rewards for successful schools and districts in the first accountability cycle. This amount equaled $26,108,840. Schools and districts that exceeded their improvement goals by exactly 1 point were to receive a maximum of 5% of the average annual salary of certified staff in the five highest paying school districts in the state for each certified staff member in that school or district. Schools and districts that exceeded by 1 point twice the number of points needed to meet their improvement goals were to receive a maximum of 10% of the average annual salary of certified staff in the five highest paying school districts in the state. Between those two extremes, schools and districts would get a proportionate reward. This formula led to potential rewards exceeding the available money because more people than anticipated shared in the rewards. The minimum and maximum dollars were adjusted accordingly. Still, rewards varied between $1,300 and $2,600 per certified staff member.

Assistance

The current accountability system assigns trained educational consultants (called distinguished educators), who are on loan from local districts, to schools whose accountability scores have declined. In addition, such schools get planning grants. Schools whose scores go up but do not reach their improvement goals are required to develop improvement plans, which are reviewed and approved by the state. Schools whose scores go up for two accountability cycles in a row but do not reach their original improvement goals also receive the services of consultants and planning grants.

State Takeover of Administration of Schools

Current legislation, the implementation of which was postponed until 1997, requires a trained educational consultant (distinguished educator), who is on loan from a local district, to take over the management of any school whose accountability scores dropped by 5 or more points. Such a school is designated a "school in crisis." The distinguished educator is responsible for all normal personnel, curriculum, and program implementation in a school in crisis. In addition, the distinguished educator must evaluate all staff every 6 months. Personnel decisions by the distinguished educator must allow all legal due process but are binding on the district. No parents are required to send their children to a school in crisis.

Some people, including the authors, have suggested that perhaps accountability scores in and of themselves should not place a school in crisis but rather should trigger a detailed evaluation of the school. That investigation, with appropriate appeals opportunities, would lead to a state takeover of the school. The state board began discussions of this option in December 1995. Such an approach would require legislative modification of existing statutes.

Instructional Consequences, Preliminary Results

Several researchers using small case studies or broader surveys have documented that significant changes are occurring in Kentucky classrooms. Teachers are working longer and harder. Their stress levels are elevated. Students are writing much more than they ever did before. Applications and solving of concrete problems are receiving increased attention in more classrooms. Matthews (1995), in a study of 32 randomly selected schools, found the following.

- "KIRIS is having a major impact on the use of performance assessment in the classrooms."

- "Nine of ten teachers reported using oral and written, open-ended questions on a regular basis, and eight of ten teachers reported using portfolio tasks within units of instruction."
- "Accountability grade (non-K-3) teachers make more extensive use of performance assessments."
- "High implementors of performance assessment use assessment to drive instruction, use technology and hands-on manipulatives more frequently, [and] provide challenging and engaging assignments."

Koretz, Barron, Mitchell, and Stecher (1996, pp. x-xi), in a survey of 4th- and 8th-grade principals and teachers, found the following:

- "Although most teachers (about 80 percent) value the information the multiple-choice items provide about student and school performance, virtually none (6 percent) reported these items have had a great deal of positive effect on instruction. In contrast, about 40 percent of teachers reported that the open-response questions and portfolios have had a great deal of positive effect."
- "Large majorities of teachers reported making instructional changes consonant with the goals of the program."
- "Although KIRIS has led to an increase in teachers' expectations for most students, more teachers (24 percent) reported that expectations had increased a great deal for high-achieving students than for low-achieving (16 percent) or special-education (12 percent) students."

The Western Michigan University Evaluation Center (1995, p. 61) found the following:

- "Students experienced more writing and group work under reforms. Teachers, district assessment coordinators, and superintendents report almost unanimously that writing has improved, and the writing improvement was over and above what would have been expected of most schoolchildren of the same age."

In a study of 13 schools, the Appalachian Educational Laboratory (1994, pp. 1-2) found the following:

- "For most teachers, the state assessment program—which emphasizes portfolios and open-response questions— appeared to be the driving force behind their instructional changes."
- "The major changes at both accountable and nonaccountable grades was an increased emphasis on writing and the writing process. At the 13 schools, we saw and heard about writing activities that required students to think and create. Interviews with teachers, principals, and students indicated this emphasis on writing was relatively new, in most cases."
- "Although the only across-the-board instructional change appeared to be the emphasis on writing, we saw and heard about a wide spectrum of other instructional strategies."

Changes in KIRIS Scores

Table 18.1 presents statewide results for the first accountability cycle, covering the years 1991-1992 through 1993-1994.

Clearly, scores have increased considerably. The question remains open to what extent these score increases reflect (a) significant broadly generalizable increases in student academic achievement, (b) significant generalizable increases in student ability to communicate knowledge while responding to open-ended questions regardless of the academic content, (c) increased nongeneralizable ability to respond to open-ended questions (i.e., testwiseness or other test-taking strategies), and (d) increased motivation for students to try their best when responding to KIRIS questions. A fifth possibility, widespread cheating by students or teachers, has been investigated by the Kentucky Department of Education and has been discounted as a significant factor at the state score level.

Changes in Other Indicators of Student Performance

Table 18.1 shows large gains in accountability scores during the first several years of the assessment and accountability programs. On the other hand, external measures of academic achievement are not showing commensurate score increases.

TABLE 18.1 Accountability Index Scores by Content Area, Grade, and Year

Grade Level	Year	Reading	Math	Science	Social Studies	Writing	Academic Index	Non-Cog. Index	Total Index
4	91-92	21.9	18.1	20.5	28.6	15.9	21.0	96.4	33.6
	92-93	32.9	20.8	22.9	29.6	31.3	27.5	96.4	39.0
	93-94	39.4	28.5	26.0	32.9	37.5	32.9	96.5	43.5
8	91-92	36.9	23.8	15.6	30.0	20.2	25.3	96.7	37.2
	92-93	40.0	29.3	17.7	26.7	28.3	28.4	97.0	39.8
	93-94	46.7	35.2	20.9	38.3	31.3	34.5	96.8	44.9
12	91-92	29.0	28.0	29.4	29.1	27.7	28.6	93.0	39.4
	92-93	23.5	27.8	26.2	23.3	41.6	28.5	94.0	39.4
	93-94	38.8	37.9	33.0	35.8	39.4	37.0	94.4	46.6

- Fourth-grade National Assessment of Educational Progress (NAEP) reading scores were flat from 1992 to 1994.[8,9]
- American College Testing scores have been flat from 1991 to 1995.
- Fourth-grade NAEP mathematics scores went up slightly from 1990 to 1992.
- The number of students taking advanced placement tests have gone up about 5% a year for 2 consecutive years, and the number of students scoring 3 or higher has gone up about 10% in the last year. The increase in test takers is slightly below the national average, whereas the increase in high scorers is somewhat above the national average.
- California Test of Basic Skills test scores went down from 1990 to 1994 in a number of districts administering the test in both years, but this was a nonrepresentative sample in which teachers knew the 1990 test results would be published and prepared students to take the tests, whereas in 1994 they did not.

It is not surprising that scores would go up much faster on KIRIS than any other test given that the purpose of the accountability program was to focus teachers on the content and methods in the test. Furthermore, psychometric characteristics of the accountability score scale can affect results. That is, student improvement within a performance category leads to no score change (all novices are worth 0 points toward the accountability index), but small student improvement across performance categories (e.g., from very high novice to very low apprentice) leads to a 40-point score change.

Regardless, some people believe it is reasonable to expect other indicators to show increased achievement 2 to 4 years into Kentucky's educational reform program.

Change Is Hard

Educational reform takes place in a highly politicized environment. The daily work of a change agent includes dealing with many individuals and constituency groups that have dramatically different agendas. These discussions are not necessarily logic or fact based. Agendas often are hidden. Many factions want to weaken or disband public education, some because they are confused or misled regarding educational jargon; for example, they believe critical thinking means teaching children to criticize parents.

Often, we get calls from parents who have heard from their children's teachers (or teachers that have heard from their principals) that KERA requires that they do not use phonics as part of reading or that all classroom instruction must be done in small groups and be aimed at the level of the lowest achieving student. These misunderstandings and rumors, like others regarding KIRIS, are untrue; all instructional decisions are left to local schools and teachers.[10]

Kentucky is a relatively conservative state. Some citizens and legislators have expressed concern that the test has a liberal slant. One example of this is a problem in which students were asked to use mathematics to answer questions about a newsletter. The title of the newsletter was *Environmental Newsletter*. This was taken as evidence of a pro-environmental bias, even though the question did not ask anything about the environment or environmental issues. Sensitivity reviews now require that controversial issues only be assessed as required by curricular issues. So, as of 1995, environmental questions may appear on the science test, but the environment no longer will be used as a context for questions in other subjects.

The public feelings whipped up by the politicians culminated in KIRIS becoming a major issue in the 1995 gubernatorial campaign.

Ten days of Republican television advertisements against KERA and KIRIS ran until a week before the election. Because of the public furor, the Democratic candidate advertised that he was going to fix KIRIS. This is particularly noteworthy because the governor has no direct control over the testing program (he or she can veto the entire state budget that includes money for the testing program or cut departmental staff but has no other constitutional control), yet this became one of the two largest issues of the campaign.

Despite (or because of) this political controversy, Koretz et al. (1996) found that about 60% of principals and half of 4th-grade teachers supported the program as a whole. Almost three quarters of the principals felt that KIRIS was a moderate or great burden on schools. Particularly burdensome was the need to retrain staff and deal with staff stress as well as the need for rapid instructional change. Koretz et al. noted,

> The majority of principals who perceived the program as burdensome, however, said that the benefits of the program balance or outweigh the burdens it imposes. . . . Moreover, 65 percent of the principals said the program has become easier to accommodate in their schools in the several years it has been in place. (p. 10)

Conclusion

There is no quick fix for our educational problems. Schools are dynamic. Students, educators, parents, and the public react and change in response to new programs—and often in unintended ways. Any plan for dramatic educational improvement also must be dynamic. Kentucky has implemented such a plan by simultaneously empowering teachers and parents with local decision making and pressuring educators with a strong accountability system.

Notes

1. The term "severe learning impairment" applies to students who are not expected to be capable of attaining diplomas or living

independently after school (e.g., profoundly retarded). Fewer than 0.5% of students are eligible to submit alternative portfolios.

2. On the other hand, even these grizzled veterans believe that it would have been reasonable to spend a year designing and implementing the program to minimize the rate of change over the next several years. However, doers must concentrate on the here and now, not on the past.

3. As indicated in separate analyses conducted by the *Lexington Herald* and the Kentucky Department of Education, overall this approach has had the desired effect; during Accountability Cycle I, regardless of whether schools are in wealthy or poor districts, they received rewards in about the same proportion.

4. Because the scope of reform was so comprehensive, it would have been unfair to hold all schools in Kentucky immediately responsible for the academic expectations that require special programs or facilities.

5. Between November 1995 and February 1996, the Department of Education involved tens of thousands of citizens in the process of establishing the core content guidelines.

6. Multiple-choice questions were administered between 1992 and 1994 but did not count as part of the accountability index.

7. Also, the use of an underlying score scale will address psychometric considerations.

8. Note that the 1994 test was administered immediately after the worst snowstorm in 25 years had closed most Kentucky schools for as many as 2-5 weeks. Also note that, despite the adverse testing conditions, there was a statistically significant increase in the proportion of students scoring at or above the NAEP proficient level.

9. Note, however, that despite the dramatic increases in KIRIS scores, KIRIS results showed that only 13% of Kentucky 4th-grade students were scoring proficient or above; using NAEP standards and results, 26% of Kentucky 4th-grade students were scoring proficient or above.

10. Local autonomy has one important exception: The multiage primary program is mandated.

References

Appalachian Educational Laboratory. (1994, December). Instruction and assessment in accountable and non-accountable grades. *Notes From the Field*, pp. 1-2.

Kentucky Department of Education. (1995). *KIRIS Accountability Cycle I technical manual.* Frankfort, KY: Author.

Koretz, D., Barron, S., Mitchell, K., & Stecher, B. (1996). *Perceived effects of the Kentucky Instructional Results Information System (KIRIS).* Santa Monica, CA: RAND.

Matthews, B. (1995). *Implementation of performance assessment in Kentucky classrooms.* Frankfort: Kentucky Institute for Education Research.

Western Michigan University Evaluation Center. (1995). *An independent evaluation of the Kentucky Instructional Results Information System (KIRIS).* Frankfort: Kentucky Institute for Education Research.

CHAPTER 19

Measurement Quality of the Kentucky Instructional Results Information System, 1991-1994

RONALD K. HAMBLETON

In 1990, the Kentucky Legislature passed an education bill that was intended to substantially redesign educational goals, services, and programs in the state. The Kentucky Education Reform Act (KERA) requires that new and ambitious goals for education be set and that curricula, instruction, and school administration be reorganized in the state to ensure that all students in the Kentucky public schools meet these new goals. Schools are held accountable for student learning through a system of rewards and sanctions. Educational tests serve as the primary basis for assessing student learning.

A major component of the education reform initiative in Kentucky is the Kentucky Instructional Results Information System (KIRIS). KIRIS is the accountability and assessment system of KERA that (a) produces annual results on the performance of schools, districts, and the state in relation to the new goals of Kentucky education in five subject areas; (b) holds schools accountable for achieving the new goals of Kentucky education; (c) results in schools being given rewards and sanctions based on student performance at selected grades in relation to expected levels of academic performance; and (d) provides student performance results in five subject areas to students, parents, and their teachers.

In the previous chapter, Kingston and Reidy provided some details about the philosophy underlying KIRIS and the interrelated roles of educational policy, measurement technology, and instructional practices. KIRIS has many important features; for example, the rewarding and sanctioning of schools based on student performance makes KIRIS a high-stakes accountability system for schools, and the assessment of student academic progress is *performance based*. Both of these features are innovative, are controversial, and place Kentucky at the leading edge of educational reform in the United States. Many states appear to be watching the educational, policy, instructional, and legal outcomes in Kentucky prior to writing their own educational reform legislation. From a researcher's perspective, Kentucky is a big educational experiment that will influence educational directions in the coming years not only in Kentucky but also in the rest of the nation. Therefore, careful research on the impact of KERA and KIRIS on education is needed.

Because of (a) the importance and centrality of KIRIS to the Kentucky education system; (b) the newness of the philosophy, concepts, and approaches to accountability and student assessment in Kentucky education; and (c) the introduction of new curricula in Kentucky emphasizing higher level cognitive performance, the Office of Educational Accountability of the Kentucky Legislature formed a Technical Review Panel of measurement specialists in the fall of 1994 to answer two broad questions:

1. Is the measurement quality of KIRIS sufficient to support the intended uses of the KIRIS results and the actions taken by the Kentucky Department of Education (KDE) and the legislature?
2. To the extent that shortcomings in KIRIS are identified, what changes would need to be made to improve the accountability and assessment system?

Members of the Technical Review Panel (hereafter referred to as "the panel") were Richard Jaeger, Daniel Koretz, Robert Linn, Jason Millman, Susan Phillips, and myself. The department itself and the contractor already were conducting an ongoing evaluation of KIRIS, and other outside evaluation groups were active too (see, e.g., Western

Michigan University Evaluation Center, 1995). Our panel, however, was the only evaluative group in Kentucky that was focused exclusively on the measurement quality of KIRIS.

The purpose of this brief chapter is to focus attention on six specific measurement questions that were addressed by the panel and that pertain to the accountability portion of KIRIS by (a) describing the six measurement questions, (b) providing information about how the questions were addressed, and (c) summarizing several of the findings and recommendations in relation to the six questions. Readers are referred to the report by Hambleton et al. (1995) for the details of the research study.

The panel used the 1985 *Standards for Educational and Psychological Testing* that were developed jointly by the American Educational Research Association (AERA), the American Psychological Association (APA), and the National Council on Measurement in Education (NCME) (see AERA, APA, & NCME, 1985) as a frame of reference for its work. These professional standards for the construction and use of educational and psychological tests provide a basis for reviewing accountability and assessment systems such as KIRIS. For aspects of KIRIS not covered directly by the test standards, the panel used the performance assessment guidelines provided by Linn, Baker, and Dunbar (1991) and also applied its collective professional judgment.

1. Are the Cognitive Tests Built Soundly Enough to Support the Assessment and Accountability Tasks of the Kentucky Instructional Results Information System?

To answer this question, the panel reviewed the educational goals in Kentucky along with the efforts of Kentucky educators to operationalize those goals into instructional initiatives and then considered the assessments that were produced to address the initiatives. How were the assessments developed, and can the developments be improved? The concern here was that if the educational assessments fell short in quality, then the whole accountability system would be questionable. A review of technical documentation as well as some of the assessments themselves provided the basis for answering this question.

One of the main findings was that the test specifications were underspecified in that they failed to adequately communicate what the assessments were measuring. Improvements in this area over the first 4 years of the project may actually have been responsible for some of the growth in performance that was observed because the initial test specifications provided little guidance to schools about the content and cognitive processes on which to focus in instruction. The later test specifications were considerably clearer. Still, although the changes in the clarity of the test specifications complicated the interpretation of achievement growth over time, we enthusiastically supported efforts to clearly articulate the test specifications and the related curricula from which the test specifications were derived.

Recommendations to improve assessment development focused on the use of more multiple-choice items to enhance coverage of the curriculum frameworks, more and better documentation of assessment development procedures, and construct validation investigations to determine what actually was being measured with the performance assessments. Each of these recommendations would strengthen any inferences about achievement growth.

The recommendation by the panel to support multiple-choice test items was not intended to discourage innovations in assessment; rather, it was intended to capitalize on the strengths of the multiple-choice format for assessing some portions of the five subject areas covered by KIRIS. Then, extra resources and time would be available to develop and validate the assessment of other outcomes where performance assessments would be needed.

2. For the School Accountability System: How Accurate Is the Classification of a School Into One of the Accountability Categories (Eligible for Reward, Successful, Improving, Decline, in Crisis)?

Evidence regarding this question could be obtained by considering the size of changes that might take place if one assessment were replaced by another of the same kind (e.g., a randomly equivalent form) in the accountability index. Obviously, little confidence in the accountability system could exist if the classification of schools depended, to a considerable extent, on (a) the particular choice of tasks for the assessment, (b) the particular persons who were assigned to rate student papers, or (c) the cohort of students enrolled in a school. This question was addressed by reviewing generalizability and decision consistency results provided by the KDE.

Our research found that a number of schools were being assigned to performance categories other than the ones deserved, and this was particularly true for the smaller schools. One recommendation would be to include multiple-choice items in the accountability index to increase the precision with which schools were assessed. Interestingly, such items were included in the assessments themselves but were excluded from the accountability index (Chapter 21).

Another recommendation of the panel was that reliability studies incorporating not only errors due to the sampling of student cohorts but also errors due to the collection of tasks in an assessment and raters were needed for a full evaluation of the reliability question. KDE studies of the reliability of school classifications were limited to the study of a single source of error. A fuller reliability assessment would provide valuable information for judging the stability of the school accountability indexes. Without strong evidence of the reliability of school classifications to the performance categories, little confidence could be given to the classifications, and they could hardly serve as a basis for rewarding and sanctioning schools.

3. Are Kentucky Instructional Results Information System Scores Equivalent Across Administrations?

The equivalence of educational assessments from one administration or year to the next becomes particularly important when the focus of analysis is on the measurement of growth or change. Nonequivalent educational assessments require that statistical adjustments (for nonequivalence) be made prior to any investigations of growth or change over time. Failure to correct for nonequivalence, or to correct for nonequivalence in improper ways, could lead to problematic indications of the effects of the instructional program on school, district, and state results. Available technical documentation and some new analyses were used to investigate this question.

What we found from our review were problems such as (a) changing equating procedures from one year to the next, (b) repeated use of ad hoc (i.e., nonreplicable) equating procedures, (c) the use of less optimal equating designs, and (d) exclusion of the multiple-choice items from the equating (such information would have stabilized some of the equating results and reduced the equating errors). The panel went on to make some specific recommendations for improving the equating of forms from one year to the next.

Recommendations included expanding sample sizes at the school level, selecting one suitable item response model (see Hambleton, Swaminathan, & Rogers, 1991, for an introduction to item response models and score equating) and sticking with it, linking all new forms to a base form, eliminating all ad hoc procedures, improving the linking design, and so on. The preponderance of available evidence appeared to suggest that less than optimal equating of forms may be contaminating the comparisons of assessment results from one year to the next and from one form to the next within a given assessment. Such contaminations undermine the validity of KIRIS and other such accountability systems.

4. Are the Performance Standards Defensible?

KIRIS is a criterion-referenced assessment system, and therefore performance standards are needed for the purpose of interpreting the performance of individual students in particular subjects and schools. In Kentucky, students are classified as novice, apprentice, proficient, or distinguished, and the percentage of students in each category over time is the primary component in the accountability index that drives school rewards and sanctions. It is essential, then, that a defensible method for standard setting be adopted and implemented. A review of available documents and some new analyses conducted by the panel provided a basis for addressing this question.

The panel felt that there were a number of areas in which standard setting could be improved. More and better documentation of the process was needed, a larger sample of assessment material was needed (the sample of assessment material used was believed to be too small to lead to stable performance standards), and a method was needed that had been shown or could be shown to lead to defensible standards. Evidence also was available showing that any sizable movement of the performance standards resulted in school reclassifications; hence the placement of performance standards had an operational impact on schools and how they were judged. Basically, the panel's recommendation was that the process of standard setting be substantially reconsidered, that a method of standard setting be selected that draws less heavily on statistical estimation (i.e., set judgmental standards on all aspects of the assessment that are used in the accountability index, not just a small sample), and that the performance standards be reset as soon as possible. Clearly, the current standard-setting method used in KIRIS did not meet with approval from the panel.

5. Are the Reports of Accountability and Assessment Results Prepared for Policymakers, Administrators, Educators, Students, and Parents Clear and Understandable?

To the extent that any interested groups may be misinformed because of the types of report forms used or the scales on which results are reported, KIRIS cannot achieve its stated goals. Clearly, persons who are misinformed about the results cannot use the information properly in considering program accountability. This question addressing the clarity and appropriateness of reports about results was addressed by the panel by reviewing a sample of score reports.

The panel's review suggested that score reporting was generally being well done. Still, a few recommendations were made. Communicating information to policymakers, educators, and the public about errors of measurement and sampling was one suggestion for improvement. Readers of reports not only need to be aware of the presence of measurement and sampling errors in score information being reported but also need some sense of the size of those errors and their impact on key interpretations. Another suggestion was that the KDE would benefit from field testing all score reports on appropriate audiences much as it does from field testing assessment material. A final suggestion was to improve the *Interpretive Guides* that are distributed with accountability reports. Readers are not conversant with things such as accountability indexes and scaled scores, and so clear explanations and examples are needed.

6. To What Extent Do Any Gains in Kentucky Instructional Results Information System Scores Reflect Real Improvements in Student Learning?

Large gains in KIRIS assessment scores have been reported by the KDE. Are the gains real in that they represent practically significant improvements in student learning, or are these assessment score increases due to factors such as teaching students to be better test takers? The panel was able to analyze limited data from other sources, in particular the National Assessment of Educational Progress (NAEP) and the American College Testing Program (ACT) college admissions test, to address the question.

An analysis of the 1992 and 1994 NAEP Grade 4 reading scores in Kentucky failed to show gains of any size, let alone gains as large as those being reported from KIRIS by the KDE. Given the overlap in reading curricula frameworks and content between KIRIS and NAEP as well as the emphasis in KIRIS on reading instruction at the lower grades, some correlation in findings was expected. At the high school level, gains in school achievement as reflected by the KIRIS assessments were substantial. An analysis of ACT scores for 12th-grade Kentucky students for 2 years showed no gain.

Certainly, there are many possible explanations for these NAEP and ACT findings, but these findings—tentative as they are—do raise some questions about the school and state achievement gains being reported based on the KIRIS assessments. Clearly, what is needed is additional research to document student learning beyond the evidence provided by KIRIS.

Conclusions

The panel concluded its review of the measurement quality of KIRIS by recommending a number of changes for the future, and there is ample evidence in the 1996 version of KIRIS that many of these recommendations were accepted. In fact, the KDE accepted nearly all of the panel's major recommendations.

Perhaps the point should be emphasized that the panel did not suggest that the educational reform movement in Kentucky was a failure or that educators were not working hard to implement KERA. On the contrary, the panel indicated that KIRIS had flaws that needed to be corrected as Kentucky moved into the second accountability cycle.

While suggesting many changes to the measurement system to support school accountability, the panel also applauded the KDE for encouraging research and evaluation pertaining to KIRIS and for encouraging and facilitating independent research by third parties unconnected to the department or its contractor. The panel also was very impressed by the department's willingness to improve KIRIS when there was evidence that measurement changes were desirable. The department's acceptance of our report was an excellent example of this point, but there were many other examples as well.

Perhaps the measurement problems that were identified by the panel were due to unrealistic expectations set originally by the KDE and its contractor to deliver an accountability and assessment system that would meet all of the essential test standards within a short period of several years. Substantial progress was made, and everyone who worked on KIRIS and its implementation deserves credit for the efforts and substantial accomplishments that have been made. On the other hand, as is clear from our report (Hambleton et al., 1995), there are important measurement areas in need of improvement if KERA, KIRIS, and the Kentucky school accountability index are to achieve the goals for which they were designed.

References

American Educational Research Association, American Psychological Association, & National Council on Measurement in Education. (1985). *Standards for educational and psychological testing.* Washington, DC: APA.

Hambleton, R. K., Jaeger, R. M., Koretz, D., Linn, R. L., Millman, J., & Phillips, S. (1995). *Review of the measurement quality of the Kentucky Instructional Results Information System, 1991-94.* Frankfort, KY: Office of Educational Accountability.

Hambleton, R. K., Swaminathan, H., & Rogers, H. J. (1991). *Fundamentals of item response theory.* Newbury Park, CA: Sage.

Linn, R. L., Baker, E. L., & Dunbar, S. B. (1991). Complex, performance-based assessment: Expectations and validation criteria. *Educational Researcher, 20*(8), 15-21.

Western Michigan University Evaluation Center. (1995). *An independent evaluation of the Kentucky Instructional Results Information System.* Frankfort: Kentucky Institute for Education Research.

CHAPTER 20

Overview and Assessment of the Kentucky Instructional Results Information System

DANIEL L. STUFFLEBEAM

Kentucky provides a high-profile case of a state in the forefront of modern trends in assessment. It has focused assessment of schools on student outcomes. It has deemphasized multiple-choice testing and initially replaced it with performance tests. It has used student performance test results to make decisions about schools. These sweeping reforms were ushered in after the Kentucky Supreme Court in 1990 declared the entire Kentucky system of public elementary and secondary schools to be unconstitutional due to inequitable distribution of public funds for education. There is much to learn about issues in assessment by studying the Kentucky education reform experience.

This chapter examines the Kentucky Instructional Results Information System (KIRIS). The chapter gauges progress of KIRIS through 1994, highlights its strengths and problem areas, and points up lessons learned that may be applicable in other states. It reflects an external evaluation of KIRIS reported by the Western Michigan University Evaluation Center[1] in early 1995 and a review of the description of KIRIS that Kingston and Reidy submitted for inclusion in this book (Chapter 18).

The Kentucky Instructional Results Information System

KIRIS is Kentucky's legislatively mandated effort to develop a state-of-the-art, high-stakes student assessment system that is primarily performance based, that is, one that assesses student learning based on a variety of students' performances of tasks instead of on multiple-choice tests. It is the core of the Kentucky education reform and is its most controversial component. Kentucky education officials designed this new system to drive curriculum, instruction, and school administration to ensure that all schools meet the "goals for the commonwealth's schools."

Through KIRIS, the commonwealth set out to (a) annually assess the performance of Kentucky students at selected grade levels, (b) hold each school accountable for achieving reform goals, (c) use the results to administer economic rewards and penalties, and (d) help teachers make performance assessment an integral part of classroom instruction. The Kentucky Education Reform Act (KERA) required that KIRIS be usable to grant economic rewards to schools that showed the greatest improvement over a threshold level and to deliver state assistance and sanctions to schools that showed little or no improvement. The rewards and sanctions made the Kentucky education reform a high-stakes program and KIRIS a high-stakes test. They also spawned much of the controversy surrounding KIRIS.

The Kentucky Instructional Results Information System Accountability Index

The state described a school's accomplishment by the KIRIS accountability number. It was a composite of six equally weighted component scores. In the initial year of the program, 1991-1992, five of the components were cognitive: reading, mathematics, social studies, science, and writing. The sixth component was itself a composite. It consisted of attendance, retention, dropout rate, and transition to adult life. This noncognitive component counted as one sixth of the total score on the accountability index.

Difficulty of Implementing a New and Innovative Performance-Based Assessment System

The KIRIS assessment system was a result of major investment and intense effort by the Kentucky Department of Education (KDE) and its outside test contractor, Advanced Systems in Measurement and Evaluation (ASME). Performance assessments have not been widely used in large-scale assessment systems. Neither education and testing organizations nor the measurement profession have solved many of the technical and operational problems with large-scale use of performance-based assessments. The KDE and ASME might have preferred to go slowly when carrying out the new performance assessment system. However, in the face of the legislative mandate and the press for reform in Kentucky, the KDE and ASME postponed much of the needed research and development. They rapidly developed and applied KIRIS. Moving too quickly is a pitfall that many states seem unable to avoid when setting up new programs. Paying too much attention to political forces and not enough to validation processes probably accounts for many failed experiences in the early years of education reforms, including accountability systems.

The KDE and ASME had only since 1991 to design, develop, set up, explain, and obtain stakeholder acceptance of the new performance assessment system. During that time, they had to orient the participants and work through the inevitable problems of developing, administering, scoring, and reporting performance-based assessments.

The KDE had to (a) work out the logistics concerning the new assessment (open-ended questions, performance events, portfolios), (b) train teachers to prepare students to submit portfolios, (c) develop a system to train teachers to evaluate portfolios, (d) set standards without a history of pertinent data, (e) define successful students, (f) develop guidelines for the participation of special education students, (g) develop the weights for the accountability index, (h) establish thresholds, (i) develop a rewards system, (j) develop the criteria for sanctions, (k) deal with other issues mandated by the legislature, and (l) develop technical and educational justifications for their design decisions.

Given the crash time schedule, they might have labeled their task "Mission Impossible."

Impacts of the Kentucky Instructional Results Information System

Impacts on Students

Students experienced more writing and group work under the reforms. Teachers, district assessment coordinators, and superintendents reported almost unanimously that writing had improved and exceeded their expectations of most school pupils of the same age.

Impacts on Teachers

The state keyed KIRIS to the state's instructional goals and sought to have teachers integrate the assessment work into the regular instructional process. The time and effort that the KDE invested in training teachers and that teachers spent marking KIRIS portfolios seemed reasonable and probably were useful as in-service education for the teachers.

Many teachers wanted timely feedback with direct relevance for improving classroom activities. However, the state did not design the accountability index (or KIRIS reports) to provide such feedback. Also, the state did not achieve the legislative intent of integrating assessment and feedback into the instructional process at every grade level.

Impacts on Schools

Stakeholders disagreed on whether the KIRIS system of rewards and sanctions would help improve the quality of Kentucky schools. District assessment coordinators judged that rewards and sanctions would help improve schools. Results for superintendents varied by survey. Some school leaders expressed concerns about whether the administration of KIRIS rewards and sanctions was fair to schools with large numbers of economically disadvantaged students, high turnover rates, or very small numbers of students. The state provided little evidence in response to this important question. Teachers surveyed by the Kentucky Institute for Educational Research said the rewards and sanctions would *not* help improve education. Although the state delayed administration of the envisaged sanctions during our study, the stigma of being a no-reward school was a kind of sanction.

Impacts on the State Education System

Coupled with the report of some incorrect accountability indexes that the state had to retract, the system's rewards and sanctions component was quite embarrassing to state officials. When the state awarded money to the winning schools, some of the schoolteachers argued about which teachers had produced the winning results and which ones should share in the funds. No one stressed that the distribution of about $26 million in reward money would greatly improve the quality of instruction. In my judgment, the state paid dearly for the confusion and controversy that this feature of the assessment generated, and the students and families probably got little in return.

Overall, Kentucky's teachers, students, and schools benefited too little from the extensive accountability features of KIRIS. The early experience showed that the state was "putting the airplane together while trying to fly it," as one Kentucky education official stated, and was investing heavily in the enterprise. The effort confused and displeased many educators and parents. For the most part, teachers were not integrating assessment into their instructional practices. It was no small achievement, however, that many students improved their writing skills.

Technical Adequacy of the Kentucky Instructional Results Information System Assessment

Construction of Assessment Devices

On the whole, KIRIS assessment tasks were well constructed. The questions were clear and appropriate for the age group. The scoring rules were appropriate. Instructions were easy for students to follow. The open-ended questions (those requiring written answers) generally met currently accepted technical item-writing standards for open-ended questions. Thus the state's assessment experts and their external contractor had competently developed performance assessment tools with good technical features.

Reliability of Assessment Devices

The reliability of the accountability index was problematic. The KDE reported impressive reliabilities that reached or exceeded .90, a level generally considered acceptable for high-stakes decisions. However, because of the particular statistical model employed, there were unresolved questions about whether the reliability estimates were spuriously high. These concerned, for example, the adequacy of the reliability of the components of the index and how they take chance agreements among raters into account.

Considered by themselves, two of the three cognitive components of the KIRIS accountability index were not sufficiently reliable for use in a high-stakes assessment. These two components were the writing portfolio and performance events. In the face of the low reliability of these assessment components, the state probably should not have initially excluded multiple-choice test results from the accountability index because typically they yield high reliabilities.

Validity of Assessment

The 1993-1994 KIRIS assessment included several modes: extended answer open-ended tasks, shorter answer open-ended tasks, portfolios, and performance events. This diversity of approaches was a strength of the scheme. Education assessment specialists support uses of multiple modes of assessment to increase the prospects for valid results. The state enhanced validity by allowing students opportunities to demonstrate their abilities in a variety of ways over a range of knowledge and skills.

Despite the employment of multiple measures, one cannot hope to reap the potential validity benefits if the individual measures are unreliable. The unreliability of the writing portfolios and performance events deterred the commonwealth from obtaining a valid index for administering rewards and sanctions to schools. The state needed to fully address issues of the stability of the index and assure all stakeholders that it provided a dependable basis for administering rewards and sanctions. This was not done. The state nevertheless used the unvalidated KIRIS index to rank schools and administer rewards.

Failure of the Accountability Index

The accountability index proved to be a dysfunctional part of the Kentucky reform. The definition of the index kept shifting and was thus confusing. It was not defensible on technical grounds. Although portfolios of students' written work evidenced instructional authenticity, scores varied considerably depending on who scored each portfolio. These scores were less reliable than other forms of assessment and were not defensible for use in high-stakes decision making. The index did not discriminate fairly among advantaged and disadvantaged schools. It generated much controversy.

Factors beyond a school's control influenced the accountability index, but the state interpreted the index without considering these factors. Among the factors not considered were adequacy of resources, changes in the economic climate of a community, and changes in student mobility. However, the state maintained a mechanism by which a school's authorities could appeal such matters if they believed failure was due to factors beyond the school's control. The state made no corrections, however, for false positives when schools passed the state assessment because of environmental factors rather than the quality of instruction.

Problems With the Longitudinal Assessment Design

The state's cohort approach to tracking a school's progress proved controversial. The district assessment coordinators and the superintendents preferred a longitudinal approach (tracking the same group of individual students as they progress through the grades) over the cohort approach (comparing each group of 4th graders to those of previous years) for assessing a school's growth or change. Longitudinal analysis would give a better picture of what happens to a group of students as it goes through the education system, although implementing it is more difficult and costly. Use of the cohort approach could disadvantage (or advantage) schools whose student populations change significantly during the assessment period. Effective use of the longitudinal approach would require that the state administer assessments to students at every other grade level or preferably at every grade level.

Credibility Gap

All the reviewed evidence suggested that principals, coordinators, superintendents, teachers, school council parents, public school parents, legislators, and the public had serious questions concerning the legitimacy, validity, reliability, fairness, and usefulness of the KIRIS assessment. The groups surveyed reported that student performance on the KIRIS assessment is the measure *least* likely to provide a reliable indicator of student learning compared to other commonly available indicators such as high school completion rates. The KDE still needed to convince Kentucky educators of the validity of KIRIS to make this system a valued and integral part of the education reform process.

Lessons Learned

The preceding assessment of strengths and weaknesses denotes that Kentucky needed to improve and validate KIRIS before using it for high-stakes decisions. The following is a list of a set of assessment program criteria suggested by the evaluation of KIRIS.

1. Establish and maintain a collaborative approach to developing the assessment system.
2. Employ multiple measures.
3. Validate the assessment program.
4. Establish the program's instructional utility.
5. Summarize the assessment results in indexes and other forms that are meaningful to the users.
6. Keep the press releases on a professional plane.
7. Train the participants.
8. Budget adequately for the assessment system.

Conclusion

The KDE assumed an important and challenging responsibility to inform Kentucky citizens about the outcomes of KERA. Its goal of developing more effective ways in which to inform the public, education policymakers, and educators about the progress of students clearly is important and has relevance in other states.

The Kentucky legislature, the state school board, the KDE, and the KIRIS developers, ASME, are to be commended. They mounted a bold experiment aimed at breaking the mold of using only multiple-choice tests to assess school outcomes. Instead, they installed a novel open-ended, performance-based assessment system aimed at driving education reform. Much of KIRIS was conceptually consistent with the aims of the authorizing legislation. The KDE also involved educators in every public school in the state to use assessment to improve curriculum and classroom instruction. The state keyed the effort to helping all students in Kentucky to meet the state's standards for education achievement.

Nevertheless, this bold experiment in performance assessment was fraught with difficulties and mistakes. The main deficiency was moving quickly to apply unvalidated assessment results to high-stakes decisions.

Note

1. The evaluation team included Mark Fenster, Anthony Nitko, William Wiersma, and Daniel Stufflebeam (study director).

CHAPTER 21

The Kentucky Instructional Results Information System Meets the Critics

A Little Light and Much Heat

NEAL KINGSTON

ED REIDY

The Kentucky assessment and accountability programs have been the subjects of numerous research and evaluation studies. Two early studies were those conducted by the Kentucky General Assembly's Office of Educational Accountability (OEA) panel (Hambleton et al., 1995) and the University of Western Michigan Evaluation Center (1995). These studies were headed by Ron Hambleton and Daniel Stufflebeam, respectively. Chapters 19 and 20 present summaries of those studies rather than evaluations of the current program, which we describe in Chapter 18.

Both evaluations took place in an intensely political environment that put a strain on all parties. Although evaluators may consider themselves impartial professionals, those responsible for the programs evaluated know that every aspect of the evaluation process will be dissected and that every individual word will be quoted out of context by both critics and supporters of public education. Also, professional evaluation standards (and common sense) require ongoing dialogue between the evaluators and those responsible for the programs being evaluated. Yet political considerations require that people responsible for the program be kept out of the loop lest they might apply pressure to influence the evaluation results.

In the case of the Western Michigan study, there was relatively little contact—perhaps 15 hours—between the evaluators and the Kentucky Department of Education (KDE). Although this may not seem little at first blush, the Kentucky Instructional Results Information System (KIRIS) is an extremely complex and multifaceted program; it took the first author of this chapter 6 months working full-time before he felt he understood well the basic aspects of the program. As another comparison, the Kentucky technical advisory committee spends about 30 hours a year discussing and evaluating just a limited number of components of KIRIS. The result of the Western Michigan evaluators' cursory overview was a draft report that required a KDE response of more than 100 pages to indicate the factual and conceptual errors. To this day, the Western Michigan evaluators apparently fail to understand Kentucky's assessment and accountability programs, as is demonstrated later in this chapter.

The OEA panel evaluation process began with much more dialogue. The panel met with members of the KDE and its testing contractor for a presentation of key data. Most unfortunately, soon afterward, the OEA ordered the KDE to cease all direct communication with panel members and to communicate only through OEA staff. Discussion of complex theoretical formulas and nuances of generalizability theory would have to be filtered through OEA staff who had no background in the subjects. This requirement stifled all dialogue and diminished the ability of the OEA panel to understand certain aspects of the programs.

The final OEA report contained a large number of useful recommendations, most of which have been implemented. Unfortunately, it also contained much intemperate language that fueled a political movement to reverse the commonwealth's school improvement efforts. But there was a much more significant flaw in the OEA panel evaluation—a flaw outside the purvey of the evaluation panel. The OEA instructed its panel to evaluate only the psychometric issues of the assessment. But a multifaceted school improvement program, such as Kentucky's, is a series of compromises among psychometric,

instructional, curricular, administrative, policy, and political considerations. In theory, a separate evaluation could have been done for
each area. In isolation, each evaluation would have failed to acknowledge the crucial context of multiple considerations (as did the
OEA panel psychometric evaluation). In that limited view, every
compromise forced by those considerations would appear as a flaw
or poor decision rather than as a reasonable response to various com-
pelling circumstances.

Properly established objective external evaluations are a critical
aspect of any education reform effort. Regardless of the best intentions of all involved, partial evaluations or evaluations that forego
communication between evaluators and program administrators are
bound to create much heat without shedding a commensurate
amount of light.

Rejoinder to Hambleton

Hambleton presents a thoughtful summary of the results of the
OEA panel evaluation of the psychometric quality of the KIRIS assessments. We structure our comments around four of the six questions he uses to organize his chapter.

Are the Cognitive Tests Built Soundly Enough to
Support the Assessment and Accountability Tasks of
the Kentucky Instructional Results Information System?

The recommendations in this section are sound. All have been
implemented.

For the School Accountability System: How Accurate
Is the Classification of a School Into One of the
Accountability Categories?

Hambleton indicates that "a number of schools were being assigned to performance categories other than ones deserved." This is
not surprising and is not due to any inherent deficiencies in KIRIS.

In his history of standard setting, Zeiky (1995) asks, "What has history taught us?" He concludes,

> We have learned that standard setting will lead to errors of classification.
>
> Implicitly or explicitly, the standard is a manifestation of the value judgments inherent in determining if it is preferable to pass an examinee who deserves to fail or if it is preferable to fail an examinee who deserves to pass. Because no tests can be perfectly reliable or perfectly valid, such mistakes in classification will be made if people are to be split into passing and failing groups. When setting standards it is impossible to reduce one of the types of mistakes without increasing the other type. (p. 29)

Hambleton's recommendation is to "include multiple-choice items in the accountability index to increase precision" (p. 213). Although we believe that multiple-choice items should be included in the index (and are now including them), we do not want to falsely raise anyone's expectations. For both Cycles I and II, about 80% of the school accountability index error variance is due to students (KDE, 1995). No decrease in task variance due to the mix of item types will lead to a practically significant increase in the precision of school classification.

Some people appear to think it counterintuitive that multiple-choice questions would not increase decision accuracy, but it is easy to show why this is so. In the 1st year of the first accountability cycle, school scores were based on 60 open-response questions. In the 2nd and 3rd years, school scores were based on 116-120 open-response questions. Although the administration time for multiple-choice questions is much shorter than it is for Kentucky's open-response questions, each open-response question contributes about 3.5 times as much to test reliability as does a multiple-choice question. This stems from each multiple-choice question differentiating but two levels of student performance (0-1), whereas each open-response question differentiates five levels (0-4). Thus, in the 2nd and 3rd years, school scores were based on the equivalent of more than 400 multiple-choice items. At this point, additional multiple-choice items cannot provide much reduction to task variance and can provide no reduction to student variance.

Hambleton argues that we should have explicitly modeled task and rater variance in our study of decision accuracy. We agree. Kentucky had to break new methodological ground to estimate decision accuracy. Whereas in 1995 the KDE modeled student variance (the primary variance source of measurement error) (Kingston & Dings, 1995), in 1996 task and rater variance also were modeled (Dings & Kingston, 1996).

Are Kentucky Instructional Results Information System Scores Equivalent Across Administrations?

It is unfortunate that halfway through the evaluation procedure, communication between the KDE and the OEA panel was summarily cut off. To this day, we do not understand many of the recommendations related to equating. On the surface, they appear to go strongly against industry standard practice. For example, Hambleton claims that equating procedures should not change over time. Yet, for example, at Educational Testing Service, the organization at which most equating procedures used in the past 40 years were developed, procedures for a given testing program change with some frequency. The appropriateness of any equating procedure varies based on the feasibility of particular data collection designs and the statistical relationships among different data elements. The latter usually is unknown until data are collected. An equating study is complex research, not merely data analysis, and it cannot be structured in a way that precludes researcher judgment.

Particularly troubling is the recommendation that multiple-choice items be used to equate the open-response tests. Although this *might* not be particularly troublesome for a within-year equating, it would be quite problematic for a cross-year equating. Equating is only meaningful for tests that are essentially unidimensional in the population of interest.[1] If some schools stress instructional activities (e.g., writing) that are likely to improve performance more on open-response items, then in theory including the equating data from multiple-choice items is likely to lower the quality of the equating. For testing programs designed to have instructional consequences, multiple-choice and open-response sections probably should be equated separately.

Are the Performance Standards Defensible?

Zeiky (1995) said,

There are so many variables involved in an operational standard setting and so many opinions and theories about each variable that some aspects of any study will always be open to attack if critics are unhappy with the results and wish to undermine the study. A standard setting study that is planned and carried out by recognized experts can be severely criticized by yet other recognized experts. (p. 31)

Nonetheless, we agree substantially with the recommendations in this section. That is, we believe that documentation of process could have been better and that larger sample sizes would have been desirable. But these are not significant issues. The real issue is whether Kentucky's performance standards are reasonable. To answer this question, Kentucky conducted a large-scale validation of the existing standards using more than 300 parents, teachers, administrators, policymakers, and business representatives (Advanced Systems in Measurement and Evaluation, 1996). Results were highly similar across the various constituencies and strongly supported the reasonableness of Kentucky's standards.

Rejoinder to Stufflebeam

Stufflebeam's chapter is filled with errors of commission and omission. We address the more egregious ones here, organized under the headings Stufflebeam used in his chapter.

Impacts on Teachers

In this section, Stufflebeam claims, "Many teachers wanted timely feedback with direct relevance for improving classroom activities. However, the state did not design the accountability index (or KIRIS reports) to provide such feedback" (p. 221). On the contrary, one of the many reports produced for each school was the curriculum report, which broke down school scores into various subareas of the school curriculum. Another report that many schools found useful was a summary of the strengths and weaknesses of student writing as found in a sample of school writing portfolios. Neither of these reports is described or critiqued by Stufflebeam, but both are vehicles that many teachers reported to us were useful in improving curriculum and instruction.

Impacts on Schools

Here Stufflebeam states, "Some school leaders expressed concerns about whether the administration of KIRIS rewards and sanctions was fair to schools with large numbers of economically disadvantaged students, high turnover rates, or very small numbers of students" (p. 221).

The concerns of these school leaders were not necessary. Table 15.5 in the *KIRIS Accountability Cycle I Technical Manual* (KDE, 1995) shows that the percentage of students eligible for free and reduced-price lunch correlated only .06 with the percentage of improvement goal attained. Thus school wealth explained less than 0.5% of school success under the accountability system. Furthermore, in 1995, the *Lexington Herald Leader* performed its own analysis (also reported in the technical manual) based on taxable property value per student and concluded in its article headline, "Poor Schools as Likely as Rich to Hit KERA Goals, Earn Rewards."

Similarly, the KDE reported a correlation of −.24 between school size and percentage of goal reached as well as a −.20 correlation between school size and a school's reward category. Thus small schools clearly were not disadvantaged.

Stufflebeam also reports, "Teachers surveyed by the Kentucky Institute for Educational Research (KIER) said the rewards and sanctions would *not* help improve education" (p. 222). Inexplicably, in this section he ignores all reports (summarized in Chapter 18) of positive impacts on students, teachers, and schools.

Impacts on the State Education System

Stufflebeam claims, "The system's rewards and sanctions component was quite embarrassing to state officials" (p. 222). Nowhere does he indicate who these alleged embarrassed officials were. As the two state officials most directly responsible for the accountability program, neither we nor any other state officials of whom we are aware was embarrassed. The system has done exactly what was expected of it and as well as was expected. Also as expected, the experience of Kentucky educators and more than 20 completed and ongoing studies by researchers across the country (conducted with the encouragement of the KDE) have revealed a number of desirable improvements that have since been implemented. The assessment and accountability systems were designed to be dynamic; they will continue to undergo improvements as we learn more from the systems and as schools continue to respond to them.

Reliability of Assessment Devices

This section is perplexing. Statements appear crafted to be misleading or provide unduly negative headlines. For example, Stufflebeam states, "*Considered by themselves*, two of the three cognitive components of the KIRIS accountability index were not sufficiently reliable for use in a high-stakes assessment" (p. 223; emphasis added).

This statement is tailor-made to be quoted as "Two of the three components of KIRIS . . . were not sufficiently reliable for use in a high-stakes assessment." The full quote, with the "considered by themselves," at least prepares a reader for the obvious response, "But of course, these components were not used by themselves; they were but parts of the index." It is akin to a banker saying, "Considered alone, your income from stocks and bonds is not enough to support your mortgage." But that banker would be doing a poor job of evaluating your creditworthiness. A competent banker would look at your total income (including salary as well as interest and dividends) and conclude that it was well within guidelines.

The discussion of reliability is, in fact, quite confused. Stufflebeam correctly points out that, early in the program, questions were raised regarding reliability estimates. He incorrectly characterizes these questions as being about the adequacy of the reliability of components and taking into account chance agreement among raters. We have no memory of, and have found no written record of, there being any unresolved questions regarding these issues. The critical question raised around 1994 regarded the appropriate sources of measurement error to include in reliability analyses. The KDE responded to these questions by producing reliability estimates (based on a generalizability study) treating student and task variance as both fixed and random (Table 13-2 in the aforementioned technical manual).

For schools with 48 students[2] (across 2 years of data), results were an average reliability index of .94 when students and tasks were considered fixed effects and .89 when students and tasks were considered random effects.

Validity of Assessment

Here Stufflebeam argues, "The unreliability of the writing portfolios and performance events deterred the commonwealth from obtaining a valid index for administering rewards and sanctions to schools" (p. 223). This argument is specious and misleading. It is tantamount to saying that because the reliability of a single multiple-choice item is very low, no multiple-choice test can be valid. Hogwash! Again, the critical concern is the reliability and the validity of the composite index, not the reliability and validity of any component of the index.

Furthermore, two critical flaws invalidate Stufflebeam's declaration that the accountability index is invalid. First, the declaration includes no supporting data. Second, the conclusion is drawn as if validity were an all-or-none quality—a position completely incompatible with the last 20 years of research on the philosophical and methodological underpinnings of test validation. For example, the standards for educational and psychological testing (American Educational Research Association, American Psychological Association, & National Council on Measurement in Education, 1985) refer to test validity as "the appropriateness, meaningfulness, and usefulness of inferences made from test scores" and to test validation as "the process of accumulating evidence to support such inferences" (p. 9). More recently, Messick (1989) and others have added evidence regarding the consequences of the use of test scores as part of the validation process.

Regardless, the KDE addressed validity in two chapters of the technical manual, a small portion of which is summarized in Chapter 18 of this book. Inexplicably, Stufflebeam ignores all this evidence in his declaration of the index's invalidity.

Failure of the Accountability Index

The poor scholarship in Chapter 20 culminates in this section, where Stufflebeam declares, "The accountability index *proved* to be a dysfunctional part of the Kentucky reform" (p. 224; emphasis added). Stufflebeam provides no data to support this allegation. He does, however, level several accusations in an attempt to support this statement. Following is a sentence-by-sentence analysis of Stufflebeam's allegations.

Allegation: "The definition of the index kept shifting and was thus confusing" (p. 224). For each accountability cycle, the definition of the index was set once and once only by a state board regulation.

Allegation: "It was not defensible on technical grounds" (p. 224). Despite critics' use of unsubstantiated allegations from the Western Michigan report, for 6 years the assessment and accountability systems have survived all legal and political challenges. Furthermore, Stufflebeam seems to believe it appropriate to hold Kentucky to higher technical standards than he holds himself and his colleagues when they make high-stakes admissions, scholarship, and hiring decisions.

Allegation: "Although portfolios of students' work evidenced instructional authenticity, scores varied considerably depending on who scored each portfolio" (p. 224). This is true but incomplete. The portfolio-scoring accuracy of Kentucky teachers has improved considerably each year of the program. Moreover, writing portfolios carried only a 16.7% weight in the first accountability cycle and a 14.0% weight in the second cycle.

Allegation: "These scores were less reliable than other forms of assessment and not defensible for use in high-stakes decision making" (p. 224). This is false and highly misleading. First, many forms of high-stakes assessment—such as many personality tests used in employment selection, college admission essays, and unstructured job interviews—have lower reliability than do writing portfolios. Second, the reliability of one component of an index is not relevant to the defensibility of the total index. (Remember that unreliable single test item we mentioned earlier.)

Allegation: "The index did not discriminate fairly among advantaged and disadvantaged schools" (p. 224). In his section titled "Impacts on Schools," Stufflebeam complains that the state provided no information related to performance of advantaged and disadvantaged schools. Now he claims that even without data, he knows the index was unfair. In reality, the program did provide pertinent data. As described in the technical manual and earlier in this chapter, the data showed the index to be fair.

Allegation: "It generated much controversy" (p. 224). True, but at best it is irrelevant to Stufflebeam's argument. As we stated in Chapter 18, "In this spirit, the test component of the accountability system was designed to be dramatically and controversially different from any previous testing program" (p. 194). Extreme controversy is characteristic of many elections. Based on this observation, would Stufflebeam conclude democracy is dysfunctional?

Allegation: "Factors beyond a school's control influenced the accountability index, but the state interpreted the index without considering these factors. Among the factors not considered were adequacy of resources, changes in the economic climate of a community, and changes in student mobility. However, the state maintained a mechanism by which school authorities could appeal such matters if they believed failure was due to factors beyond the school's control" (p. 224). Although it is true that the state *calculated* the accountability index without consideration of the factors he mentions, as Stufflebeam himself shows in the third sentence, these factors were considered in the *interpretation* of the index. That is, the state had an appeals system, and several schools were exempted from negative categorization based on successful appeals.

Allegation: "The state made no corrections, however, for false positives when schools passed the state assessment because of environmental factors rather than the quality of instruction" (p. 224). The state did make negative adjustments for changes in school district sending patterns that occurred within an accountability cycle. Similarly, negative adjustments were made in the case of intentional or inadvertent inappropriate testing practices. Surprisingly, one school did successfully appeal that it was a false positive and should have its scores lowered for environmental reasons beyond its control.

Problems With the Longitudinal Assessment Design

The title of this section is puzzling given that Stufflebeam correctly points out that Kentucky did not use a longitudinal design and then goes on to present a case as to why we should have. Stufflebeam appropriately discusses the problems with cohort comparison designs but makes no mention of the reasons Kentucky rejected a longitudinal design (as described in Chapter 18). If Stufflebeam disagrees with those reasons, then he should present his case, but it seems inappropriate for an evaluator to ignore those reasons.

Notes

1. For tests to be equated requires that it be a matter of indifference to examinees as to which test they receive (Lord, 1980). Imagine a test that is half reading and half math. Further imagine two forms of the test, Form A in which the math questions are hard and the reading questions are easy and Form B in which the math questions are easy and the reading questions are hard. Even after equating, a student good in math will be advantaged if he or she takes Form A.

2. Note that this is 48 students across 2 years of testing. Virtually all middle and high schools and most elementary schools in Kentucky are considerably larger than this. Thus this is an underestimate of the reliability of the school index.

References

Advanced Systems in Measurement and Evaluation. (1996). *KIRIS standards validation study*. Dover, NH: Author.

American Educational Research Association, American Psychological Association, & National Council on Measurement in Education. (1985). *Standards for educational and psychological testing*. Washington, DC: APA.

Dings, J., & Kingston, N. (1996, April). *Effects of students and tasks on gain scores used in complex school accountability decisions*. Paper presented at the annual meeting of the National Council for Measurement in Education, New York.

Hambleton, R. K., Jaeger, R. M., Koretz, D., Linn, R. L., Millman, J., & Phillips, S. (1995). *Review of the measurement quality of the Kentucky Instructional Results Information System, 1991-94*. Frankfort, KY: Office of Educational Accountability.

Kentucky Department of Education. (1995). *KIRIS Accountability Cycle I technical manual*. Frankfort, KY: Author.

Kingston, N., & Dings, J. (1995, April). *Estimating the accuracy of complex school accountability decisions*. Paper presented at the annual meeting of the National Council for Measurement in Education, San Francisco.

Lord, F. (1980). *Applications of item response theory to practical testing problems*. Hillsdale, NJ: Lawrence Erlbaum.

Messick, S. (1989). Validity. In R. L. Linn (Ed.), *Educational measurement* (3rd ed., pp. 13-103). Washington, DC: American Council on Education.

Western Michigan University Evaluation Center. (1995). *An independent evaluation of the Kentucky Instructional Results Information System (KIRIS)*. Frankfort: Kentucky Institute for Education Research.

Zeiky, M. (1995). A historical perspective on standard setting. In *Proceedings of joint conference on standard setting for large-scale assessments* (pp. 1-38). Washington, DC: Government Printing Office.

PART VI

Synthesis and Perspectives

CHAPTER 22

How Do I Judge Thee?

Let Me Count the Ways

Jason Millman

If nothing else, the four approaches highlighted in this book are intended to link rewards and sanctions to the assessed effectiveness of teachers and schools. The approaches all measure effectiveness, and hence hold teachers and schools accountable, by measuring their students' learning. In this chapter, I offer four criteria for judging how well these systems carry out this accountability function.

Because developers of all four systems claim that their systems also foster teacher improvement, the chapter also considers a criterion uniquely suitable for that claim.

Criteria for an
Accountability System

Any method of evaluating teachers and schools with an eye toward making them accountable should be fair to the teachers and schools, should be comprehensive in terms of the types of learning objectives measured, should be competitive in relation to other methods of evaluating teachers and schools for an accountability purpose, and should not cause undesirable effects when used properly. I discuss each criterion in turn.

Fairness

The single most frequent criticism of any attempt to determine a teacher's effectiveness by measuring student learning is that factors beyond the teacher's control affect the amount students learn. These factors range from those at the student level (e.g., student ability) to those at the classroom (e.g., class size) and school and community levels (e.g., district wealth). Educators want a level playing field and do not believe such a thing is possible. Many people would rather have their fortunes determined by a roulette wheel, which is invalid but fair, than by an evaluation system that is not fair.

It is no wonder that the designers of all four systems have given much attention to the question of fairness. They all attempt to level the playing field by using past levels on the factors to predict end-of-year levels for students in a given teacher's classroom or for students in a given school. Deviations above and below the predicted level are attributed to the teacher or school being evaluated. For example, the Kentucky program

> was designed to be more fair and equitable than most previous programs used to make judgments about schools. Traditional programs have compared schools on resources . . . or on academic success . . . without regard to any history of inequities in school funding or the financial means of the local community and parents. KERA [Kentucky Education Reform Act] changed this by judging schools based on their progress toward state-set goals that were based on the schools' initial academic scores and thus eliminated many potential sources of inequity. (Chapter 18, p. 197)

The Dallas accountability system

> controls for preexisting student differences in ethnicity, gender, language proficiency, and socioeconomic status . . . and prior achievement levels. Additionally, the hierarchical linear model . . . employed controls for school-level variables. (Chapter 8, p. 82)

For Oregon's work sample methodology,

Pre- to postinstructional gain scores are calculated on a student-by-student basis, with separate analyses required for initially high- and low-scoring pupils. . . . Descriptors of classroom, school, and community context variables accompany all measures of learning gain. (Chapter 3)

The complexity and size of the Tennessee program are due in part to its tracking, for 3 different years, individual students in a given teacher's classroom. The ensuing longitudinal analyses are intended to level the playing field. To date, implementation of the Tennessee model indicates that using a single factor, the prior achievement of students, is sufficient for this task.

Comprehensiveness

This criterion refers to the degree the range of intended learning outcomes are represented in the assessment measures. Schools in general and teachers in particular have an ambitious set of objectives. The tests that are used in these accountability systems cannot possibly capture entirely the richness of these objectives. The subject matter knowledge, the learning skills, the testing formats, and the noncognitive outcomes that are targeted by the reformers/educators are greater than the information accessible by testing. The systems reviewed here are more or less successful in closing the gap between the ideal measures and the practical indicators.

Why is comprehensiveness important? Tests, especially those reflecting on teachers, drive the curriculum. Teachers inevitably will attempt to prepare their students to do well on the assessment measures. Their instruction will emphasize the subject matter, the intellectual skills, and the testing formats that appear on the test. If noncognitive variables are part of an accountability index, then these will be heeded as well.

Teachers may find themselves faced with disincentives to follow their perceived best practices if doing so would detract from student performance according to the accountability system. It is in teachers' best interest to teach to the objectives measured by the test. Advocates of linking student learning to teacher effectiveness counter such criticism by claiming that the measures of student learning are in step with contemporary reform movements in education and that the accountability system will thereby enhance instruction and teaching.

Competitiveness

Although measuring teacher success via student performance has found favor with the public, especially parents, it often is vehemently opposed by teachers, partly for the reasons mentioned in the preceding. However, to date, other alternatives for evaluating teacher performance, such as assessment by school principals, have proven to be even less desirable or credible. Given that teacher assessment via student performance usually is not considered the sole indicator of teacher excellence and that no foolproof method of teacher evaluation exists, this method of teacher evaluation is competitive in relation to other methods.

Consequential Validity

The system for measuring teacher effectiveness could be 100% accurate and still have undesirable side effects. It is not enough that teachers succeed in producing measurable quantities of student learning if that is accomplished at the expense of other valued resources such as teacher morale (see Chapters 10 and 23).

It is useful to distinguish between consequences that arise when the approach is used as intended and those that arise from misuse of the approach. Linking teacher effectiveness to student learning inevitably will create some undesirable side effects. For example, suppose it is found that applying one of the approaches described in this book consumes a lot of teacher time and detracts from the overall creative effort of teaching. It is essential to determine whether these consequences are the result of misusing the method. When the method is used properly and still creates undesirable effects, this is good reason for a negative evaluation of the method.

Criterion for a Teacher Improvement System

The four systems described in this book all are accountability systems in that they are used for making decisions that affect teachers and schools. The users of these systems, however, suggest that they are appropriate for serving other purposes as well. For example,

> [The Teacher Work Sample Methodology] also carries with it the aim of *improving instruction and learning* that is common to the alternative assessment movement. (Chapter 3)

> However, the real value of TVAAS [Tennessee Value-Added Assessment System] lies in its ability to serve as a data source for formative evaluation purposes. (Chapter 13)

> The primary goal of Kentucky's school-based accountability system is to motivate educators and the public to dramatically improve student learning. This goal is paramount and takes precedence over the strategies and tactics associated with the accountability system. (Chapter 18)

> Internally, at the campus and classroom levels, relative effectiveness is identified, rewarded, and used as a model for improvement. . . . The entire system is focused on continuous improvement. (Chapter 8)

How should we judge these four systems for their contribution to teacher improvement? On the one hand, one could argue that any information is valuable, including information on what students know and can do. On the other hand, merely describing the product (what students know and can do) provides scant information on what the teacher did or should have done to yield better results. Such an assessment is similar to the old-fashioned process-product research in which the explanatory goodies are kept in a mystical black box.

It has been my observation that when an assessment system tries to serve two purposes, the accountability and improvement functions, the system is less than optimum for accomplishing either purpose. The systems that focus on teacher improvement (e.g., Western Oregon) or educational reform (e.g., Kentucky) seemingly do so at the expense of their accountability efforts.

CHAPTER 23

Toward What End?

The Evaluation of Student Learning for the Improvement of Teaching

LINDA DARLING-HAMMOND

There are all kinds of technical quarrels that can be raised about student achievement measures and their use in various indexes, regression models, or teacher evaluation systems. However, the bottom-line questions for any assessment system that purports to measure the quality of schools or teaching are two:

1. Is it real? Is the system really measuring the quality of schooling or teaching? Or is it measuring something else, such as changes in student population or artifacts of the assessment methods?

2. What are the effects? Does it improve teaching and learning? Conversely, does it do any harm?

In this response, I examine the systems reviewed in this book through the lens of these two questions. Unless the answers to both of them are positive, researchers may be amusing themselves or satisfying the whims of policymakers, but they are doing little to help teachers and students improve their collective work. I conclude by suggesting what we might ideally want to see in an assessment system that can both evaluate the quality of teaching and support educators in their efforts to improve.

The Kentucky Instructional Results Information System

Kentucky's experience illustrates how a good idea for improving curriculum and student assessment can be undermined by a bad idea for "accountability"—one that fails to measure the quality of schooling and undermines teaching in the process.

In many respects, Kentucky's efforts to create and implement a new performance-based assessment system in a short period of time might be viewed as nothing short of heroic. Evaluations of the student assessments themselves point to work that is needed to improve scoring reliabilities, but many analysts also note that the assessments have begun to influence instruction in positive ways, especially in encouraging much more extensive and higher quality student writing (Appalachia Educational Laboratory [AEL], 1996; Whitford & Jones, in press; also see Stufflebeam's contribution to this book [Chapter 20]). My own review suggests that tasks on the early Kentucky instruments were more authentic than those on traditional standardized tests; most were well constructed and provided useful indicators of student learning.

The Kentucky Department of Education was criticized by some for eliminating multiple-choice items from the tests and for continuing to use portfolios despite low reliabilities in scoring. (Recently, multiple-choice items have been reinstated and the mathematics portfolio has been shelved.) Certainly, the concern for adequate reliability in a high-stakes system is justified. However, as performance assessments evolve, it is increasingly possible to score them reliably, and Kentucky eventually should be able to benefit from the accumulated wisdom of other states. In recent work in New York, for example, we have obtained interrater reliabilities for performance assessments in reading, writing, and mathematics consistently above .85 and often above .90 (Pecheone, Falk, & Darling-Hammond, in press), even though these include extended tasks and no multiple-choice items.

Even where such results have not yet been obtained, however, I believe the Department of Education's original decisions can be defended on the grounds of both consequential and construct validity. The consequential validity case is strengthened as reports of significantly improved instruction accompany the use of performance assessments and portfolios in states as far-flung as Vermont, New York, and California as well as Kentucky (AEL, 1996; Darling-Hammond & Falk, in press; Koretz, Stetcher, & Deibert, 1992; Murnane & Levy, 1996).

In terms of construct validity, it is time to demand serious answers to the question of what multiple-choice responses really measure, when they can be answered with guesswork rather than knowledge, and when they give no indication of the ability to apply information in a performance context. The critique of multiple-choice tests for their failure to measure complex performance skills is well known (see, e.g., Resnick, 1987). However, even straightforward factual knowledge may be poorly measured by such items. One study that asked students to reply to the same set of questions posed in multiple-choice and short-answer formats found that scores were 43% higher when students were able to pick answers out of a list than when they had to produce the answers themselves. Furthermore, many of the constructed responses were so far off the mark that it was clear the "correct" multiple-choice answers measured anything but genuine learning (Shea, 1993).

We may be asking the wrong questions about the relationship between assessment methods and stakes. Rather than limiting the range of assessments because of the stakes attached to them, perhaps we should be limiting the range of stakes to meet the demands of educationally useful assessments. If assessments are created that produce improvements in teaching and learning, then we should ask whether stakes that undermine these influences are warranted and defensible.

This brings me to the fly in the Kentucky ointment: its poorly conceived accountability system. As reviewers in this book and elsewhere have noted, there are many technical problems with the accountability index: the arbitrary reduction of many dimensions to a single score; unresolved questions about its reliability; the arbitrary setting of expected improvement levels from schools in continuous, linear fashion; the failure to take into account differences in student populations and community conditions; and the failure to allow for cohort analyses of the same students over time, a particularly problematic shortcoming.

However, the most egregious limitations of the accountability system are the fact that it does not measure school quality in a meaningful way and it undermines high-quality teaching in a number of ways. The use of cross-sectional rather than cohort analyses of performance means that annual scores are as likely to be an artifact of changes in the population of students taking the test as in the quality of teaching they experience. For example, one Kentucky elementary school of 200 students, a reputedly excellent school visited by many educators seeking to understand good practice, found itself on the "merit school" list one year and, with a small change in the students enrolled, on the "deficient" list the following year without having undergone any change in school practices. Five out of nine schools on the "deficient" list this year were "in rewards" last year (Whitford & Jones, in press). This common occurrence destroys the credibility of the so-called accountability system, which clearly is not measuring school quality at all.

As Stufflebeam's analysis suggests, studies have found that educators in many schools, particularly small schools and those with large numbers of disadvantaged students or high turnover rates, feel victimized by the accountability system because it does not measure the actual progress of their students and evaluates them unfairly (AEL, 1996; Whitford & Jones, in press). Furthermore, the rewards and sanctions scheme assumes that the real problems of schools are caused by teachers who are holding out on their students; That is, that they will only teach well out of greed or fear. According to reports from the field, this offends many educators while it heightens their anxiety, which they pass on to their students by applying negative pressure, creating rewards and sanctions for students, and narrowing their teaching to test-related drills that are becoming narrower as the tests become less authentic and performance oriented (Whitford & Jones, in press). Some evidence suggests that, because of these pressures, increased scores a result of better test taking rather than genuinely improved learning (Hambleton et al., 1995).

The accountability system never sought to improve learning directly by investing in teachers' abilities to teach more effectively. Furthermore, it undermines the teacher learning and enhanced teaching quality that might result from more instructionally valid and powerful assessments, which are now being removed from the system because they are not scored reliably enough to support high-stakes decisions. Finally, the high-stakes nature of the assessments has minimized teacher involvement in the assessment development and scoring process, which would increase knowledge about how to teach. Costly external contractor scoring eliminates the potential learning about curriculum, assessment, and teaching that teachers could get from being involved in moderated scoring of student work. This may account for the finding that teachers have not integrated assessment into their instructional practices (see Chapter 20), and it may lead to the ironic outcome that the nation's most ambitious plan to overhaul curriculum and teaching was short-circuited by the very policy that was supposed to make schools pay attention to it.

The Dallas Value-Added Accountability System

Unlike Kentucky, the Dallas accountability system (which was proposed but not ultimately implemented) at least strives tried to evaluate value-added learning by measuring individual student test scores using prior scores as controls. This intention confronts a major Achilles' heel in the approach used in many states and districts, although, as Thum and Bryk note in their contribution to this book (Chapter 9), a gain score analysis would be preferable to the use of residuals that introduce error and reduce expectations for many students.

However, the proposed Dallas system seemed to have little to do with either the appropriate evaluation of teaching or its improvement. According to the accounts of school people in Dallas, neither administrators nor faculty understood the system, thus making it irrelevant to the improvement of teaching. As John Cole, Texas Federation of Teachers president, noted,

> I do not believe we will motivate employees to work harder or to improve their skills by implementing an accountability program which is so complex that no one understands it. If the administration cannot even explain how it works, how do we expect school principals to advise teachers on what teaching behaviors to change in order to improve performance? (Cole, 1995)

Other important concerns included the mismatch between Dallas's curriculum and the test measures used, the absence of measures for many subject areas, and the fact that the existing measures bear little relation to the kinds of higher order learning most policymakers and educators now feel are essential (see Sykes's contribution to this book [Chapter 10]). By raising the stakes for scores on these limited measures, the accountability system would only increase the negative effects of teaching to the test, especially for low-scoring schools or students (Madaus, West, Harmon, Lomax, & Viator, 1992).

Finally, despite the use of statistically complex, test-based accountability systems in Dallas for more than a decade (this one was only the latest in a string of such efforts), the schools there are widely acknowledged as poor, and they continue to perform badly both nationally and regionally. This may have to do with the fact that the district has expended more effort perfecting its indicator systems than it has improving schools or attracting, supporting, and keeping well-qualified teachers and other staff.

Unlike other Texas cities, such as San Antonio, that have focused on improving the training, recruitment, and mentoring of teachers, Dallas continually hires large numbers of untrained teachers and runs an alternative route to certification that produces less effective teachers than do university-based teacher education programs (Gomez & Grobe, 1990). Professional development is thin and typically focused on implementation of packaged programs rather than on skillful analysis of teaching and learning. Rather than develop professional competence and accountability, Dallas clings to bureaucratic methods—a top-down, "mechanical" approach to management (see Chapter 10) of which such accountability systems are a centerpiece. Among teachers in Dallas these approaches to accountability are seen not as a spur to better practice but rather as a spur for those with talent and options to leave for the suburbs as quickly as possible (J. Cole, personal communication, 1994).

Even if Dallas were to address all of the statistical concerns that might ever be raised about its regression equations, the question would remain: Why bother? Teaching and learning in Dallas would most likely be substantially better off without this kind of "accountability."

The Tennessee Value-Added Assessment System

The "why bother?" question is a bit easier to answer for the Tennessee assessment system, which already has proven itself useful for addressing some important research questions. The finding noted in Sanders, Saxton, and Horn's contribution to this book (Chapter 13) that students lose ground on achievement when they move into the lowest grade in a new school is made possible by the longitudinal measures that the system uses to track student learning. These measures are a major strength of the system, along with the use of analytic tools that allow greater use of existing data. As a research tool, the Tennessee Value-Added Assessment System (TVAAS) has clear value.

To their credit, Sanders and colleagues note that "schools, school systems, and teachers cannot be assessed solely on the basis of TVAAS" (Chapter 13, p. 139). I would underscore their warranted caution. There are many reasons why TVAAS is inappropriate for evaluating teachers, and there are even more reasons why it is an unsound basis for the kind of incentive scheme Walberg and Paik propose (Chapter 15).

First, the realities of schools, classrooms, and communities— along with the limits of the TVAAS measures—make it inappropriate to attribute measured gains in learning to the skills and competence of specific teachers. As Darlington notes in his response (Chapter 14), students are not assigned randomly to teachers; some teachers routinely get more difficult students, either because they can "handle" them or because they rank low in the school pecking order. Furthermore, students in many U.S. schools are routinely tracked, as are their teachers (Darling-Hammond, 1995; Oakes, 1985). It is, of course, easier for those teachers who are assigned "high-track" students to get learning gains from students who teach themselves than it is to do so with students who need high levels of teaching skill and personal attention.

Home factors and personal learning needs or difficulties also make a difference in student performance independent of teaching skill. The large numbers of students who experience divorces, homelessness, violent crimes, hunger, or the deaths of relatives are, of course, affected by these experiences. Children who experience many of these things are not randomly distributed across classrooms or schools, as anyone who gets close to the real world of schooling knows. Even where troubled or educationally needy children are more rare, their presence in a class can have a major effect on how the energies of the teacher are deployed and on how other children respond. If TVAAS were to be used as the basis for personnel evaluations or, heaven help us, for rewards and firings, the already existing incentive in schools to avoid "problem" children would be exacerbated. More teachers would try—as many already do—to offload such children on their colleagues with less clout: new teachers, those who are less skilled, and those who have less political power. Children with the greatest needs would become educational lepers, and their needs would be even less well served than they are today.

For large-scale research, the methods used by TVAAS to handle missing data and to partial out the presumed effects of different teachers are unobjectionable. However, for personnel evaluations, such methods would be indefensible. No person should be evaluated for high-stakes decisions based on statistical assumptions rather than on actual information. In addition to the obvious problems of substituting mean scores for missing data, especially for high-mobility or low-attendance schools and classrooms, is the problem of attributing gains to specific teachers. The assumption of the TVAAS system is that, over time, the influence of previous teachers on a current score can be expected to decrease. This is not necessarily true. Particularly in the early elementary grades, the efforts of teachers who emphasize conceptual teaching and the building of higher order thinking skills often are not captured by traditional standardized tests until several years later, when more conceptual material and higher level performances are measured.

The limitations of the tests used constitute another obvious shortcoming of the TVAAS system as a tool for teacher evaluation. In addition to all of the concerns I raised earlier about what current standardized tests measure—and do not measure—they have low ceilings, making assessment of gains for high-achieving students especially problematic. Use of such measures for research does not pose the same problems that such use would pose for personnel evaluation tied to sanctions. Research already has well documented the incentives that would be created for teaching to the test and neglecting more complex work—research, projects, extended writing, experimentation—from the attachment of stakes to such measures. Not only would teachers who teach toward these important goals not be acknowledged, they would be discouraged from continuing to focus on these activities at the expense of drilling for the test (Darling-Hammond, 1991; Madaus et al., 1992; Shepard, 1991).

Finally, to whatever extent the tests measure useful learning, there always will be attribution problems. In some schools, students' gains in writing are actually produced by the social studies teacher who assigns regular research papers, and students' gains in mathematics are the product of the science teacher's efforts because he or she uses mathematics in contexts that encourage deeper understanding—or vice versa. Without looking at practice, inferences about what teachers are actually doing simply cannot be made from statistical methods that make assumptions that are functional for highly aggregated analyses and unwarranted for drawing individual conclusions.

Some years ago, Susan Stodolsky (1984) wrote a piece titled "Teacher Evaluation: The Limits of Looking," which described why observations of teachers alone were inadequate for the purposes of teacher evaluation. The subtitle for the TVAAS system might well be "The Limits of Not Looking" to acknowledge the shortcomings of black box approaches to the evaluation of teaching.

The Oregon Work Sample Methodology

The Oregon work sampling approach has this to commend it: It actually looks at teaching, and it does so in the context of teachers' goals, classroom contexts, and student learning, measured in ways that attempt to link learning to the educational goals being sought. In these respects, it stands head and shoulders above all of the other approaches in this book as a means for providing sound evaluations of teaching that might also be useful in helping teachers improve.

As the responses by Airasian (Chapter 4) and Stufflebeam (Chapter 5) note, there are areas of further work to be done to make this a useful tool for formative evaluation of student teachers or veteran teachers. In my view, the most important areas for improvement concern the measures of outcomes used, the measures of practice used, and the approach to evaluating the effects of practice on outcomes.

In terms of measuring student learning, the Teacher Work Sample Methodology (TWSM) is dependent on the quality of assessments teachers can devise, which could be highly variable and fail to evaluate important kinds of learning well. As Stufflebeam notes, "It matters little whether ratings of teacher performance are associated with pupil gains in work sample performance if the teachers employ biased outcome measures or assess low-level knowledge and skills" (Chapter 5, p. 57). Furthermore, TWSM still envisions very limited kinds of performances that can be tested with a batch of items to produce a "percentage correct" score rather than more complex performances that support higher order learning, such as designs for experiments, mathematical models, research papers, extended essays, oral presentations, or debates. In theory and in practice, these kinds of measures can be scored and improvements measured over time, but the methods of evaluation must extend beyond percentage correct indexes if they are to be used.

TWSM's measures of practice are not well described in the chapter, and they may be better developed than this brief chapter suggests. However, the self-referential quality of the TWSM system means that the teaching observed will only be that associated with the objectives the teacher has selected rather than a sample of performance assessed against some professional standard of practice. As Airasian notes, "Although it is important to align objectives, instruction, and assessment to one another, it also is important that the objectives themselves be meaningful and worthwhile" (Chapter 4, p. 47). This is equally true of the nature and quality of practice evaluated. My own experience with the evaluation of teachers for purposes of licensing and certification also leads me to wonder about the extent to which observers are applying common criteria for assessing appropriate practice, especially because the chapter makes no reference to common standards, measures, or training. Finally, there is presently no means within TWSM to link teaching practices to student outcomes. This limits the learning that can emerge from the system for teacher educators and teachers alike.

These critiques made, there is value in an approach to teacher assessment that points practitioners to the careful evaluation of practices, contexts, and outcomes, including the systematic consideration of student and teacher work. I have no doubt that this encourages teachers to reflect on their work in ways that are extremely productive for developing diagnostic habits of thinking as well as specific practices.

In this respect, TWSM resembles the new approaches to certification and licensure testing developed by the National Board for Professional Teaching Standards (NBPTS) and the Interstate New Teachers Assessment and Support Consortium (INTASC). These assessments also use work sampling methods to examine teachers' plans, instructional practices, assessment of student work, and feedback in the context of student work samples for several students whose progress is followed over time. The assessments already are in use for decisions about advanced certification (NBPTS) and initial licensing (INTASC methods are used in Connecticut). However, they differ from TWSM in some key respects that make them more appropriate for these high-stakes decisions.

First, the assessment tasks are substantially standardized: English teachers must conduct literary discussions and submit videotapes of the lessons and their analyses of them, and they must show how they teach writing by presenting several assignments with student work samples and feedback over time. Middle grade teachers must outline and conduct several-week interdisciplinary units that tie several fields of study together. Mathematics teachers must show how they teach small group lessons using technology or manipulatives and large group lessons that focus on mathematical discourse. Second, as these descriptions suggest, the tasks and their evaluation are pegged to clear standards of practice that were developed by expert teachers, linked to emerging student standards, and validated in the field. Third, the examinations include both on-demand performance tasks (e.g., critique of a textbook or piece of educational software against criteria indicated in a task) and samples of work that derive more directly from the teachers' own work. Like other certification decisions, it is important to have some tasks preset so that evaluators can determine whether candidates have certain skills commonly accepted as essential for success in the field.

Fourth, the scoring systems are highly developed and have been validated and tested for reliability. They evaluate important dimensions of teaching and are administered by trained assessors who must achieve reliable levels of scoring ability. Fifth, a careful process of standard setting has been undertaken and validated. Finally, the examinations and scoring systems have been thoroughly vetted for evidence of bias, a critical concern for high-stakes testing, especially when the identity of candidates is known to evaluators. Whereas all of these features are important, perhaps most important is the fact that teachers who have undergone the portfolio and performance assessment processes of the NBPTS and INTASC assessments, or who have served as assessors, consistently cite their experience as the most powerful professional development of their careers. They believe they are better teachers as a result of this work. This claim cannot be made of the systems in Kentucky, Dallas, or Tennessee.

TWSM is not yet close to meeting these standards for high-stakes use as a method of licensure or merit pay. However, that does not make it unuseful. As it evolves, it could be a valuable tool for preparing and assessing both beginning and veteran teachers. I suspect that teachers find it helpful in inquiring into their teaching. We should be mindful that many tools are *more* useful when they are not tied to stakes than they become when they have overreached their appropriate uses. Indeed, growing evidence suggests that policymakers' overreliance on high stakes often undermines reform rather than supporting improvements in practice. All of the assessment systems reviewed in this book would be used more productively in a low-stakes environment than for the high-stakes purposes that have been proposed for them.

The Seduction of Statistics and Stakes

Americans have a love affair with "hard" data and, increasingly, with tough-nosed approaches to school accountability. Policymakers and researchers who spend little time in schools and have even less knowledge of the realities of teaching and learning are wont to crank up numbers that appear to justify "taking names and kicking butt," as one eloquent analyst put it recently. A growing number of states and districts have gambled that education will improve if consequences for students and schools are attached to achievement measures.

More than a decade's worth of evidence shows, however, that simply setting test score goals and attaching sanctions to them does not result in greater learning—and sometimes produces destructive side effects. In many states and school districts, test-based sanctions have created incentives for schools to keep out or push out the most educationally needy students; large numbers of students have been retained in grade so that their scores look better, placed in special education so that their scores do not count, denied admission, or pushed out of schools to keep average scores up (Allington and McGill-Franzen, 1992; Darling-Hammond, 1991; Orfield & Ashkinaze, 1991; Smith, 1986). These strategies lead to lower levels of student learning and higher dropout rates in the long run, even though test scores appear to improve (Holmes & Matthews, 1984; Shepard & Smith, 1986). Similar outcomes have occurred in medicine. In one state that decided to rank cardiac surgeons based on the outcomes of their surgeries, many doctors began to turn away the most difficult cases or to refer them to physicians in other states because they would detract from the outcome measures.

These results are predictable when accountability schemes assume that all clients are alike or that punishments are the best way to produce change. As policy analyst Bill Clune has noted, "beating the dog harder" does not lead to meaningful reform. If educators do not have the knowledge or resources to achieve higher outcomes, simply telling them to do so cannot work. In New York, for example, test-based accountability reforms of the early 1980s have caused the state's graduation rates to drop to 45th in the nation while overall achievement has declined because mandates for testing were not coupled with investments in improved teaching. If we really want accountability that works for students—rather than primarily for politicians—then we need to attend to the conditions that would actually produce better schooling and more responsive teaching.

Solving the Real Problems
of Underachievement

For those closely engaged in work with schools, it is clear that the failures of recent reforms are due not to schools' unwillingness to improve but rather to the fact that most educators do not know how to teach so that all students can learn and that the systems within which they work are not structured to help them do so. If today's focus on higher standards is to result in greater student learning rather than greater levels of failure, it will need to be coupled with accountability policies that ensure that teachers and other educators have the knowledge and skills they need to teach effectively and that help schools evaluate and reshape their practices.

Achieving these goals will require approaches to assessment and accountability that incorporate at least the following.

- *Methods for examining the work of teaching and schooling,* including the work of students, using standards of practice that can propel learning and change. These include strategies such as the Oregon TWSM and assessments such as those of the NBPTS and INTASC. They also include school assessment strategies such as the school quality reviews that practitioners have found to be helpful in California, Illinois, and New York

(Ancess, 1996) as well as opportunities for teachers to collectively evaluate student work and their own practice (Darling-Hammond & McLaughlin, 1995; Murnane & Levy, 1996).

- *Measures of student learning* that are sufficiently sophisticated to assess higher order thinking and performance skills and that can allow for longitudinal evaluations of individual student progress rather than aggregated cross-sectional school scores that reflect changes in student populations more than gains in learning or improvements in teaching.

- *Means for linking assessments of learning to assessments of teaching and schooling* in meaningful ways. This will require a merger of qualitative and quantitative measures of schooling processes and "outcomes" that is grounded in an understanding of professional standards of practice as well as appropriate statistical techniques.

Perhaps in the next round of work on school accountability, we can develop tools that support student learning and the development of quality teaching as they clarify what students and teachers are doing to achieve their goals.

References

Allington, R. L., & McGill-Franzen, A. (1992). Unintended effects of educational reform in New York. *Educational Policy, 6*, 397-414.

Ancess, J. (1996). *Outside/inside, inside/outside: Developing and implementing the school quality review.* New York: Columbia University, Teachers College, National Center for Restructuring Education, School, and Teaching.

Appalachia Educational Laboratory. (1996). Five years of reform in rural Kentucky. In *Notes from the field: Educational reform in rural Kentucky* (Vol. 5). Charleston, WV: Author.

Cole, J. (1995, April 17). Letter to Sandy Kress, president, Board of Trustees, Dallas Independent School District. Used with permission.

Darling-Hammond, L. (1991). The implications of testing policy for quality and equality. *Phi Delta Kappan, 17*, 220-225.

Darling-Hammond, L. (1995). Inequality and access to knowledge. In J. Banks (Ed.), *The handbook of research on multicultural education.* New York: Macmillan.

Darling-Hammond, L., & Falk, B. (in press). Policy for authentic assessment. In A. L. Goodwin (Ed.), *Assessment for equity and inclusion: Embracing all our children.* New York: Routledge.

Darling-Hammond, L., & McLaughlin, M. W. (1995). Policies that support professional development in an era of reform. *Phi Delta Kappan, 76,* 597-604.

Gomez, D. L., & Grobe, R. P. (1990, April). *Three years of alternative certification in Dallas: Where are we?* Paper presented at the annual meeting of the American Educational Research Association, Boston.

Hambleton, R., Jaeger, R., Koretz, D., Linn, R., Millman, J., & Phillips, S. (1995). *Review of the measurement quality of the Kentucky Instructional Results Information System 1991-1994.* Frankfort, KY: Office of Educational Accountability.

Holmes, C. T., & Matthews, K. M. (1984). The effects of nonpromotion on elementary and junior high school pupils: A meta-analysis. *Review of Educational Research, 54,* 225-236.

Koretz, D., Stetcher, B., & Deibert, D. (1992). *The Vermont Assessment Program: Interim report on implementation and impact, 1991-92 school year* (CSE Technical Report 350). Los Angeles: University of California, Los Angeles, Center for Research on Evaluation, Standards, and Testing.

Madaus, G., West, M., Harmon, M., Lomax, R., & Viator, K. (1992). *The influence of testing on teaching math and science in Grades 4-12.* Boston: Boston College, Center for the Study of Testing, Evaluation, and Educational Policy.

Murnane, R., & Levy, F. (1996). *Teaching the new basic skills.* New York: Free Press.

Oakes, J. (1985). *Keeping track: How schools structure inequality.* New Haven, CT: Yale University Press.

Orfield, G., & Ashkinaze, C. (1991). *The closing door: Conservative policy and black opportunity.* Chicago: University of Chicago Press.

Pecheone, R., Falk, B., & Darling-Hammond, L. (in press). *Technical report on the 1996 pilot assessments in New York State.* New York: Columbia University, Teachers College, National Center for Restructuring Education, Schools, and Teaching.

Resnick, L. (1987). *Education and learning to think.* Washington, DC: National Academy Press.

Shea, J. H. (1993). Deceiving oneself and others with multiple-choice exams. *The Physics Teacher, 31,* 8.

Shepard, L. (1991). Will national tests improve learning? *Phi Delta Kappan, 73,* 232-238.

Shepard, L., & Smith, M. L. (1986, November). Synthesis of research on school readiness and kindergarten retention. *Educational Leadership*, pp. 78-86.

Smith, F. (1986). *High school admission and the improvement of schooling*. New York: New York City Board of Education.

Stodolsky, S. (1984). Teacher evaluation: The limits of looking. *Educational Researcher, 13*(4), 11-18.

Whitford, B. L., & Jones, K. (in press). Assessment and accountability in Kentucky: How high stakes affect teaching and learning. In A. Hargreaves, A. Lieberman, M. Fullan, & D. Hopkins (Eds.), *International handbook of educational change*. Netherlands: Kluwer.

CHAPTER 24

The Moth and the Flame

Student Learning as a Criterion of Instructional Competence

W. JAMES POPHAM

When I was growing up, while hearing older family members discuss a younger family member, I sometimes heard them remark that "he [or she] was attracted to her [or him] like a moth to a flame!" Even back then, I thought it was a wonderful expression. It signified the attraction of Person A for Person B, who, it was thought, would not be good for Person A. An attraction was clearly there. (Most moths apparently find flames quite appealing.) Even so, there was danger at hand. (Singed wings, it is believed, can really ruin a moth's day.)

Well, for my entire career, I have been almost neurotically fascinated by the possibility of evaluating teachers on the basis of whether they were able to promote student learning. Moth-like, I have been tantalized by the appeal of student learning as the chief criterion for determining an instructor's competence.

An Attraction Spawned in Graduate School

In retrospect, I am quite sure that I was first afflicted by this morbid fascination during my initial year in graduate school. My first assignment as a research assistant had been to assist in the preparation of an annotated bibliography about quantitative efforts to evaluate a teacher's instructional skill. That assignment obliged me to read a huge number of empirical studies dealing with the appraisal of teachers' competence. Teacher evaluation, I quickly discerned, has been a question of importance almost since the days of Socrates. I was astonished, and sometimes annoyed, by how much had been written about the appraisal of teachers.

When I had finally finished my semester-long review of the teacher evaluation literature through the late 1950s, I was convinced that the most important criterion by which to appraise teachers simply had to be the degree to which they were able to promote student learning. Although none of the studies that I had read and abstracted for the annotated bibliography had come close to solving the problem of how to use student learning as a criterion for judging teachers, most of the authors whose work I was reviewing had taken the general position that *pupil growth is the ultimate criterion by which teachers must be evaluated.*

The idea that student learning ought to be the big-bopper indicator of a teacher's skill was quite appealing to me because, before heading for graduate school, I had been a high school teacher and had thought quite a bit about whether I was doing a good job. And as I reviewed my years as a high school instructor, I realized that my instructional efforts had only been as good as the effects I was able to have on my students. If my students had learned loads, then I was an instructional winner. If I had simply bored or even entertained my students and they really had not learned all that much, then I was an instructional loser.

Well, ever since graduate school, I have sporadically devoted major chunks of my life to the quest for a serviceable scheme of evaluating teachers on the basis of student learning. I dipped in and out of this quest because, as I wrestled with the problem of how to evaluate teachers on the basis of their students' growth, the problem invariably won the wrestling match—usually quite decisively.

On a half dozen distinct occasions, I have traveled down different research trails trying to appraise teachers by seeing how well their students learn. On each of these occasions, one of which took me 9 full years before I packed in my teacher evaluation tools, I have returned from the teacher evaluation battlefield as a wounded and often whining warrior. And after each of these fruitless evaluative quests, I have pledged that I would never again mess around in the teacher evaluation arena. More often than not, cursing creatively, I would vow never to even utter the phrase "teacher evaluation," much less read or think about it.

A Seductive Invitation From Ithaca

And so it was that I was experiencing a blissful abstinence from the travails of teacher evaluation when I received an invitation from Cornell University's Jason Millman to write a chapter in a book he was putting together about the use of student achievement as a measure of teacher and school effectiveness. Little did my friend realize that he was thrusting temptation squarely in front of a recovering teacher evaluator. Unknowingly, he was quite surely stoking my addiction. He was waving that frustrating flame right in front of a fried-wing moth. And, of course, I fluttered forward to do battle once again, albeit briefly, with my special nemesis.

In the remainder of this chapter, therefore, I will do what I was asked to do after having read the book's earlier chapters. I was requested by genial Jason, as was Linda Darling-Hammond, to supply an answer to the following question: Where should student achievement-based measures of teacher and school effectiveness go from here? As you might suspect, I have some battle-biased views on that topic. Yet please regard the following paragraphs as what they are— nothing more than the musings of a frequently frustrated evaluator who, having tried on numerous occasions to solve the problem of how to use student achievement as the cornerstone of an instructional appraisal system, is loath to give more than one chapter's consideration to that neurosis-inducing challenge.

To be honest, I have not seen a tremendous amount of advancement in the teacher evaluation game since I read all those musty studies during graduate school. There has been effort aplenty, of course, and this book contains four solid examples of attempts to employ student learning as an indicator of instructional effectiveness. But I believe our progress on that front during the past few decades has been decidedly meager.

Four Coins in the Fountain

The bulk of this book is devoted to the four major chapters in which folks from Oregon, Tennessee, Kentucky, and Dallas (apparently a city with state-level aspirations) describe how they are tackling the task of ascertaining instructional competence using student achievement as an important evaluative criterion. Although I enjoyed reading the four chapters and then the excellent reviews of these chapters, I simply am compelled to offer a few comments about the four appraisal schemes. After all, how often does one get an opportunity to write the final chapter of an edited book and thus have almost certain knowledge that the only rejoinder possible might be the book's index?

Evaluative Focus

Oversimplifying somewhat, as is the certain privilege of a final-chapter author, it is possible to consider the four systems on the basis of the evaluative foci of the different approaches. This can be seen in Table 24.1, in which we are reminded that only two of the appraisal systems—namely, those in Tennessee and Dallas—attempt to use student achievement as a criterion for both school-focused and teacher-focused evaluation. Oregon's Teacher Work Sample Methodology clearly is aimed at evaluating individual teachers, whereas Kentucky's accountability system is deliberately focused only on school-level effects rather than on a teacher's contribution to those school effects. I want to emphasize the differences in evaluative foci among the four appraisal systems because I subsequently argue that the way in which we must employ students' achievement results should differ if the evaluator is scrutinizing a single teacher's effects rather than a school-based aggregation of many teachers' effects.

Assessment Devices Employed

There also are other differences in the four appraisal systems that are quite important. One of these differences consists of the kinds of achievement tests used in the systems. Both the Kentucky and Dallas schemes use a variety of student achievement tests. Kentucky employs a diverse array of state-developed assessments intended to be primarily performance based. Kentucky also uses other indicators such as dropout rates. Dallas employs students' scores on a nationally standardized norm-referenced achievement test (the Iowa Tests of Basic Skills), a state-developed criterion-referenced test, about 150 end-of-course criterion-referenced tests, and standardized college aptitude examinations.

Table 24.1. Evaluative Foci of the Book's Four Instructional
Appraisal Systems

Appraisal System	School-Focused Evaluation	Teacher-Focused Evaluation
Oregon	No	Yes
Kentucky	Yes	No
Tennessee	Yes	Yes
Dallas	Yes	Yes

In Oregon, ad hoc criterion-referenced assessment devices are developed in accord with a teacher's intended instructional outcomes. In Oregon, therefore, the evidence of student achievement is collected via decidedly idiosyncratic assessment instruments that are, it is hoped, accurately aligned with a teacher's instructional aims.

Tennessee, by contrast, has opted exclusively for norm-referenced tests, that is, as Sanders, Saxton, and Horn say in Chapter 13, "the norm-referenced portion of the Tennessee Comprehensive Assessment Program" (p. 138). After consulting other sources, I learned that the assessment "portion" referred to by the authors is the Comprehensive Tests of Basic Skills.

So, it is clear there is a good deal of variability in the numbers and kinds of assessment instruments that are used in the four appraisal systems to gauge student learning. To unthinkingly lump these assessment tools together would be, tautologically but truly, unthinking.

Statistical Enshrouding

Although all four of the appraisal systems quite naturally employ numbers to help arrive at indicators of instructional effects, two of the systems are positively swimming in statistical formulas. The Tennessee Value-Added Assessment System employs a mixed-model methodology that is so statistically complex that even its originators concede the model is not easily explained. As one critique of the Tennessee appraisal system asserted, "The complexity of the model makes it difficult to convince those most affected by the evaluation that it is an appropriate and reliable means of measuring the impact educators have on student learning" (Baker & Xu, 1995, p. iii).

The Dallas Value-Added Accountability System uses a two-level hierarchical linear model that, to most of those educators being evaluated by it, must appear more than mildly opaque. The technical adequacy of the Dallas statistical approach has, of course, been seriously questioned by Thum and Bryk earlier in this book (Chapter 9).

Although less complicated than the statistical gyrations embodied in the Tennessee and Dallas models, some of the numerical manipulations employed in the Kentucky appraisal system (e.g., the gap reduction improvement minima required of the state's schools) and the Oregon appraisal system (e.g., the stipulated Index of Pupil Growth expectancies) also have raised questions of reviewers.[1]

It seems clear that the more statistically and numerically convoluted the appraisal system is, the more open it will be to attacks based on the way in which it uses its numbers and statistics. Teacher evaluation systems that are regarded as obfuscative are not apt to be widely applauded and, hence, widely used.

Thumbnail Reactions to the Four Systems

Before turning to my Delphic-like prophecies about the future of instructional evaluation based on student learning, I offer my own snippet-size reactions to the four appraisal systems.

I like the Oregon system's potential for the evaluation of individual teachers in situ. Of the three appraisal systems in this book that strive to evaluate individual teachers, Oregon's approach is, to me, the most promising because it is attentive to contextual variables.

I also like Kentucky's school-focused accountability program, although it is quite clear that some substantial rethinking will need to be done about certain aspects of the program. There already have been meaningful modifications in several aspects of the Kentucky system. Kentucky's approach is straightforward enough for most educators to comprehend what is evaluatively afoot.

The folks in Dallas are to be commended for trying to employ a wide variety of assessment devices in their evaluative scheme. The more valid the inferences yielded by these varied assessment devices, the better. I hope, therefore, that the district and state criterion-referenced tests are just as solid as they can be. I do not believe, however, that the Dallas approach is apt to be very effective for evaluating teachers. With some massaging of its statistical approaches, it may do the job in evaluating school-level effectiveness.

I really am least enthused about the Tennessee appraisal system. It is an approach that has bet all of its assessment marbles on results of a national norm-referenced test even though increasing numbers of measurement specialists concede that such tests often are insensitive to detecting the effects of teachers' instructional efforts. Beyond that fatal flaw, the Tennessee folks have adopted an almost incomprehensible statistical system to provide both school-focused and teacher-focused evidence. There is an old saying that "data gathered with a rake should not be analyzed with a microscope." I think that in Tennessee the rake-collected data are being analyzed with a mystery microscope. The folks at the University of Tennessee Value-Added Research and Assessment Center ought to (a) employ other and/or additional assessment devices, (b) restrict their evaluative attention to schools rather than teachers, and (c) either figure out how to explain their statistical machinations or choose other statistical machinations or procedures that can be understood by those being evaluated (Baker & Xu, 1995).

All of the architects of these four appraisal systems deserve solid applause for their stalwart efforts. But effort does not always yield a successful consequence. Because we are dealing here with instructional competence, and because ineffectual instructors are apt to harm children, we need to maintain stringent standards when any instructional appraisal scheme is put under the spotlight.

Where From Here?

Where do we go, then, with student achievement as an index of instructional competence? Well, as I have implied in my previous remarks, I believe it is imperative to differentiate the evaluation procedures that should be employed to judge teachers from those that should be employed to judge school-level effectiveness.

School-Level Evaluation

When we attempt to determine the effectiveness of the staff in a given school, the benefits of aggregation allow us to spread out the impact of certain contextual variables that can dramatically influence the appraisal of an individual teacher. Thus I believe that the general methodological strategies reflected in the Kentucky, Dallas, and Tennessee approaches do, indeed, have potential for school-level evaluation. For such school-focused evaluation to be successful, I think it is imperative to employ the most instructionally sensitive assessment devices possible. So I certainly would want to supplement norm-referenced tests with criterion-referenced tests well aligned to a given school's district-sanctioned or state-sanctioned curriculum. Without decent assessment devices, the use of student learning as a criterion of instructional competence is foolish.

In addition, unless the statistical procedures that are employed can somehow be defensibly explained to those being evaluated, I would back up and start again. Even though we are dealing with school-level evaluation, the stakes are high here. Statistical methods surely will need to be employed to compensate for school-to-school differences on important variables. But statistical procedures must be selected that are at least intuitively comprehensible to those who are evaluated. And those procedures, once intuitively understood, must be regarded by educators and policymakers as sensible ways in which to level the evaluative playing field.

I believe that for school-level evaluation of instructional quality, we should continue to seek ways that will make student achievement results not the *only* evaluative criterion but rather the *most important* such criterion by which a school staff is judged.

Teacher-Level Evaluation

Turning to the evaluation of teachers, I think the ground rules regarding the evaluative role of student learning must be altered substantially. Because a given teacher must function in the midst of a highly individualized context, it is imperative to employ an evaluative approach that takes full cognizance of such contextual variables.

In my own thinking about the evaluation of teachers, I have moved toward much greater reliance on data-based professional judgment. I recommend teacher evaluation schemes in which well-trained educational professionals consider a wide variety of relevant data, the most important of which usually should be student learning, and then make a carefully documented in-context judgment about a teacher's instructional competence. I have described this judgment-based approach to teacher evaluation elsewhere (Popham, 1988).

This is why I found much to commend the Oregon approach. There is a clear effort to particularize the evaluation of a specific teacher. The several measures that were created to characterize the context in which teaching and learning occur make it clear that the Western Oregon State College researchers realize that a particular teacher's skill must be appraised in the multivariate setting in which that teacher functions.

I am quite fearful, however, that the Oregon gang may go overboard in their quest for quantifiable precision. I am dismayed by the almost overwhelming array of Oregon's measures, scales, and numbers. That is a common problem when researchers get very involved in studying a complex phenomenon. They start understanding the phenomenon's nuances so well that they want to delineate those nuances for all to see. But it is more than possible to inflict nuance overload on others, and I think Schalock, Schalock, and Girod have just about crossed that overload line (Chapter 3). Yes, the teacher evaluation world is complex, and surely the evaluators need to understand its complexity. But the mark of a first-rate presenter is to simplify an exposition so that the essence of complex phenomena can be understood. It is time for the Oregon researchers to start staking out a comprehensible essence or two.

Because I would like student achievement results (almost always) to play the pivotal role in determining a teacher's skill, I worry, as does Airasian (Chapter 4), about the quality of the assessment devices employed in any sort of contextually based teacher evaluation scheme. It will be especially important to have nonpartisan reviewers judge the caliber of the assessment devices used in contextualized judgments of a particular teacher's skill.

While I am on that point, I believe that we should be collecting anonymous self-report data from students about their school-related attitudes (e.g., how much they like mathematics) and out-of-school behaviors (e.g., how many books they read volitionally).[2] When I refer to student learning, it includes not only cognitive outcomes but also affective, behavioral, and psychomotor outcomes.

To repeat, I believe that, now and in the future, student learning should be the most important criterion by which we evaluate teachers and school staffs. I think we can tackle the school-level use of student learning via methods that attempt to compensate for variability among schools. For teacher-level evaluation, I believe the student learning data must be employed only after taking into consideration the entry behaviors of a particular teacher's students as well as other relevant contextual variables.

Complexity Calls the Shots

The older I get, the more I realize how complex the instructional phenomena we study really are. We are studying one human's efforts to bring about worthwhile changes in a flock of other (usually smaller) humans. Humans are so confoundingly complicated that I fear our aspirations for evaluative precision almost always exceed our evaluative capabilities.

Remember, when we evaluate something as complicated as instruction, we do not need to come up with a flawless set of evaluative procedures. Flawless we will not get. But it is reasonable to design instructional evaluation systems that at least improve the quality of the decisions we make about many teachers and school staffs. Realistic expectations have a chance of being realized. Unrealistic expectations sometimes can cause us to jettison procedures that, albeit not perfect, might lead to modest educational improvements.

When it comes to the employment of student learning as a criterion for appraising instructional competence, I urge its use but in a modestly ambitious manner. Come to think of it, it might be easier to evaluate moths.

Notes

1. The Kentucky system was vigorously criticized by Hambleton and colleagues (1995) as part of a recent review commissioned by the Kentucky State Office of Educational Accountability. Oregon's work sample methodology is on the receiving end of some insightful questions posed by Airasian in this book (Chapter 4).

2. I recently described such approaches (Popham, 1996) in a series of unoffical suggestions to Department of Defense Education Activity educators.

References

Baker, A. P., & Xu, D. (1995). *The measure of education: A review of the Tennessee Value-Added Assessment System.* Nashville, TN: Office of Education Accountability.

Hambleton, R. K., Jaeger, R. M., Koretz, D., Linn, R. L., Millman, J.,
    & Phillips, S. (1995). *Review of the measurement quality of the Kentucky Instructional Results Information System, 1991-94.* Frankfort,
    KY: Office of Educational Accountability.

Popham, W. J. (1988). Judgment-based teacher evaluation. In S. J.
    Stanley & W. J. Popham (Eds.), *Teacher evaluation: Six prescriptions
    for success* (pp. 56-77). Alexandria, VA: Association for Supervision and Curriculum Development.

Popham, W. J. (1996). *Collecting SIP indicators-of-success evidence for
    the 1996-97 school year.* Los Angeles: IOX Assessment Associates.

Author Index

Advanced Systems in
Measurement and
Evaluation, 232
Alexander, K., 133
Allington, R. L., 259
Almaguer, T. O., 120
American Educational Research
Association, 211, 235
American Psychological
Association, 211, 235
Ancess, J., 261
Appalachia Educational
Laboratory, 204, 249, 250, 251
Aschbacher, P. R., 18
Ashkinaze, C., 259
Associated Press, 134

Babu, S., 89
Baker, A. P., 268, 270
Baker, E. L., 67, 211
Barron, S., 203, 206, 207
Bearden, D. K., 89
Bembry, K. L., 86, 89, 91, 121
Bereiter, C., 121
Berk, R. A., 4
Bixby, J., 18
Bloom, B., 79
Bock, R. D., 107
Bryk, A. S., 102, 105, 106, 107, 142

Cherland, M., 112, 113

Clune, B., 260
Cole, J., 252
Congdon, R. T., 107
Corns, R., 185
Cowart, B., 44
Cowart, B. F., 68
Cronbach, L. J., 110

Dallas Public Schools, 88, 93
Darling-Hammond, L., 116, 249,
250, 254, 255, 259, 261
Davis, D., 133, 135
Deabster, P., 102
Dearden, B. L., 140, 141
Deibert, D., 250
Dings, J., 231
Draper, K., 112, 113
Dunbar, S. B., 67, 211

Easton, J. Q., 102
Edelsky, C., 112, 113
Education Improvement Act,
134, 135
Estes, N., 75, 76

Falk, B., 249, 250
Fisher, T. H., 107
Forgione, Pascal, 188

Gardner, H., 18, 112
Gearhart, M., 18

Gitomer, D. H., 18
Glass, G. V., 4
Glenn, J., 18
Gomez, D. L., 253
Grobe, R. P., 253

Haertel, E., 4
Hambleton, R. K., 210, 211, 214,
    217, 227, 251, 273
Hamilton, R., 190
Hanushek, E. A., 170
Harmon, M., 114, 115, 253, 255
Harville, D. A., 145
Henderson, C. R., 145
Herman, J. L., 18
Holmes, C. T., 259
Horn, S., 102, 107, 140
Horn, S. P., 133, 135, 140, 141,
    174, 175

Jaeger, R., 210, 211, 217, 227, 251,
    273
Jones, K., 249, 251

Katz, V., 12
Kentucky Department of
    Education, 191, 230, 233
Kerbow, D. W., 102
Keisling, P., 12
Kifer, E., 188
Kingston, N., 231
Kitzhaber, J., 12
Kohn, A., 112
Koretz, D., 203, 206, 207, 210, 211,
    217, 227, 250, 251, 273
Koziol, S. M., 66
Kruse, S. D., 117

Levy, F., 250, 261
Lindquist, E., 79
Linn, R., 67, 210, 211, 217, 227, 251,
    273
Lomax, R., 114, 115, 253, 255
Lord, F., 238
Louis, K. S., 117
Luppescu, S., 102

Madaus, G., 114, 115, 253, 255
Matthews, B., 202
Matthews, K. M., 259
Maughan, B., 116
McGill-Franzen, A., 259
McLaughlin, M., 117
McLaughlin, M. W., 261
McLean, R. A., 135, 138, 145, 175,
    176, 177
Meier, D., 112
Mendro, R. L., 82, 86, 91, 120, 121
Messick, S., 67, 235
Meyer, R. H., 102
Millman, J., 4, 7, 25, 210, 211, 217,
    227, 251, 266, 273
Minnick, J. B., 66
Mitchell, K., 203, 206, 207
Mortimore, P., 116
Murnane, R., 250, 261

National Council on Measurement
    in Education, 211, 235
Newmann, R., 116, 117

Oakes, J., 254
Olson, G. H., 81, 120, 121
Orfield, G., 259
Organization for Economic
    and Cooperative
    Development, 170
Orsak, T. H., 86, 91, 121
Ouston, J., 116

Pankratz, R., 186
Patterson, H. D., 160
Pecheone, R., 249
Perkins, D., 112
Peters, T., 194
Phillips, S., 210, 211, 217, 227,
    251, 273
Popham, W. J., 271, 273

Raudenbush, S. W., 105, 106,
    107, 142
Redfield, D., 188
Resnick, D. P., 67
Resnick, L., 114, 250

Resnick, L. B., 67
Rogers, H. J., 214
Rottenberg, C., 112, 113
Rowan, B., 116
Rutter, M., 116

Sanders, W. L., 102, 107, 133, 135,
    138, 140, 141, 145, 174, 175,
    176, 177
Saxton, A. M., 140, 141
Schalock, D. H., 44, 53, 62
Schalock, M., 44, 53
Schneider, J. F., 140, 141
Schuhmacher, C. C., 122
Schulman, L. S., 36
Scriven, M., 94
Searle, S. R., 156
Shea, J. H., 250
Shepard, L., 110, 114, 255, 259
Sherman, M. A., 66
Shinkfield, A. J., 3
Shulman, L. S., 67
Smith, A., 116
Smith, F., 259
Smith, M. L., 112, 113, 114, 259
Socrates, 265
Staebler, B., 44
Stecher, B., 203, 206, 207
Steinberg, L., 112
Stetcher, B., 250
Stodolsky, S., 256
Stroup, W. W., 145
Stufflebeam, D. L., 3, 171

Swaminathan, H., 214
Sykes, G., 7

Talbert, J., 117
Tennessee Business Round-
    table, 134
Tennessee Small School Systems v.
    McWherter, 133
Thompson, R., 160
Thum, Y. M., 102
Travers, R. M. W., 4
Tyler, Ralph, 79

Viator, K., 114, 115, 253, 255

Webster, W., 76, 77, 78, 81, 82, 86,
    91, 93, 120, 121, 122
West, M., 114, 115, 253, 255
Western Michigan University
    Evaluation Center, 203,
    211, 227
Whitford, B. L., 249, 251
Wiggins, G. P., 18
Wiggins, Grant, 188
Wilkenson, Wallace, 186
Winters, L., 18
Wolf, D. P., 18
Wolfe, R., 107
Wright, S. P., 140, 141

Xu, D., 268, 270

Zeiky, M., 230, 232

Subject Index

Accountability system:
competitiveness of, 246
comprehensiveness of, 245-246
consequential validity of, 246
criteria for, 243-246
fairness of, 244-245
framework of accountability
for, 111
See also Dallas Value-Added
Accountability System;
Kentucky Instructional
Results Information
(Improvement) Systems
(KIRIS); Teacher Work
Sample Methodology
(TWSM); Tennessee
Value-Added Assessment
System (TVASS)
Advanced placement tests, 205
Advanced Systems for
Measurement in Education
(ASME), 189, 220, 226
Alternative assessment move-
ment, 18
American College Testing scores,
205, 216
Assessment/accountability
approaches:
factors required, 260-261
See also specific assessment/
accountability approaches

Authentic assessment, 17, 67, 115
criticism of, 126
impracticality of, 122
See also Teacher Work Sample
Methodology (TWSM)

California Basic Educational Skills
Test, 12
scores, 205
Career Ladder (Tennessee), 181
Classroom Effectiveness Indexes,
128, 129
Classroom effects, 164, 165, 168
Classrooms:
development diversity in, 28
multiage, 28
Cohort effects, 164, 165, 168
Commission for Educational
Excellence (Dallas), 81, 89
intent of, 88
Council for Better Education
(CBE), 185
Council on School Performance
Standards (CSPS), 186
Curriculum:
damaging through tests, 122
representation of knowledge in,
114-115

Dallas Independent School District
(DISD), 75, 76, 77, 78

Dallas Public Schools, 81, 82, 92, 100, 101, 120, 127
  basic duties of teachers, 95
  performance money awarded by, 88
  See also Dallas Value-Added Accountability System; School Effectiveness Indexes; Teacher Effectiveness Indexes
Dallas Value-Added Accountability System, 5, 101-106, 111, 266
  Accountability Task Force, 82-83, 88, 123, 124, 127
  advantages, 102
  analysis strategy, 103-106
  assessment devices, 267
  bureaucratic conception of organization and management, 115
  continuous improvement as controlling philosophy, 79, 128
  criticisms, 110-118, 252-253, 269
  evaluative focus, 267
  fairness, 244
  hierarchical linear modeling (HLM), 79, 82, 85, 86, 87, 91, 92, 105, 106, 121, 123, 124, 125
  identifying effective schools, 82-89
  identifying effective teachers, 89-92
  multifaceted nature, 82
  multiple regression model, 85
  school effectiveness and fairness, 82-85, 102-103
  school-level evaluation, 270
  standardized test scores, 101
  statistical complexity, 269
  statistical models, 85-88
  tests, 112
  update, 120, 127-129

Education Act for the 21st Century (Oregon), 12, 13, 18, 28, 53
Educational process, organization and management of, 115-116

Educational reform, politics and, 205-207, 227
Educational Testing Service, 231
Education Improvement Act (EIA) of 1992 (Tennessee), 139, 140, 161
  TVAAS's primary purpose in, 139
Formative evaluation use, 4

Hierarchical linear modeling (HLM), 79, 82, 85, 86, 87, 91, 92, 105, 106, 121, 123, 124, 125 of TWSM, 47

Index of Pupil Growth, 25, 48, 49, 70, 269
  appropriateness of as learning gain measure, 65
  sensitivity of as learning gain measure, 65
Interstate New Teachers Assessment and Support Consortium (INTASC), 257, 258, 260
Iowa Test of Basic Skills (ITBS), 112, 127, 267

Joint Committee on Standards for Educational Evaluation, 171

Kentucky Department of Education (KDE), 198, 210, 213, 216, 217, 220, 226, 228, 233, 249
Kentucky Essential Skills Test (KEST), 56
Kentucky Institute for Educational Research (KIER), 190, 222, 233
Kentucky Instructional Results Information (Improvement) System (KIRIS), 5, 189-190, 206, 209, 217, 218-221, 266
  accountability assessments, 188
  accountability index, 219
  accountability index failure, 224, 235-237, 250-251

Kentucky Instructional Results
    Information (Improvement)
    (*continued*)
  accuracy of school
    accountability
    categorization, 212-213,
    229-231
  advantages, 269
  as open-ended, 226
  assessment devices, 267
  assessment devices
    construction, 222-223
  assessment devices reliability,
    223, 234-235
  assessment validity, 223-224, 235
  changes in scores, 204
  complexity, 228
  continuous assessments, 188
  credibility issues, 225
  criticisms, 249
  defensibility of performance
    standards, 214-215, 232
  description, 192
  design, 188-189
  distinguished educators, 202
  equivalency of scores across
    administrations, 213-214, 231
  evaluative focus, 267
  grade placement of tests, 199
  impacts on schools, 221-222, 233
  impacts on state education
    system, 222, 233-234
  impacts on students, 221
  impacts on teachers, 221, 232-233
  implementation difficulties,
    220-221
  independent evaluations, 190
  informal assessments, 188-189
  key features, 194-202, 210
  longitudinal assessment design
    problems, 224-225, 238
  multifaceted nature, 228
  multiple-choice questions, 199,
    218, 231, 250
  noncognitive data, 200-201
  noncognitive goals, 189
  open-response questions, 199

  performance-based, 197-198,
    210, 218, 226
  performance standards, 199-200
  portfolios, 189, 198
  primary goal, 191-192, 247
  report clarity, 215
  results/consequences, 202-204
  scheduled restricted 2D
    response items, 189
  schedules performance tasks, 189
  School Accountability Index, 190
  school-level evaluation, 270
  "schools in crisis," 202
  soundness of cognitive tests,
    211-212, 229
  technical adequacy, 222-225
  test component of, 194
  test scores, 205
  test scores and student learning
    improvement, 216
Kentucky Legislative Task Force
    for Education Reform, 187
Kentucky Office of Education
    Accountability (OEA),
    190, 210
  report, 190, 227, 228
Kentucky Reform Act (KERA),
    187-188, 191, 197, 199, 200,
    206, 209, 210, 216, 217, 219,
    233, 244
Kentucky schools, evolution as
    model of change in, 193

Mentor Teacher Act (Oregon), 12
Mentor Teacher Program
    (Oregon), 12
National Assessment of
    Educational Progress
    (NAEP) scores, 205, 216
  math, 205

National Board for Professional
    Teaching Standards
    (NBPTS), 58, 257, 258, 260

Oregon Board of Higher
    Education, 12

Performance-based assessment:
    impracticality of, 122
    new forms of, 115
Personnel assessment, evaluation
    and standards of, 171-172
Personnel assessment policy, 180
    field conditions and, 170
    policy context of, 170-171
    value-added performance
    and, 170

Restructured schools, 17

School:
    as community, 117
    as culture, 116-117
School Effectiveness Indexes, 89,
    91-92, 96
    Campus Improvement Plan
    and, 94
    District Improvement Plan
    and, 94
School effects research, learning
    gains and school
    effectiveness and, 6
School evaluation for account-
    ability and organizational
    control, learning gains and
    school effectiveness and, 7
Schooling, student learning as
    objective of, 11, 47
School system, American:
    indictment of, 14
Special education, inclusive edu-
    cation movement and, 28
Standardized tests, effect of on
    teachers and teaching, 113-114
Standardized tests, student per-
    formance on:
    as criterion of school success, 14
    as criterion of teacher success, 14
    criterion-referenced, 118
    heavy reliance on, 16
    norm-referenced, 118, 127
    value of, 126-127
Student learning criterion:
    gains in student achievement, 3

measures of teacher knowledge/
    skills and, 3
Summative evaluation use, 4
    of TWSM, 47

Teacher and school evaluation,
    performance contracting
    and, 7
Teacher Effectiveness Indexes, 89,
    90-91, 92, 96, 128
    addressing all teachers, 93
    concentration of resources, 93
    in teacher evaluation, 92-96
    meshing with other district
    processes, 93, 94
    teachers without, 94
    timing of, 93
Teacher effects research, learning
    gains and teacher effective-
    ness and, 6
Teacher evaluation, historical, 3-5
    payment-by-results system, 3-4
    weaknesses of, 5
Teacher evaluation, learning gains
    and, 265
    contemporary approaches to
    using, 5
    See also specific approaches
Teacher evaluation cycle (Dallas), 97
Teacher evaluation for merit pay/
    career advancement, learn-
    ing gains and teacher effec-
    tiveness and, 7
Teacher Evaluation Task Force
    (Dallas), 93, 96, 127-128, 129
Teacher improvement system
    criterion, 246-247
Teacher Standards and Practices
    Commission (TSPS), 12
Teacher Work Sample Methodol-
    ogy (TWSM), 5, 13, 15, 147,
    247, 256-259, 260, 266
    adaptations required by
    context, 28
    adaptations required by
    purpose, 28-29
    advantages, 47, 57, 61, 256, 269

Teacher Work Sample Methodology (TWSM) (continued)
applied performance approach issues, 34
as authentic applied performance approach, 17
as "close-to-a-teacher's work" methodology, 17
as complex applied performance approach, 17
as context-dependent theory, 18, 19, 53, 54
as measurement approach, 18-19
as outcome-based theory, 18, 47, 53, 54
assessment devices, 268
as standards-based approach, 19
as teaching vehicle, 18
calculating learning gains by pupils taught, 22, 24
cheapness, 51
conceptual narrowness, 56
construct-defined measures, 22, 23-24
criterion-referenced measures, 16
critique, 47-49
critique of for linking pupil learning to teacher performance, 49-50
demonstrated value, 55
design, 17-28
empirical support, 29-34, 37, 57
establishing work sample performance standards, 25-26
evaluation functions, 17
evaluative focus, 267
evolving nature, 46
fairness, 244-245
feasibility of implementation, 26-37, 51
importance, 54-55
licensure functions, 17, 28-29, 54, 60, 257
limitations, 256-257
measures derived from, 19, 22, 38-43

overview, 18-19
practical guidelines, 57
predictive validity, 36, 67
procedures, 16
professionalization of teaching, 38
pupil assessment test quality, 47-48
reliability issues, 34, 35-36, 55
research functions, 17
reasonableness, 36, 51
school restructuring, 17
serving multiple purposes, 37, 51, 68
soundness of as theory, 55-57
steps, 19, 20-21, 47
strengths of as instruction vehicle, 67-68
teacher-level evaluation, 271-272
teacher training and, 17, 28, 47, 50, 56, 59
technical merits of as measurement approach, 66-67
trade-offs, 69
traditional concerns, 35-36
unfinished nature, 46, 63
validity issues, 34, 35-36, 48-49, 55
value of for formative/developmental purposes, 57-58
value of for improving teacher preparation, 59-60
value of for informing high-stakes decisions, 58-59
See also Index of Pupil Growth (IPG); Work sample profiles
Teach for America, 58
Teaching:
conditions, 16
professionalization of, 14, 38
"Teaching the test," 56
Tennessee Business Roundtable, 134
Tennessee Comprehensive Assessment Program (TCAP), 135, 138, 268
test results, 136
Tennessee Education Association, 136

Tennessee Value-Added Assessment System (TVASS), 5, 107, 133, 247, 266
  accuracy standards, 172, 173, 176-177
  adaptability, 161
  as dynamic process, 161
  as least of bad systems, 171
  as results-based, 169
  assessment devices, 268
  as state-of-the-art, 169
  "blocking factors," 138, 142, 180
  "building change phenomenon," 141
  complexity, 181
  computer programs for, 167
  criticisms, 169, 254-256, 270
  database, 138, 157, 247
  description, 135, 137, 163-164
  early testing of, 135
  efforts to inform groups about, 140-141
  encoding fixed effects, 149-151
  encoding random effects, 152-155
  evaluative focus, 267
  feasibility standards, 172-173, 176
  flexibility, 161
  goal, 161
  Henderson's mixed-model equations, 143, 144-146, 165, 167
  longitudinal data and, 138, 142, 161, 171, 173
  methodological advantages, 179
  model equations used, 146-149
  personnel evaluation standards, 174-177
  properties, 142-144
  proprietary standards, 172, 174
  raw data, 138
  regression models versus, 165-168
  research initiatives as priority, 141
  school-level evaluation, 270
  statistical claims, 144
  statistical complexity, 268
  statistical methodology, 142-157
  statistical models and encoding, 144-157
  support for, 140-141
  use of mixed-model methodology, 137
  utility standards, 172, 175
  value as research tool, 139-140, 254
Texas Assessment of Academic Skills, 112, 126, 127
Texas Education Agency, 78
Texas Teacher Appraisal System, 95

U.S. Office of Education, 75
Underachievement, solving real problems of, 260-261
University of Tennessee Value-Added Research and Assessment Center (UT-VARAC), 140, 141, 160, 163, 165, 167, 270

Western Michigan University, Evaluation Center at, 190, 227, 228, 236
Western Oregon State College, 5, 12, 15, 26, 69, 272
  faculty, 19, 53, 54
  See also Teacher Work Sample Methodology (TWSM)
Work sample profiles, 26
  as needs assessment tools, 59, 60
  focusing on
    "easy-to-accomplish" learning goals, 64
  preparation, 26-28, 53, 56

CORWIN
PRESS

The Corwin Press logo—a raven striding across an open book—represents the happy union of courage and learning. We are a professional-level publisher of books and journals for K–12 educators, and we are committed to creating and providing resources that embody these qualities. Corwin's motto is "Success for All Learners."

Printed in the United States
215925BV00001B/65/A

9 780803 964020